Academic Departments

Problems, Variations, and Alternatives

Dean E. McHenry
and Associates

Academic Departments

/ 08480

 Jossey-Bass Publishers

San Francisco • Washington • London • 1977

ACADEMIC DEPARTMENTS
Problems, Variations, and Alternatives
by Dean E. McHenry and Associates

Copyright © 1977 by: Jossey-Bass, Inc., Publishers
615 Montgomery Street
San Francisco, California 94111
&
Jossey-Bass Limited
44 Hatton Garden
London EC1N 8ER

Library of Congress Catalogue Card Number LC 76-11896

International Standard Book Number ISBN 0-87589-307-4

Manufactured in the United States of America

JACKET DESIGN BY WILLI BAUM

FIRST EDITION

Code 7706

The Jossey-Bass Series
in Higher Education

Preface

This book deals with the elemental part of academic life and administration that lies between individual faculty members and the deans of an institution's schools or colleges. In American higher education, this area traditionally is occupied by departments, of which faculty members of a given discipline are members. No organizational problems besetting American colleges and universities affect the education of students more critically than those arising from this traditional structure. Thus, it is important to assess the strengths and weaknesses of these departments as they now exist and then to examine some departures from the conventional pattern.

The reasons for seeking other ways to organize academic institutions are several. Excessive departmentalism tends to narrow one's outlook and emphasize specialization to the neglect of the possible contributions of other disciplines. In scholarship, as in farming, the most fertile soil may be that under the fences rather than at the center of long-established fields. Especially in undergraduate work, there is a need for a breadth of study that comes not only from a student taking courses in departments other than his own, but also from associating with faculty members and other students who read and think and talk in multidisciplinary ways. In more advanced study and research there is increasing recognition that many of our most complex problems, such as the quest for clean air and pure water, cannot be solved without engaging the talents and approaches of people from diverse fields of the several academic cultures.

Yet despite these considerations, the disciplinary department continues to dominate. Small professional schools in such areas as business, social welfare, and public health may operate as single departments, including all instructors who serve the profession without consideration for their disciplinary or professional specialty. But larger professional schools are typically departmentalized according to the various components of professional practice—for example, engineering is divided into civil, electrical, mechanical, and other sections or units. Some professors may hold joint appointments in two or more departments; but only a few are allowed to teach without being attached to any department—among them, the "university" professors of a limited number of institutions.

Most important, virtually all institutions rely exclusively on departments to initiate proposals for the appointment of new faculty members and for the advancement of existing faculty members as well as suggest changes in course offerings and course content. In almost all American colleges and universities, courses are offered mainly, if not exclusively, by departments, and students are expected to concentrate their work in departmental majors. Those institutions with graduate programs rely almost entirely on departments to teach, examine, and certify candidates for advanced degrees. Departments normally supply the stenographic, telephone, duplicating, and other services needed by faculty members, and the academic advising and counseling needed by students. Some have authority over travel funds and research and recommend members for grants or affiliation with other institutions and centers, as well as provide a modicum of accounting assistance and research assistants to professors.

In short, the disciplinary department is firmly established as the predominant body in the college and university firmament. Moreover, the departmental system has ancient roots, not easily disturbed. In the United States, as Andersen records in Chapter One, both Harvard and the University of Virginia were departmentalized by 1825; and as Dressel and his associates have indicated, within the past seventy-five years the departmental system has become ubiquitous: "By the 1880s Cornell and Johns Hopkins had succeeded in establishing autonomous departments, but the real solidification of departmental structure and the academic rank system came in the 1890s. Harvard moved decidedly toward departmentalization about 1891–1892. Columbia was thoroughly departmentalized by the late nineties, with Yale and Princeton only somewhat slower in adopting this organizational style" (Dressel, Johnson, and Marcus, 1970, p. 5). Thus, "By the first decade of the twentieth century, the department, with all its inherent strengths and weaknesses, was firmly entrenched in the American university" (Dressel and Reichard, 1970, p. 394).

Nevertheless, as the subtitle of this volume implies, the disciplinary department is not universally accepted as the best of all possible modes of academic organization. The major criticism, as I have already suggested, is that conventional departments foster a specialization and particularism that narrows the horizons of both students and professors. Some observers regard these characteristics as positive assets to graduate education, but many others view them as harmful not only to undergraduate education but to research. Thus, although academic departments exist for the purpose of facilitating teaching and research, their critics are increasingly questioning their value in facilitating learning and the application of new knowledge.

In the only other book of the past decade devoted specifically to this problem—*The Confidence Crisis: An Analysis of University Departments*—Paul Dressel, Craig Johnson, and Philip Marcus concluded that to provide adequate liberal education in the future, American universities might need to establish alternatives to traditional departments. In the present volume, my colleagues and I weigh the pros and cons of that idea, but more important, we show how several American colleges and universities have already moved in that direction. Here we go beyond the consideration of possibilities to the description of actual alternatives—and to an assessment of the implications of these recent experiments for higher education at large. As a result, we hope that this book will be useful to several categories of readers: university and college administrators who want to know what changes are occurring in the academic organization; students of higher education who seek to find out what organizational options exist and how others have gone about choosing them; trustees and regents who need to formulate the right questions about academic departments; and faculty members who wonder whether the single-discipline department provides the optimum environment for learning and growth, for themselves as well as students.

To achieve our purpose, my associates and I have divided our volume into three major sections.

In the first four chapters, four expert observers of colleges and universities and participants in higher education consider the strengths and weaknesses of departmentalism as we now know it. Kay Andersen begins with a careful review of its evolution and its importance in academic governance. His former position as an academic dean of Church College, Hawaii, and his present one as executive director of the Western Association of Schools and Colleges (the regional accrediting association that serves California, Hawaii, and Guam) give him a valuable perspective. He makes a few concessions to the critics of conventional departments, but basically he states the case for retaining them as they are and improving them mainly by strengthening the administrative hand of the department chairman.

In Chapter Two, Martin Trow deals mainly with the large multipurpose university and shows the utility of its disciplinary departments in graduate education and in the recruitment and promotion of academic staff. He views departments as the indispensable link between the university and the organized bodies of knowledge and specialized methods of extending knowledge that characterize the academic disciplines. Yet as a long-time sociological student of higher education (and editor of the recent book for the Carnegie Commission on Higher Education, *Teachers and Students,* 1975b) and professor of sociology in the School of Public Policy at the University of California, Berkeley, he recognizes that general undergraduate education suffers under present-day arrangements— and he suggests that a more appropriate division of labor within and among departments could provide more attention to the teaching of undergraduates.

In Chapter Three, Louis Benezet looks at departments from a vantage point which few, if any, other American educators have had—that of a former president of four colleges and universities, three private and one public, three small and one large. A psychologist by training, he balances departmental advantages and disadvantages and concludes with more doubts about their serviceability than either Andersen or Trow. Making a distinction between college and university departments, he agrees that college faculty members can well use their departments as home base for creative teaching but believes university departments suffer from a preoccupation with their faculty's standing in research. He sees little promise in abolishing departments; instead, he favors providing incentives to them for cooperating in interdisciplinary programs.

In Chapter Four, Fred Harrington finds more weaknesses than strengths in present arrangements from his perspective as a historian and university administrator, and especially as a past president of the University of Wisconsin. Noting that departments foster loyalty to the discipline at the expense of the institution, block needed curricular change, seem unable to deal with current and recent problems (such as overenrollment, student militancy, and faculty collective bargaining), and demonstrate an inability to detect and correct their own decline in quality, he advocates a variety of supplements and alternatives to them.

The five chapters that form the second part of the book present and evaluate examples of these supplements and alternatives. Four of them focus on new American institutions; in each case they are written by the founding or current head, and they provide data that can be used for comparisons and contrasts among various possibilities. The authors of all four case studies either state or imply that their experiments are still too young for final judgments on the validity of their administrative arrangements, but all see promise in their efforts to eschew conventional departmentalism. From that point on, however, diversity takes over: three are state institutions, one is private; two have a tenure system, two do not; and two are parts of a larger system while two stand alone. They vary in enrollment from one thousand to six thousand; they vary in years of full operation from five to eleven.

In Chapter Five, Edward Weidner describes the "problem-based" departments of the University of Wisconsin–Green Bay, which are organized around broad areas of human concern, such as population dynamics and regional analysis, rather than the traditional disciplines as such. A political scientist, Weidner became the first chancellor at Green Bay after broad experience in public administration as well as higher education.

In Chapter Six, I explain the academic organizational "matrix" that evolved at the University of California, Santa Cruz, where I served for thirteen years as founding chancellor after previous experience as a political scientist and university dean of academic planning. At Santa Cruz, the faculty hold membership not only in disciplinary "boards of studies" but also in co-equal nondisciplinary "colleges."

Next, Charles R. Longsworth, initial vice-president and now president of Hampshire College in Massachusetts, describes the academic organization of this innovative new college which stemmed from the partnership of Amherst, Mount Holyoke, Smith, and the University of Massachusetts in the Connecticut River valley. A participant in the meticulous planning that resulted in Hampshire's nondepartmental curriculum, Longsworth shows how it employs four interdisciplinary schools as its basic academic units.

In Chapter Eight, Charles McCann tells the story of the widely watched administrative experiments at The Evergreen State College in Washington. McCann prepared for a career in English teaching but "fell" into administration as chairman and dean before assuming the founding presidency of Evergreen; and rather than recounting its well-known curricular innovations, he here explains the organizational and administrative structure behind them—a structure that avoids any remnants of departments as commonly conceived.

As a foil to these four American case studies, in Chapter Nine F. M. G. Willson presents an overview of academic organization in British universities and, in particular, at the new "plate-glass" institutions organized on bases other than the single-subject department. Willson draws on his proven skill as a political scientist and analyst of governmental administrative problems, his service as dean, provost, and vice-chancellor in African as well as American universities, and his present perspective as principal of the University of London to give a comprehensive yet concise account of how British universities are meeting challenges similar to those facing American institutions.

The final two chapters of the book seek to synthesize the

themes of earlier chapters. In Chapter Ten, J. Douglas Brown, the economist widely known as author of *The Human Nature of Organizations* (1973) and as dean of the faculty and provost emeritus of Princeton University, reviews the ways that a university can maintain its effectiveness as an organization and its humane climate, regardless of organizational arrangement. He concentrates on the personal and philosophical characteristics of academic statesmanship, whether in conventional departments or new arrangements. He bases his analysis on Princeton and its departments, but his ideas about leadership relate to nontraditional institutions as well.

Finally, in Chapter Eleven, I offer my own conclusions about the variety of reforms open to departments and about the potential of the alternatives explored in the previous chapters, both for long-established institutions and for the next generation of institutions.

At this point, I wish to make quite clear that my associates and I, by participating in a book on *organization*, do not hereby imply that administrative structure is all-important. On the contrary, as J. Douglas Brown implies and most other contributors agree, we are inclined to quote with approval Alexander Pope's couplet:

> For forms of government let fools contest;
> Whate'er is best administered is best.

Nonetheless, organization and structure do make some difference. They determine, to a considerable extent, who has adjacent working spaces, whom one sees most frequently, and whether conversations turn most often to narrow specialties or broad problems. An academic structure that mingles colleagues of diverse disciplines can stimulate joint enterprises in teaching and research and, at the very least, serve to broaden horizons, whereas an opposite structure can inhibit cross-fertilization despite the good will and good intentions of individual faculty members and administrators.

Each of the ten contributors to this book has experienced as faculty member and administrator the frustrations and satisfactions of dealing with academic problems through various organizational forms. In their chapters, several roads to the New Jerusalem of balanced academic organization are mapped out. And the terrain, often rough, is reported by some of us who have survived the journey. We would be among the first to warn against a precipitate dash into reorganization without counting ten several times. Vested interests are nearly always on the side of the status quo. Almost all academic men and women were trained in graduate programs based on disciplinary departments; and it is far easier and safer to accept the accustomed form than to ship out on an uncharted sea. But for anyone who questions the perfection of contemporary academic organization and who seeks to learn about new territory and unfinished adventures, this book should give some guidance.

In my role as navigator and editor, I wish to thank several people who helped with suggestions: Peter H. Armacost, Ottawa University; V. R. Cardozier, the University of Texas of the Permian Basin; Paul L. Dressel, Michigan State University; Karl A. Lamb, the University of California, Santa Cruz; and Arthur Levine, the Carnegie Council on Policy Studies in Higher Education.

I owe an exceptional debt of gratitude to JB Lon Hefferlin of Jossey-Bass, Inc., for good counsel, to Sandy Crain for able stenographic services, and to Virginia Campbell, my long-time assistant, for turning bibliographer and girl Friday for this project.

Santa Cruz, California   DEAN E. McHENRY
January 1977

Contents

The Authors

Dean E. McHenry *is chancellor emeritus and professor of comparative government emeritus of the University of California, Santa Cruz.*

After receiving his Ph.D. from Berkeley, McHenry began his teaching career at Williams College and spent 1937–1939 at The Pennsylvania State University. He joined the faculty of the University of California, Los Angeles, in 1939, and subsequently served as department chairman, divisional dean, and secretary of the academic senate.

In 1961 President Clark Kerr and The Regents of the University of California invited him to plan and launch a new campus at Santa Cruz. The campus opened in 1965 and had grown to 5500 students when McHenry retired in 1974.

McHenry has written numerous articles and books, mainly in political science; the most well-known work, of which he is co-author, is The American System of Government *(13th ed., 1977).*

Since retirement, McHenry has divided his attention between farming-gardening and writing about higher education and government problems. He lives with his wife, Jane Synder McHenry, on a farm in the Santa Cruz mountains.

Kay J. Andersen *is executive director of the Western Association of Schools and Colleges and executive secretary-treasurer of the Western College Association. Previously he served as academic dean of the Church College of Hawaii (now Brigham Young University, Hawaii).*

Louis T. Benezet, *professor of human development at the State University of New York, Stony Brook, was formerly president of Allegheny College, Colorado College, the Claremont University Center, and the State University of New York, Albany.*

J. Douglas Brown *is provost and dean of the faculty, emeritus, Princeton University, a trustee of the University of Rochester, and a former member of the Federal Advisory Council on Social Security.*

Fred Harvey Harrington, *Vilas research professor, University of Wisconsin, and program associate for the Ford Foundation in India, served as president of the University of Wisconsin and earlier taught at the University of Arkansas.*

Charles R. Longsworth, *president of Hampshire College, was formerly vice president and chairman, Hampshire College Educational Trust, and assistant to the president of Amherst College. He is president-elect of the Colonial Williamsburg Foundation.*

Charles J. McCann, *president of The Evergreen State College in Washington State was formerly dean of Central Washington State College.*

Martin Trow *is professor of sociology in the Graduate School of Public Policy, University of California, Berkeley. A former editor of* Sociology of Education, *he previously taught at Columbia University and Bennington College.*

Edward W. Weidner, *chancellor, University of Wisconsin–Green Bay, was formerly vice chancellor of the East-West Center, Hawaii, and has taught at University of Minnesota, University of California at Los Angeles, Michigan State University, and University of Kentucky.*

F. M. G. Willson, *principal, University of London, has served as dean of social studies at the University College of Rhodesia and Nyasaland; provost of Stevenson College at the University of California, Santa Cruz; warden of Goldsmiths College, London; and was previously affiliated with Oxford University.*

Academic Departments

*Problems, Variations,
and Alternatives*

1 Kay J. Andersen

In Defense
of Departments

N‌o administrative unit within the college or university has been so important, misunderstood, and maligned as the academic department. Prominent observers of the American scene have both castigated it for fragmenting higher education and extolled it for developing new knowledge. All of them, however, have agreed that departmentalization has played a dominant role in the evolution of higher education. I will analyze this role by establishing a definition of the department, tracing its evolution in the United States and its medieval antecedents in continental Europe and the British Isles, and weighing the writings of its supporters and critics.*

* More support and criticism of departments has occurred than solid research about them. The highlights of the research literature over the past thirty-five years include less than a dozen entries. In 1941–1942, McGrath, Nystrom, and Patmos (1943) sampled 350 liberal arts colleges (122 of which had a division structure) and attempted to justify the division as a means of correlating the work of related departments. In 1950–1951, Doyle (1953) surveyed 33 private and church-related colleges to ascertain the status and functions of the department chairman. Later, McKenna (1957) studied the interpersonal relationships among forty-seven department chairmen and their faculties; Murray (1964) developed a theory of departmental development based on visits to twenty-two universities; Shuart (1966) made an exhaustive search of the literature bearing on academic department chairmen as background for research on their personal values; and Darkenwald (1970) examined the chairman's role in relation to the social organization and "in-

1

To encompass the diverse functions of departments in a tidy definition poses problems, but as a start let us consider the academic department as the basic administrative unit of the college, housing a community of scholars that is relatively autonomous and responsible for instruction and research within a specialized field of knowledge. Whitehead claims that "the whole point of a university, on its educational side, is to bring the young under the intellectual influence of a band of imaginative scholars. There can be no escape from proper attention to the conditions which—as experience has shown—will produce such a band" (1929, p. 100). Largely because of the academic department, these conditions have existed at various times and places during the evolution of higher education, and they are now extant in varying degrees in most institutions. But current attempts to blunt departmental influence by the excessive centralization of power, the crude consolidation of departments, and the insistence on ill-defined institutional commitments could undercut them once again.

American Precedents and Antecedents

To properly understand the present role of the academic department, one must be aware of the historic confluence of forces, both American and European, that contributed to its development. Let us begin with the earliest reference to something called a department in Harvard College in 1739. Josiah Quincy records the encroachment of an overzealous board on department prerogatives: "The zeal and anxiety of the board of Overseers at this period, ex-

---

stitutional differentiation" of fifty-four colleges and universities. Dressel, Johnson, and Marcus (1970) reported an intensive analysis of the impact of seven departments within fourteen universities on institutional achievement and concluded that departments were "out of control" (p. 232). Two years later, Dressel and Faricy (1972) analyzed the possible constraints on departmental autonomy that might be necessary to regain control over institutional resources. The same year, Ikenberry and Friedman (1972) reported responses from the directors of more than 125 university institutes and centers and traced the origins and importance of these quasi-departmental units before making recommendations for their improvement. And during 1974–1975 Waltzer (1975) conducted more than eighty interviews with department personnel of Miami University in Ohio in an attempt to understand the expectations and realities of the department chairmanship and make the job more manageable and satisfying.

tended not only to the religious principles held by the Professors and Tutors at the time of the election, but also to the spirit and mode in which they afterwards conducted their respective departments" (1840, II, p. 28).

Departmentalization became necessary in these early years when it proved impossible for one tutor to teach a single class in all subjects. Even after assigning a particular subject to a single tutor, the increase in enrollment brought together several professors who were engaged in teaching within a particular discipline (Thwing, 1906, p. 311). By 1767 Harvard had four departments: Latin, Greek, logic and metaphysics, and mathematics and natural philosophy; and on its opening in 1755, the College and Academy of Philadelphia (now the University of Pennsylvania) had two: Latin and Greek, and philosophy.

Thomas Jefferson forthrightly expressed his convictions concerning the departments of knowledge that should be included in the University of Virginia, and in 1824 the Board of Visitors accepted his recommendations calling for eight separate schools or broad courses of study, among which students would select one to enter and pursue. The expansion of knowledge and student enrollment caused the School of Law to be subdivided into two departments and the School of Ancient Languages to be expanded into departments of Latin and Greek, but Jefferson's political views accounted for the original departmentalization of the University of Virginia. He disapproved of whatever leaned toward consolidation, and in the governance of both states and institutions, his preference was always for numerous bodies moving in their own separate orbits (Bruce, 1920, pp. 325–326).

Also in 1824, a committee of seven persons appointed to study the state of Harvard presaged the modern department by recommending that professors and tutors be divided into separate departments, each embracing analogous studies and having a professor at its head responsible for the direction of studies, instructors, and students. On June 10, 1825, Harvard's Overseers accepted the committee's recommendation, and the university was divided into departments with superintendence of their own studies (Quincy, p. 346). A year later, in 1826, James Marsh, president of the University of Vermont, divided that institution into four departments and permitted students who were not seeking degrees to pursue the studies of a single department (Rudolph, 1962, p. 121). And in 1837 the University of Wisconsin provided for departments of science, literature, and the arts (Dressel and Reichard, 1970).

A detailed recital of the evolution of academic departments in American higher education would trace the impact of new fields of knowledge, the influence of German-trained professors, the full maturation of the elective system at Harvard during the presidency of Charles W. Eliot, the establishment of Johns Hopkins University in 1876, and the pressure of social forces such as those identified by Brubacher and Rudy (1958, pp. 114–115): the preoccupation of students with utilitarian education in order to take advantage of the new economy, the assistance to public institutions through the Morrill Acts that forced private liberal arts colleges to offer similar programs; and the pressure from private industry and business for specialized programs to foster their private ends.

Some analysts, such as Henderson (1960, p. 115), Kerr (1964, p. 18), and Trow (Chapter Two), suggest that American undergraduate departmentalization stemmed from disciplinary specialization in graduate education—as seen in the founding of Johns Hopkins and the model presented by the German universities in contrast to the English college system. But the evidence of early departments at Harvard, Pennsylvania, Virginia, and Vermont supports a more complex lineage from abroad. Haskins' detection of influences on American institutions provides a plausible explanation. He observes that "even in the colonial period a sense of the general university tradition survived, as seen in the charter of Rhode Island College in 1764 which granted 'the same privileges, dignities, and immunities' enjoyed by the American colleges and European universities" (1923, pp. 30–31).

Let us inspect more carefully Haskins' assumption. In the medieval university in Salerno, and more completely in the numerous universities established by the end of the Middle Ages in different parts of Europe, parallels of the modern department can be discerned in the beginnings of the specialization of knowledge and professional schools. Masters grouped themselves, spontaneously at first, into relatively autonomous faculties of arts, canon law, medicine, and theology with responsibility for setting standards for their own degrees.

Even in England, where the corporate development of these faculties never went as far as it did on the continent (Huber, 1843, I, pp. 42–53) and where both Oxford and Cambridge emphasized the residential college system instead of separate faculties, specialist influences can be detected. For example, a college was founded at Cambridge in 1316 for the special purpose of providing "clerks for the King's service" (Whitehead, p. 92), and there was an abortive attempt during the reign of Edward VI to organize at both universities a college whose fellows would all be students of civil law (Curtis, 1959, pp. 158–159). But as the Inns of Court took on instruction in secular law and the hospital schools took over instruction in medicine, Oxford and Cambridge came to focus on divinity and the liberal arts, which ceased separate organization as faculties. Neither university, as Willson notes in Chapter Nine of this volume, ever became departmentalized, although other British universities did so—Edinburgh, for example, in 1708. Even today, the colleges within the Oxbridge universities are self-governing and autonomous, but because the colleges cannot separately employ enough fellows to teach every subject, they cooperate in certain subjects; and in modern languages and science, they leave teaching and research largely to the university or university institutes. Similarly, in Canada the University of Toronto has sought to maintain the Oxbridge pattern: although each student matriculates in a college within the University of Toronto, he finds himself taking courses in other colleges and in one or more of the nineteen "university departments" not associated with any particular college.

These developments in England and Canada of faculty groupings in particular fields of knowledge, although not always functioning as separate administrative units, approach the concept of the department elsewhere. And it is evident that the American idea of the department stemmed both from indigenous needs for decentralization and from the example of other medieval and Reformation universities that had separate faculties and departments. The English college provided the general curricular model for our colonial colleges, but not the organizational or administrative model;

and only an additional, rather than initial, thrust toward American departmentalization was provided by our introduction of formal graduate programs. This thrust has continued unabated to the present time and has made strong departments the foundation of the American system of higher education.

Critics of Departments

Although function and tradition have thus given the academic department a firm position, and most persons would credit it for having developed and disseminated much knowledge, there are those who criticize it for causing certain deficiencies they see in higher education. In *The Confidence Crisis,* Dressel, Johnson, and Marcus (1970, p. 8) assert that increased departmentalism is producing serious problems within the university, including the inhibition of new fields of knowledge, the isolation of professors, and the narrow specialization of courses and research, all of which forces administrators to establish more flexible centers and institutes as competing alternatives. These authors, who question whether the department is the appropriate unit for such diverse functions as undergraduate instruction, graduate instruction, basic research, applied research, and service, conclude that although departments contribute to the basic store of knowledge, "they have become arrogant and lost the vision of service" (pp. 222–223).

Corson (1975) similarly expresses considerable ambivalence toward departments. He recognizes that they are responsible for the major work of the university and that they exert a major influence on decisions affecting the character of the institution, decisions about the content of courses, who shall teach them, the requirements for majors, the compensation and status of faculty members, and what students shall be admitted to graduate work. But he finds several faults as well. Departments' lack of planning makes it difficult for the institution to develop objectives that can be implemented. Their influence supports faculty resistance to change in terms of modifying curricula, requirements, and instructional practices. Their specialization deters the sharing of ideas among the disciplines. Their rigidity makes the reduction of instructional costs difficult. And their disabilities increase rather than decrease as institutions move from college to university status. To correct these deficiencies, Corson recommends among other remedies the increase of authority among chief academic administrators over curriculum, budget, faculty selection, and promotion. He argues rightly that this increase in central authority would reduce the finality of departmental decision making.

Riesman (1958, pp. 107–108) holds that departments, like political and social blocs that frustrate political action in the United States, operate in the intellectual realm to crush potential disciplines that might threaten their control over funds and students. Mooney (1964) contends that neither the faculty nor the administration can take leadership initiative because departmentalization has created a leadership vacuum at the institutional level. Henderson (1960, p. 24) sees the department as becoming a rigid, isolated, and self-contained community of students and scholars. And Hutchins (1953, p. 24) holds that the extreme specialization of knowledge, inevitable in the experimental sciences and fostered by departmentalism, should not be imitated by scholars in nonempirical fields, where the experimental approach has admittedly produced insignificant studies.

My associates in later chapters of this volume contribute further censure of current departmentalism, and I grant there is justification for some of these criticisms—especially those dealing with undergraduate education in the large university department. But without the particular kind of environment that departments have provided for scholars and their students throughout the ages, higher education could well be in a state that would warrant even more condemnation.

Although there undoubtedly are examples of departments that have suppressed the development of others, the burgeoning number of departments in today's universities suggests that Riesman has overrated their power to crush new disciplines. Rather than producing a leadership vacuum, as Mooney contends, departmentalization has provided untold leadership opportunities. Departments, like political and social blocs, can enhance as well as frustrate action within the institution, especially when departments bring themselves together to solve particular problems. The exponential increase of knowledge is creating new departments, often beginning as interdisciplinary programs, area studies, experimental centers, and institutes; and while at first blush this trend would appear to increase fragmentation, where parent departments remain, we have both integration and compartmentalization. What to many appears to be a threat can contribute further to the service a university must provide.

As fragmented, splintered, compartmentalized, and sterile as many claim higher education to be, the department must not be forced to assume responsibility for a condition that is largely the outgrowth of the development of knowledge itself. In fact, when was the university ever unified, or when were departments ever subordinate to it? The philosophical unity of earlier times, when the total body of knowledge represented an infinitesimal fraction of today's reservoir of information, was of the imposed, monolithic variety, restrictive rather than catalytic in the development of new knowledge. Administrative pressure for interdisciplinary programs merely to establish curricular unity or to imitate other institutions could deflect these catalytic trends. Indeed, administrative concern about structure and the unsettling diffusion of centralized authority may explain in part the preponderance of antidepartmental literature, since academicians write primarily within their own discipline rather than about institutional structure. One has only to examine the mortality of administratively instituted interdisciplinary survey courses to be convinced that structure must be subordinate to other considerations. And the price of institutional cohesiveness through increased central authority will be too high if the long-range effect is a reduction in the vitality of the department.

Advantages of Departments

Although they appear much less frequently in the literature of higher education than departmental criticisms, cogent arguments exist favoring the department.

First, throughout the history of higher education, departments have provided the milieu most suitable for the development, preservation, and transmission of knowledge. Historical and contemporary evidence supports the concept of the department as a community of teachers and scholars responsible for instruction and research within a specialized field of knowledge, and thus as the basic administrative unit of the institution.

Second, the department possesses the advantage of familiarity, formal simplicity, and a clearly defined hierarchy of authority. It provides the locus of power to which instructors and students can most easily relate themselves.

Third, it provides a milieu in which faculty members can interact with a minimum of misunderstanding and superfluous effort; and it supplies the new faculty member with a means to acquire the professional understanding necessary to adjust to his institution.

Fourth, as a unified group, it can operate more effectively in the university organization than can individual faculty members, and it affords the scholar protection from those persons both within and outside the academic community who demand more intellectually from the academician than he should be prepared to deliver (Walker and Holmes, 1960).

Fifth, a scholar's achievement and promise cannot be appraised wisely except by his professional colleagues within the discipline (Caplow and McGee, 1958, p. 252), and the department provides an understandable and workable status system within which the faculty member may orient himself and be professionally evaluated. Although academicians traditionally have tended to be considered somewhat more eccentric in behavior than the general population, members of the department are usually willing to tolerate extraneous differences in personality and behavior in making disciplinary judgments.

Although some of these conditions and functions can also be accomplished through centers, institutes, and other arrangements, it is highly unlikely that nondisciplinary units will effectively replace the disciplinary department. Even Ikenberry and Friedman (1972, pp. 14, 83, 97), in their thorough analysis of institutes and centers, conclude that departments are here to stay. And although research sponsors, especially the federal government, feel that their money can often best be utilized by units other than departments, these other units are subject to the criticism of complicating still further an already complicated organizational structure and of being oriented more toward profit than learning. Indeed, despite the proliferation of institutes and centers during the past two decades, academic departments have, if anything, enlarged their power base. Waltzer (1975, p. 20) sees them properly, not as the bottom administrative rung on the ladder of delegated responsibilities but instead as the setting for the primary business of the university.

Improving Departmental Operations

New departments, and the increased delegation of administrative authority to them, portend greater decentralization of responsibility. Although this trend may be slowed by restrictions in funds and reduced growth, it can provide a quantum jump in university services. That outcome will depend largely on the formation of a workable partnership among departmental faculties, administrators, and students in identifying and striving for the realization of common values within a basically decentralized system. This partnership would be assisted by all three components' considering themselves a single community of students in the sense that they are all learners—susceptible to new knowledge and different ways of doing things.

Additional steps can be taken to improve the functioning of all departments, of whatever kind. The heart of the operation is the office of the chairman or chairperson. David Fellman, past president of the AAUP, pleads for much more attention to the importance of this position (1967, p. 5): "His is an extremely difficult job, requiring diplomatic tact, unremitting industry, close attention to detail, a regard for the feelings and needs of his colleagues, and a mastery of the complicated procedures through which complex institutions function." And Waltzer (1975, p. 4) speaks with some authority in calling for better preparation of chairmen, proposing such aids as training sessions, a chairman's handbook, overlapping periods of office for outgoing and incoming chairmen, and greater recognition of subchairmanships.

We must also recognize that the chairman's basic loyalty is of necessity to his department and discipline. Attempts to dislodge him from this commitment, in the hope that he will be more concerned about the institution, result in weakness and confusion, as do efforts at some institutions to bypass chairmen by drawing the membership of high-level policy committees from others within the departments or "using" them in a consultative manner under the guise of participatory management. If the chairman is to act like an administrator—and certainly administrative action is inescapable—then he should be treated like a first-class administrator: he should have adequate supporting services, information, and equipment; a reduced teaching load; and possibly a reduction in his oppressive committee assignments. Many large departments desperately need a full-time administrative assistant or executive secretary, perhaps one with a business management background, to save the chairman for teaching, research, and major academic decisions.

The chairman should participate with the dean in the formulation of policy. Once the budget has been approved, he should be responsible for administering it, including adjusting salaries in keeping with market conditions within the discipline. Just as salary diversity exists among colleges within the university, similar flexibility might well be needed within and among departments.

Beyond supporting the chairmanship, we should respect the department as virtually the last remnant of the community of scholars in an organization so complex as to necessitate many bureaucratic practices. In attempting to establish the proper tension between responsibility and autonomy, perhaps we should err on the side of autonomy. Allowance for departmental differences may well complicate the life of the harassed provost or president who strives for an orderly world; it may fracture the image of an army of educators marching together with singleness of purpose; and it may confuse science- and business-oriented trustees who think in terms of tight ships, exact measurements, and production units. But I hope we will heed Whitehead's caveat: "The modern university system in the great democratic countries will only be successful if the ultimate authorities exercise singular restraint" (1929, pp. 99–100).

2 Martin Trow

Departments As Contexts for Teaching and Learning

The academic department is the central building block—the molecule—of the American university. Indeed, it is not far wrong to think of the university as a kind of administrative arrangement for supporting and coordinating the activities of fifty to one hundred relatively autonomous departments. That conception has never been wholly true and is perhaps less so today than it was ten or twenty years ago: under the impact of zero or slow growth rates and tighter budgets, more authority is being drawn toward the central administration as it in turn is held more closely responsible to the public and private authorities that provide its basic support. Nevertheless, to view the university as a loosely coordinated aggregate of semiautonomous departments is a better way of understanding that peculiar institution, far closer to the realities of academic life, than the bureaucratic, hierarchical, quasi-industrial models accepted by so many politicians and workers in state and federal government.

An earlier version of this chapter was prepared for The Educational Research Symposium on Strategies for Research and Development in Higher Education, Göteborg, Sweden, 7–12 September 1975.

In discussing the academic department as a context for teaching and learning, I will for the most part be describing the department in the basic arts, letters, and science disciplines in large research universities, both public and private. The department has somewhat different characteristics in professional schools and four-year colleges, though the university academic department is a powerful model for both.

The academic department is the central link between the university and the discipline, that is to say, between an organized body of learning—a body of knowledge and characteristic ways of extending knowledge—and the institution in which teaching and learning occur. It thus links an international fraternity of scholars who carry on a tradition of work in a defined area of inquiry to an institution that supports and houses the people who are actually engaged in transmitting and extending knowledge. In the United States, not all basic scientific and scholarly work is carried on in universities: research in a number of subjects is undertaken by a variety of public and private agencies—among them, the American Museum of Natural History, The Library of Congress, the RAND Corporation, The National Bureau of Standards, and Bell Telephone Laboratories. But the disciplines from which they draw and to which they contribute are firmly rooted in universities and in their academic departments, and the map of learning would not be significantly different if they did not exist.

Emergence of Departments

Departments as we know them are a relatively late development in American academic life. Although there were units referred to as departments in some American "universities" before the nineteenth century (as Andersen noted in Chapter One), the academic department arose with the emergence of graduate education and the research-oriented university in the last three decades of the nineteenth century. Indeed the link between the department and the university in America is very close. As one observer has said, "During the nineteenth century, departmentalism was indeed a product of the same general movement toward academic reform that produced the university itself" (Storr, 1966, p. 94).

The forces that gave rise to the academic department are in large part the same as those which sustain it today, in the face of great changes in the size and scope of higher education over the past seventy-five years and also despite continuous and steadily growing criticism from academic theorists and reformers. The purely historical factor was the influence of the German university to which Americans had been going for advanced studies since the early decades of the nineteenth century. By 1914, some ten thousand Americans had studied for varying periods at German universities, and many on their return brought with them the ideas and ideals of the research-oriented university. But what they helped create was a research-oriented American university and not a copy of the German model.

Whereas in Germany the discipline was represented by the chair-holding professor and his Institute, in the United States a more democratic ethos, a wider variety of functions, and the growing size of the institutions led rather quickly to the appointment of more than one professor in the same field in the same university and to a set of salaried academic ranks that together composed the regular academic career. In this system, a full professorship became the normal expectation of every academic man or woman. Although not every instructor actually achieved this goal, it was a sign of relative failure not to do so, rather than, as in England or on the Continent, a mark of singular success to gain that rank before retirement. For this and other cultural reasons the American "professor" has never commanded the towering status of his European counterpart, either in the society at large or in the university itself. This difference has been a matter of considerable significance in the development of the department as well as in the professor's relations with his colleagues and his students.

Thus, what shaped the American academic department was largely the development of knowledge and the formation of a new university structure in this country. In the last half of the nineteenth century, the growth of knowledge broke the boundaries of the old classical curriculum and led to a specialization in scholarship that disrupted the intellectual unity reflected in the broad "schools" (corresponding roughly to the "faculties" of European universities) of the first half of the century. And as specialized knowledge grew, and disciplines emerged, so did a new research spirit, the belief in systematic and cumulative studies as the central method for extending knowledge.

The emergence of specialized disciplines coincided with the growth in size of American universities; the two together changed the role of the university president: he could no longer define the curriculum in detail and hire all the staff. The department, then, was as much an organizational as an intellectual necessity, an efficient unit for making decisions about the curriculum, student careers, and the appointments and promotion of staff, decisions that could no longer be made effectively or credibly by the president.

Today, as in its origins, the department is an arm of a specialized discipline in a university, as well as the administrative unit that legitimately applies the resources it receives from the university to performing its assigned tasks, principally teaching and research.

Functions of the Department

Graduate education. The department in most American universities has almost complete autonomy over graduate education in its discipline. The university may set limits, after discussion and negotiation, on the numbers of graduate students admitted and may also require that examining committees for the "orals," or qualifying examinations, and the committees supervising the doctoral theses include members of neighboring departments. But on the whole, the department determines the graduate curriculum and recruits and admits students. It then inducts them into the discipline, transmitting skills and knowledge and shaping and creating values and attitudes regarding what knowledge is and how best to pursue it. This component of graduate education, the socialization of graduate students into a structure of values, attitudes, and ways of thinking and feeling, is perhaps the most important single function that departments perform. The effects on students are often very strong, providing an individual with the perspective and orientations that guide a lifetime of academic teaching and research.

Departments also screen and assess students, first when they enter and then periodically throughout their careers, through grading their course work, by requiring them to take various "qualifying" examinations, and, finally and most importantly, through assessing the doctoral dissertation. Some students withdraw during the first year of their graduate work; others leave after gaining the master's degree, which is often awarded as a consolation prize for those unable for whatever reason to continue on to the doctorate. The M.A. may qualify students for teaching in secondary schools or two-year colleges; in the sciences and social sciences, it may also equip students for applied research work outside the university. But in most university academic departments, the object of the graduate training is the doctoral degree. (Professional schools other than law or medicine place greater weight on their master's degree, which is usually a more rigorous degree than that offered by the academic departments and is the basic academic qualification for practitioners in the field.) The time it takes for a student to gain a degree varies greatly both among fields and among individuals in the same department. But the chief work of the university department is preparing the new recruits, that is to say, the next generation of scholars and scientists, some of whom will be doing the research and scholarship that will advance knowledge in the field.

Although the basic forms and functions of graduate education are similar across a wide range of disciplines in the various universities, the actual processes of that education are enormously varied, among disciplines, among different departments in the same discipline, and even among subdisciplines and individual teachers and students in the same department. The training of a historian is different from that of an anthropologist or a chemist; and each type of training obviously involves the candidate in unique relations with the existing body of knowledge and with his fellow students and teachers. Some departments (often the large ones in public universities) maintain a competitive environment for students, admitting more than will gain the degree and accepting, even ensuring, high rates of attrition on the way to the doctorate. Other departments (usually smaller and in private universities) are more severely selective at entry and then "sponsor" students so that most who are admitted are brought along to eventually gain the doctorate. Though there are advantages and disadvantages to each of these departmental policies, they constitute very different "contexts for learning." Similarly, some professors who supervise doctoral theses give their students close and detailed supervision, helping them to avoid serious errors in the course of their work; others are more distant and permissive and allow students to make (and learn from) their errors, even at the cost of some of them failing to complete their dissertations.

This enormous variety in the actual processes of doctoral education is very little known or understood, even by academics themselves outside their own disciplines and especially by the administrators, politicians, and civil servants who make policies affecting academic life. These complex intellectual, social, and psychological processes of graduate teaching and learning are not well known both because they are highly variable and also because they are so esoteric. We each know something about our own relationships with our students, something less about how our colleagues relate to their students, much less about what goes on in neighboring disciplines, and little or nothing about practices in more distant fields about which we have no technical or professional expertise. If that is true for practicing academics, it is even more so for people further removed from the actual processes of graduate education.

Graduate education has two quite different components: helping students acquire "competence" in their subjects—the ability to engage in high-level teaching and applied research—and developing their capacity to do creative and original work on their own.

Originality and creativity are only partly a function of the student's own talents and quality of mind; they can be cultivated, but not through routine or standard procedures. These qualities seem to be elicited by both personal and working relationships with a creative and gifted teacher, who serves in part as a model. Because the crucial factor in stimulating students' creativity is their belief that they can in fact do significant and original work—that they can actually have ideas and not merely rearrange and apply the ideas of others—the encouragement and approval of a distinguished professor have great importance. Thus, the kind of education that engenders creative and original work is very closely linked to that

which encourages the student's own embryonic scholarship and research, often through an apprenticeship to his thesis advisor or some
other faculty member with whom he works closely.

The relatively few academics who make significant creative
contributions to their disciplines are the products of a dispropor-
tionately small number of leading graduate departments. This result
may derive from a number of factors that are very hard to disen-
tangle empirically: it may be that the "best" minds apply to and are
accepted by the leading departments; that those departments give
their students superior training and education in their disciplines;
that those departments are able to place their best students on the
teaching staffs of their own and other leading departments in their
disciplines, where the graduates have access to better students, more
stimulating colleagues, larger resources (libraries, laboratories,
lighter teaching loads); and that the prestige associated with gaining a degree from one leading department and then teaching in
another one gives an individual access to research opportunities
which in turn allow him/her to make important contributions to
the discipline. Part of this network of mutually reinforcing and favorable conditions is the heightened self-confidence that comes to the
student from associating with the leading figures in the field and
from gaining their approbation. Merely listing the conditions that
affect the emergence of creativity in academic scholars and scientists
suggests the complex interweaving of intellectual, emotional, and
institutional functions performed by graduate departments. They
select, train, and socialize students; they certify them to others and
confer status on them; and thus they affect their students' intellectual and academic life chances in a multitude of ways.

Unlike education for creativity, which is provided primarily
in a close relationship between a student and a teacher, the training
for competence in the discipline is more commonly the work of the
whole department or of a significant subdiscipline within it. Indeed,
defining what constitutes competence in the field, and how to train
for it, is one of the very few collective acts of the department. "Normally,"* the members of the department arrive at a rough consensus

---

*It is an empirical question how "normal" this is. How common is
it for a department's members to be in substantial agreement about the nature of the field and about the graduate curriculum (the two are surely closely

regarding competence in their discipline and then shape a graduate curriculum of courses and examinations designed to ensure that such competence is acquired and demonstrated. But as disciplines develop and change, and generate subdisciplines and new problems and links to other fields, even this concept of competence may not be shared consensually. Where dissensus among the departmental staff members on the nature of competence in the field is wide and deep, it may no longer be possible to create a common curriculum for the first year or two of graduate work, and different students may move through the same department gaining quite different skills and basic perceptions of the nature of the discipline. This situation, which seems to be increasingly common in recent years—more in the social than in the natural sciences, more in sociology than in economics, for example—creates a special problem both for the individual student and for the discipline. Among other things, it threatens the department's claim to a monopoly of expertise in the subject, a claim that is the ultimate basis of both its authority and its right to call on the resources of the university and the society.

Recruitment and Promotion of Academic Staff Members. The department is the locus of the academic career. In the leading universities it is the department that initiates the appointment of new members to the staff and then recommends them for promotion to higher rank. The department may have to gain the approval of its recommendations from academics in other departments and from academic administrators. But if an individual lacks the recommendation of his departmental colleagues, and especially of his senior colleagues, he will not be given the initial appointment or subsequent promotion. Nevertheless, the department does not play as decisive a role in the career of a scholar or scientist who has the doctorate as it does in the career of a graduate student, since appointments and promotions, at least in the best universities, in large part merely reflect and ratify the status that the scholar or scientist has achieved in the broader discipline through his or her published

---

linked)? What are the sources of dissensus and what are its consequences for the academic careers and scholarly contributions of graduate students? These are questions about which we need much more research. A further question calling for study is how departments arrive at such a consensus and how it is then institutionalized in the graduate curriculum.

work. Although teaching performance is, or at least is supposed to be, "taken into account" in recommending individuals for promotion, in fact the departments are judged within their disciplines largely on the national and international reputations of their members. The university, and those academic administrators who represent its broadest interests, are under cross-pressures: on the one hand, they have a responsibility to the undergraduates to maintain standards of teaching as well as of scholarship; on the other hand, they are sensitive to the reputation of the university in the broader academic community, and that standing in turn is largely determined by the aggregate status of its academic departments—that is, by the quality and quantity of their published research.

The university department seeks and rewards research productivity in its staff members and thereby strongly influences how academic men and women spend their time and energies, as well as how the department and the university are evaluated. But at the same time, it is educating and socializing its members, and especially its junior members, completing and reinforcing the socialization to the discipline that had begun in their graduate training or earlier. This function of developing appropriate habits of mind and work in what are now fully independent scholars and scientists (as they are, even as junior members) is only visible when it is performed badly, as it has been in recent years in some rather demoralized departments whose members no longer share a common sense of the nature of their discipline or of the scholar's craft and calling.

Research. Graduate university departments are commonly seen as existing largely to further the creation of knowledge through scholarship and research. And so, in a way, they do. But ironically, the department *qua* department is less significant for the furtherance of its members' research than it is as the center of graduate training and the academic career. The reason is that science and scholarship are so highly specialized that an individual is likely to have no more than one or two colleagues in his own department (and often none at all) who have any interest in or expert knowledge about his/her special area of research. The true research communities are the "invisible colleges"—the handful of people around the world working in some subdiscipline or line of inquiry. Moreover, the physical home of university research, and the source of its support within the institution (at least for natural and social scientists, though less so for humanistic scholars), is likely to be an interdisciplinary research center or institute. These institutes, unlike the "institute" in the traditional German university, are not the lengthened shadow of a single chair holder, but rather the administrative units that exist to further the work of a group of researchers, both senior and junior, drawn usually from a number of related academic departments. (Examples, though they will have different names in different universities, would be an institute for international studies, a center for the study of law and society, a center for research in higher education, a high-energy radiation laboratory, and an institute for the study of personality.) To become a full member of such an institute a person ordinarily must have full membership in an academic department, though these centers also usually have a full-time professional research staff, whose members may also play a role in the teaching and graduate programs of the academic departments. But the *department's* direct contribution to the research work of its members is, except in the humanities, likely to be less significant than the external support an individual can gain from government agencies or private foundations. And the research thus supported is administered and housed in the research institutes and centers, not in the departments. Nevertheless, the department is not insignificant in that it provides the scholar/scientist with a basic salary, time for research, and perhaps modest research funds allocated to the department by the university itself.

The increase of federal funds for research after World War II, and the way those funds were granted and administered, greatly strengthened the autonomy of the department vis à vis the university and of the individual scientist vis à vis his department. In addition, the rapid growth of enrollments in higher education, and the resulting sharp competition for able or even competent scholars and scientists, also greatly strengthened the individual professor in relation to his department. Although external research support has leveled off, it remains an important factor in the autonomy of departments and scientists, especially in the natural sciences. But the slowing of growth has sharply reduced the demand for academics and thus limited their bargaining power within their own institutions. This factor strengthens the hand both of the institution and the department in relation to the individual scholar or scientist. With few exceptions, he can no longer threaten so credibly to leave the institution if his demands for salary, teaching load, research support, and the like are not met.

Parenthetically, the reduced demand for academics also reduces the mobility of academics among institutions. Less mobility encourages the development of more stable relationships within departments, both among colleagues and between teachers and students. That result may, on the whole, be very good for the department as a context for learning.

Undergraduate Education. Up to this point, little has been said about the role of the department in teaching undergraduates. And this, of course, is the subject of its critics' major charge: that because of the department's emphasis on specialized research and the doctoral degree, it is not able to develop or usefully contribute to a nonspecialized liberal education. Liberal education, as some perceive it, aims to free students from the narrow prejudices and assumptions of region, class, and ethnic group by extending their understanding of the human condition and their range of sympathies through an exposure to literature, poetry, philosophy, mathematics, the sciences, and social sciences. Such an education is intended to refine sensibilities and strengthen the capacities for making independent and informed judgments in art, in science, and in life. But, so this argument goes, this kind of education requires that teachers seek and communicate the underlying connections among the various facets of life with which the separate disciplines deal. And a liberal education is not advanced, say its proponents, by undergraduate courses that are narrowly constrained within the boundaries of a discipline and that focus on a watered-down, elementary treatment of a discipline's own stock of certified and current research problems. It is perfectly clear that many problems do not present themselves in the convenient categories of the academic disciplines, that many of the most important questions about man and society transcend the disciplinary boundaries. The natural response to this fact is to argue against the department as the unit of organization of undergraduate education and to make attempts to organize interdisciplinary studies that are more appropriate, in their range of perspectives and intellectual resources, to the questions that students and society ask of them.

There is considerable substance to these charges. The university department may well not be the best unit for providing a liberal and unspecialized education. It recruits research-oriented specialists and rewards their specialized research. Much of the energy of its members goes into research and into their graduate program; a very large part of the actual instruction of undergraduates, especially in the big public universities, is carried on by graduate assistants who teach the small lab and lecture "sections." Insofar as the department has an interest in undergraduate education, much of that is devoted to its program of courses for the undergraduate majors who are specializing in the subject in their latter two undergraduate years. And since the number of undergraduate majors often has a bearing on the size of the department's budget, departments commonly have a stake in retaining their own majors. Thus, interdisciplinary programs may be seen by the department as competitors for students and for related resources.

At its very best, a carefully thought out program of interdisciplinary studies, involving senior professors possessing great breadth of learning across disciplinary lines, is arguably the best introduction to higher learning that able and motivated undergraduates can experience. Certainly the programs of general and interdisciplinary studies that were developed, in their several ways, at Harvard, Chicago, and Columbia after World War II were models of what undergraduate education in great research universities might be. But it is wrong and misleading to compare the rare best forms of interdisciplinary studies with the average course work offered by departments. And even those exemplary models at Harvard, Columbia, and Chicago no longer exist, at least in their early forms. Such broad programs, as contrasted with ad hoc "interdisciplinary" courses involving instructors from two or three neighboring departments, involve a measure of constraint on the students' freedom to study what they like, and students increasingly resist such constraints. This resistance has led to the dismantling of the far less coherent or integrated "breadth and depth" requirements, which were an effort by the university to expose students to a variety of subjects in the hope that they would find the links and connections among these subjects themselves. These requirements were thus a kind of half-way house between coherent interdisciplinary programs and the increasingly common system that prescribes little or no structure of studies in the first two years and a departmental major in the upper-division years.

Interdisciplinary programs require a great deal of consensus regarding what knowledge is of most worth, and such consensus is increasingly hard—in most cases, I believe, quite impossible—for a university academic staff to achieve. It is difficult enough to reach agreement on an undergraduate curriculum *within* a department, almost impossible across departments. In addition, such a program makes very large demands on the time and energies of its staff members, time and energy necessarily taken from their own research, their work with graduate students, and their more advanced undergraduate majors. Moreover, the academic reward system is still keyed to a professor's published work; for a variety of reasons, it is difficult for a university to assess and reward "teaching ability," though it may generate much rhetoric on the subject. Perhaps most important, the qualities of mind and breadth of learning and perspective that make a really strong interdisciplinary program are very rare. Very few academics, even those who have achieved great distinction in their own field, have the intellectual qualities needed by first-rate interdisciplinary teachers. When courses and programs are created in the face of these difficulties, they are very often short-lived failures; a genuine integration of perspective and knowledge around a problem or issue is rarely achieved, and such courses often descend to a relatively uninformed discussion among teachers and students, none of whom has a solid mastery of the topic or its problems. As one scholar with experience has observed: "Interdisciplinary programs are devices for bringing creative people together and arranging for them to be less creative," at least in the short run. There is some truth in that gloomy observation.

Furthermore, we may pay a considerable price for interdisciplinary studies when we substitute a richer but less systematic discussion of issues for a narrower but more systematic one. By a "systematic discussion" I mean one that results from those impersonal pressures a discipline exerts on its members, pressures to formulate problems in ways that can be addressed by evidence. Disciplines control personal bias in several ways, not the least of which are the procedures that force a confrontation with negative evidence. Interdisciplinary studies may bring a rich variety of viewpoints to bear on an issue, but my impression is that when difficult problems arise, the tendency of such courses is to look at the matter from yet another standpoint rather than confront the difficulty head on. There is also at work the well-known but little documented phenomenon of "disciplinary courtesy": we are not inclined to challenge the professional judgment or competence of colleagues in other disciplines. We are disinclined both by the norm of professional courtesy and by our own lack of specialized expertise in other fields to go behind the assertions of other disciplines to the structure of concepts and data on which they are, sometimes precariously, based.

It is not widely enough recognized that academic disciplines, and the departments that embody them in universities, constitute a kind of moral community, centering on the powerful norms implicit in the canons of verification and in our scholarly and scientific methods and procedures. These standards are perhaps most clearly manifested in our commitment to the search for negative evidence. For Max Weber this search is the central moral function of education. In his great essay on "Science as a Vocation," he asserts that:

> The primary task of the useful teacher is to teach his students to recognize "inconvenient" facts—I mean facts that are inconvenient for their party opinions. And for every party opinion there are facts that are extremely inconvenient, for my own opinion no less than for others. I believe the teacher accomplishes more than a mere intellectual task if he compels his audience to accustom itself to the existence of such facts. I would be so immodest as even to apply the expression "moral achievement," though perhaps this may sound too grandiose for something that should go without saying [1946, p. 147].

The academic disciplines embody, in their methods of work, procedures designed to force their practitioners to confront inconvenient facts. Indeed, it may be said that only the disciplines care whether an assertion is empirically or logically true and are concerned with the evidence on which it is based. Other approaches to issues, outside the constraints of a discipline, are more concerned whether a statement is plausible or interesting or morally or politically virtuous (for example, "progressive"). One might argue that universities, perhaps alone among social institutions, should ground their central functions of teaching and learning in the issues of truth, falsity, and the quality of evidence. (Of course, the nature of "truth" and its relation to evidence differ in different disciplines, but it is a central issue in each.) It is not an accident that we are most likely to see academic work highly politicized in those courses furthest removed from the restraints of the academic disciplines. And indeed, those persons who wish to politicize higher education are very often those most hostile to the autonomous norms and values of the academic disciplines, and for good reason.

To what extent are students drawn into the "moral communities" of science and scholarship, to what extent do they acquire the norms and values of the disciplines as well as their knowledge and perspectives? As I pointed out earlier, these questions have traditionally been a central concern of graduate education. (If graduate students in the department are not, for some reason, being "socialized" into the moral community—if, for example, they pursue graduate studies as a continuation of their liberal education or use their graduate study for political or other ends of their own without accepting the special research norms of science and scholarship—then departments, and perhaps the disciplines, are in some difficulty.) But the acquisition of these scholarly and scientific norms, the values of the discipline as a research enterprise, has not been stressed for undergraduates. In fact, it has often been seen as a symptom of premature professionalization or specialization. Now, however, colleges and universities are beginning to offer research seminars to introduce beginning students to the discipline as a community of seekers for knowledge. And those kinds of efforts must, inevitably, bring them at least to the borders of the discipline as a moral community. How successfully that aim is accomplished with undergraduates is a variable and uncertain matter.

We should also ask whether early introduction to the norms and values of research in a discipline need be at the expense of a "liberal education," a broad exposure to a variety of ways of looking at the worlds of man and nature, each way with its own, somewhat different, moral lessons to teach. In designing an undergraduate education, one encounters certain conflicts between the moral community of inquiry and the moral content of the major fields of learning—between, for example, what anthropology can teach about the human condition as opposed to how it goes about finding things out. Departments typically try to teach a little of both, the latter often under the rubric "methods." But while "methods" courses may tell students that there is a moral community of inquiry, it is likely that only the experience of seeking knowledge themselves through the discipline's own methods of inquiry will effectively bring students inside it.

All of the foregoing comments are not intended as a general attack on interdisciplinary studies, of which I am a warm if somewhat qualified admirer. I want only to suggest that the price we pay for their breadth of perspective may lie in the moral education of our students, at least that part of their moral education that arises from a sense of the importance of intellectual difficulties and from a personal commitment to confront these perplexities rather than evade them by dropping the question and shifting the focus to another part of the intellectual forest. The policy implication may be that interdisciplinary studies are not inherently preferable to a program of coordinated studies within departments, but need to be examined in every case on their own merits. In addition, we might pay more attention to the methodology of interdisciplinary courses and try to find ways of requiring ourselves to confront unwarranted assumptions and inadequate theories as well as to ask at strategic moments for the evidence behind assertions in other people's disciplines.

On "Change" Versus Change

It may be useful to distinguish two quite different kinds of interdisciplinary studies: those that are introduced purposefully as an academic "reform," and those that arise naturally out of intrinsic developments in the map of knowledge. The former reflect an ideological commitment to educational change for its own sake; they are often in part a response to vague but powerful pressures from the state or society that the university adapt itself to the new conditions

of society, that it be "more relevant" to social problems and to the
interests of a new mass student body. Such reforms are ordinarily
well publicized, in keeping with their public relations function of
persuading outsiders that the university really is "progressive" and
"responsive to social change." By contrast, the changes that arise out
of the inner life of a discipline ordinarily go unnoticed outside its
boundaries; they are not even perceived as change or reform in
higher education. Although the university is widely attacked as conservative, resistant to change, deeply committed to traditional forms
and practices, we have seen an enormous explosion of knowledge in
all areas of scholarly and scientific life over the past several decades.
In every area and subject I know, there have been enormous
changes in the map of knowledge since World War II, changes that
have often been accompanied by equally large changes in the forms
and contents of instruction. At the same time, new disciplines and
subdisciplines such as computer science and psycholinguistics, have
emerged and sometimes pressed for institutionalization as new academic departments. Here, in the private life of higher education,
there is constant ferment and change but little publicity (Trow,
1975a). It is the widely heralded, often short-lived academic "innovations"—instructional programs keyed to measures of "com-
petency" or to "contracts" between students and teachers; the abolition of grading; academic credit for "community participation";
courses offered through videotape or remote computer consoles, and
colleges oriented around "relevant" topics—that catch the eye of the
public and politicians and become the basis of the university's claim
that it is not as conservative as charged.

    As we observe the fashionable pursuit of educational inno-
vations, innovations that are frequently accompanied by attacks on
the "narrow, ossified, specialized disciplines," we might reflect on
the extent to which the disciplines, by providing us with external
criteria and the machinery for forcing us to confront negative evidence, serve the moral growth of students and teachers as much as
they do the growth of knowledge. We all are, for the most part, inclined to indulge our own pieties. We need the help both of critical
colleagues who are competent in our fields and of impersonal rules
of inquiry to prevent us from acquiring followers rather than teach-

ing students. Whatever their shortcomings, most discipline-based departments supply both; some other ways of organizing instruction do not. That fact, and not necessarily blind stubbornness, may at least partly account for the survival of the academic department under conditions of rapid change and in the face of widespread criticism.

Departments and Academic Research and Development

Departments, as we know, are often not hospitable to academic innovations generated outside their boundaries. They often take a jaundiced view of "institutional research," of educational "experimentation," and "reform." There are a number of reasons for this suspicion and even hostility on the part of academics toward academic R & D.

Disciplines, and the departments that represent them in the university, claim to possess a monopoly of expertise in a given area of scholarship or science. Research by outsiders on academic programs and on pedagogy in higher education, that is to say, on the forms and content of instruction, is seen as a challenge to this expertise, a claim that others can know how knowledge in "their" field should be pursued and transmitted. This threat is not a trivial matter. The claim to expertise is the basis of the department's authority over everything that is important to it: the direction of its research; its selection, training, and certification of graduate students; its appointment and promotion of its own members. Indeed, the autonomy of the university is based to a very large extent on the aggregate claims to special expertise on the part of its departments.

This suspicion of outside intervention might seem to be merely a defense by the department of its power over its own affairs. In reality departmental power ultimately rests on successful claims to a special authority in its area of work. Where that claim is weakened—either by the weakness of the department, by changes in the map of learning, or by attacks on the legitimacy of academic authority based on political or social grounds—the department (and, by extension, the weak institution) is less able to resist "academic innovations." Thus, I am suggesting that "innovations" in the organization and forms of instruction are linked to successful attacks on academic authority. Political change and academic reform are indeed closely tied, as both political and academic reformers know.

Undergraduate teaching is more often the target of academic reform than is graduate education or the organization of research. One reason is that the department's claim to expertise in undergraduate education is not as clear as it is in graduate education and research. In addition, undergraduate teaching is often a prey to boredom, the result of the repetition of relatively elementary facts or principles by teachers whose interests lie elsewhere. Academic innovations, almost regardless of their character, promise to break the crust of boredom and routine and allow the teacher to gain a fresh perspective on familiar materials and modes of presentation.

Graduate education and research are not inherently afflicted by boredom since they are linked to the incessant changes in knowledge arising out of scholarship and research. They thus do not need curricular "innovations" as an act of will, but can allow them to arise from changes in the subject itself.

Academics may also resist academic "reforms" to preserve an environment favorable to the pursuit of knowledge. Intellectual boldness and creativity require, I believe, a relatively stable and orderly institutional environment. The enormous efforts devoted to creating new forms of academic governance in French, German, and Dutch universities, for example, drain off the time and energies of teachers and students as well as destroying the delicate personal relationships that excellent teaching and research require. It is a hypothesis worth testing that research, scholarship, and teaching of the highest quality are likely to be carried on in a stable environment or at least in one insulated from the noise and turmoil of university politics and academic reform.

There is, of course, one important class of "innovations" that can only arise outside the department: that is, the new forms and structures through which access to higher education can be extended to groups who cannot already gain entrance easily. I am thinking especially of the institutions of continuing education and, where they do not exist, of such open-access institutions as community colleges or their equivalent. These *structural* reforms clearly require authority over whole systems of higher education and are part of the responsibility for broad educational and social policy that departments do not have. But these structural reforms—as much political as educational in origin and character—are quite different from reforms in the content of learning within existing institutions, which ought to be made primarily on educational and not political grounds, and thus in most cases are better left to the people who know most about them, who must ultimately put them into effect and live with their consequences.

Academic Division of Labor

My emphasis on the dominant norms and functions of university academic departments simplifies and distorts reality by implying that all the members of a department are oriented primarily to graduate teaching and to research and are performing their departmental functions in similar ways. In fact, there is a very considerable division of academic labor, both within and among departments. But this arises *informally,* and not through a formal assignment of roles and functions to different department members. Thus, the formal characteristics (and the equality) of departments and their members are preserved, while a considerable variability in individual talent, preference, and disposition allows people to actually distribute their time and energy very differently among the various functions of the department: graduate and undergraduate teaching, research, university administration, consulting, and "public service" (Trow and Fulton, 1975).

In every department some members are much more deeply interested and involved in the undergraduate program than the average member. Such people must have done enough research to have gained a tenured appointment in the university (if untenured, they risk not gaining such an appointment), and they may continue to write and publish. But informally they come to be seen as especially interested in the undergraduates and over time come to play a disproportionate role in that part of the department's work. Some of these more "teaching-oriented" academics are senior professors (especially in the natural sciences) who are no longer working at the research frontier of their disciplines; others, younger men and women, may be temperamentally drawn to the undergraduates and may accept the somewhat slower rates of promotion that accompany a lower level of research productivity. Moreover, some departments in the university—for example, English and mathematics—commit more of their time to undergraduate education than do others and therefore place a somewhat higher value on teaching-oriented professors. It should, however, be emphasized that the division of labor within departments is not absolute, sharp, or formalized: almost no academics in American university departments do nothing but teach or nothing but research. Similarly, no sharp division of labor exists between departments in the university. This overlapping prevents the emergence of formal "classes" of academics and avoids the dangers of a two-class system of teaching and research professors.

Incidentally, the diversity within departments poses a further problem for offices of academic research and development, which are often unable to recognize or to cope with this informal division of labor, preferring a formal allocation of functions to the actual processes by which departments and universities get their work done.

The academic division of labor, both among individuals and departments and, in the larger view, among different kinds of institutions, is absolutely crucial in American higher education: for example, it is central to the diversity of the system in the society as a whole. But within the university, it allows the academic department, despite its powerful orientation to research and graduate education, to actually perform a wider range of functions than would be possible if its members were more homogeneous in orientation and personal preference.

Conclusion

We can see what makes departments strong by seeing where they are weak: in small institutions, where their administrative functions are slight; in four-year colleges, where they do not organize graduate education; in academically weaker institutions, where appointments are made on grounds other than scholarly or scientific competence. But despite the dismantling efforts of some innovative universities committed to collegiate structures and interdisciplinary studies, it is extremely difficult if not impossible to keep the departments weak in universities that are big, that offer graduate work, or that place high value on the scholarly and scientific distinction of their staff.

Departments have been given a bad name; they have been the object of more abuse than analysis. Yet they have strong roots, not in the alleged conservatism of academics, but in the functions that they perform more effectively than any other academic structures. It is ironic that just when academic reformers in America were attacking departments, European universities were attempting, with variable success, to modify their old "faculty" structures in the direction of the discipline-based American departments. There are some things departments cannot do, or cannot do well; and many universities have created a variety of alternative structures to organize interdisciplinary studies and research. But the academic department remains the central organizational unit of American universities and of many colleges, and it must be given much of the credit for the extraordinary success of American higher education over the past century in extending both educational opportunities and the frontiers of knowledge.

3 Louis T. Benezet

Uses and Abuses
of Departments

Academic departments lead a double life in the minds of presidents, students, and some of their own members. For the administrator, they are an essential educational working unit with built-in centrifugal tendencies that need to be countered. For the student, they seem to tie learning together at one time and to tear it into bits at another. For untenured professors, they offer at once a ladder to a safe berth on board and a shaky perch from which one's career can be pitched into the sea—not always by natural forces.

This mixed bag of metaphors is appropriate because departments serve different roles at different times for different constituencies in different types of institutions, making generalizations about them difficult. Overall, however, the basic use of the academic department is that it permits us to order the investigation and presentation of knowledge in centers of learning. The basic abuse of the department is that we permit it to reorder knowledge into enclaves of personal privilege. This latter result might be better tolerated under the American ethic of free enterprise if energies thus turned resulted in the production of more knowledge useful to more of society. Some great departments have done this, such as the Chicago school of philosophers led by Dewey, Mead, Angell and Moore at

34

the turn of the century (Rucker, 1969). But more often in recent decades strong departments have turned into guilds whose immediate effects have included restraint of intellectual trade. For better or worse, the academic department has inherited the tasks both of preserving the privileges of scholarship and of fulfilling public obligations for which the ancient university was not conceived.

The strong, self-serving department that opposes the university's desires to advance broader aims reenacts a contest that dates to the founding of universities in the late Middle Ages. Then, as E. D. Duryea (1973) reminds us, both popes and kings entered into the creation by charter of universities as free corporations empowered to operate under rules and regulations of their own making. The corporate university invaded the guild that was represented in universities by independent associations of scholars who assembled in the *studium generale*. The university gave scholars a certain protection from local interference; still, it imposed restraints of its own.

The contest continues eight hundred years later; and the parochial interests of scholars may no more need to be checked than the aggrandizement of a modern university corporation. But what is different, after nearly a millenium, is the modern demand for scholarly efforts to serve the public interest in a variety of ways and on a scale previously undreamed of. Scholarship of necessity turns more and more to public sources for its base of support, and the price in public service must be negotiated somewhere in between scholar and taxpayer. Further complicating the scene are thousands of new-generation students whose interests are not those of the prospective professional scholar. It has become the duty of the university to meet their interests somehow within a structure still flying the pennants and tassels of medieval academia.

The College Department

During the past century the United States has lived with a double image in higher education: the conflicting models of undergraduate college and comprehensive university. Andersen and Trow, in Chapters One and Two, draw upon conventional belief (see also Corson, 1975, p. 250) in viewing the academic department as the building block in each type of organization. Yet building blocks

differ between the college and the university; the department of the
undergraduate liberal arts college is both structurally and function-
ally distinct from the structure and function of a department in a
large university offering doctoral and professional programs. The
distinctions are less apparent in catalog descriptions than in the ways
college department and university department members, respec-
tively, reflect their priorities in professional life.

The college department still shows elements of its ancestry
in early American higher education. To an extent that varies among
institutions, it reflects values dating back to the small nineteenth
century campus with its religious overtones. Most colleges before
1880 operated with a handful of professors, typically ordained min-
isters, all of whom might teach rhetoric or composition in addition
to such specialties as had been developed by then. Besides his other
duties, the president usually taught one to five subjects; coming as
he did from a similar background of seminary training, the president
often filled in for the class when a colleague was absent or ill. The
resulting climate was one of close academic exchange and a certain
restrained congeniality, not only with each other but with members
of their small student bodies.

Despite decades of growth as well as secularization in the
undergraduate college, the traces of its small-community history
remain in its stated purposes and in some of its practices. The primary emphasis, at least by precept, remains undergraduate teaching,
with a stress on individual attention to students. The smallness of
most college departments makes it easier for faculty to communicate
across the lines of disciplines. It is still not considered *infra dig* for
one professor on a college campus to talk with another professor
about the progress, problems, and prospects of liberal education.
Although opportunities are missed on too many campuses now
growing large and specialized, the tradition of talking together is an
advantage-in-being that college faculty members have over university faculties. Seen at its best, that tradition of conversation has enabled a few American colleges to provide national leadership in the
development of creative programs of undergraduate teaching. The
key to progress is the presence of enough faculty initiative to start
the conversations from within. Administrative prodding is usually
unproductive among college departments; on a university campus
it is rarely even contemplated.

The kinds of faculty conversation regarding their profession may be grouped under three interrelated topics. The first and most basic topic is common interests. Collegial talk occurs routinely among human beings who happen to be sharing approximately the same mission at the same place and time. This fundamental type of conversation is what T. R. McConnell referred to when he wrote rather glumly: "In most of our large institutions there are few evidences of an academic community; perhaps collegiality survives in the departments" (1971, p. 98). A dean or president may have little or no access to faculty conversation of this kind, at least past the point of whimsical sparring in the faculty club luncheon line.

The second subject of conversation is the improvement of teaching, a taboo topic on almost any faculty turf except the safe inner court of a departmental gathering (see, for example, Richard Meeth's "On the Dangers of Teaching Too Well," 1976). People have spent decades trying to elevate good teaching through trustee awards, all-campus conferences, and now, under the lash of retrenchment, faculty development programs. Notwithstanding all these efforts, the anatomy and physiology of teaching remain an X-rated subject for serious faculty discussion except insofar as senior department members will undertake it among their own kind. Curriculum change is traditionally the faculty's preserve. After they have moved to consider it, the college administration can aid the department, but not before, if outcomes are to be hoped for.

The third kind of department conversation concerns curriculum change. The subject itself is freely discussed in general faculty circles, but the viewpoint arrived at by each department tends to be that the other department ought to do the changing. Once again, a breakthrough typically cannot be made without intramural action. As Rodney Hartnett observed, "The likelihood of getting faculty involved in the improvement effort and generating strong interest in both the process and the outcomes is greater where they are more likely to share interests, values, perspectives and responsibilities. Thus, with the possible exception of extremely small institutions, efforts to examine and strengthen educational quality are probably optimally conducted at the department level" (1975, p. 61).

Conversation and action are particularly needed to achieve program change in the area where departmental defenses are strongest, interdisciplinary study. University departments that claim to be doing interdisciplinary work are more often talking about multidisciplinary research of a kind that has led to the growth of new superspecialties such as biomathematics or astrogeophysics. But real interdisciplinary study requires scholars cheerfully to profess ignorance about some subject matter that seems to defy classification under one or a combination of disciplines. The professor throws aside his fine-honed specialty tools and digs in with his students in order to ask questions and to learn with them. Arranging a course of that sort calls for academics who feel both personally and professionally secure. The untenured professor tackles it at his peril unless he happens to be in the rare department that itself feels secure enough to back unspecialized curiosity. Gratefully I remember a college music professor who offered to teach a general seminar in American creative arts after telling his colleagues, "I don't know much of anything about art." It helped, to be sure, that the professor was known as the foremost scholar of the early polyphonic music of Ugolino.

Beyond its function as a locus for various kinds of conversation, the college department is best used to support the creative teaching of individual students. That purpose surely does not rule out scholarly production, but such an aim gives the department a broader base than competitive university scholarship will typically allow. The abuses of college departments can come either from those who try to apply university objectives to them or from those who have fled scholarly competition and chosen the college campus chiefly for ego support. For every college department trying to grow beyond its teaching mission and become a research group, there are probably three or four that have grown content with things as they are, salaries excepted. The need to retain an emphasis on instruction is what makes decisions on the selection of chairmen and on the tenure of junior faculty members every bit as vital to the college as they are to the university. Since decisions made by college departments also involve a wider range of professional criteria than do those made by university departments, they require administrative judgment as subtle as it must be firm. The typically close personal ties in a college department do not make the chairman's task easier.

College departments may be governed tightly or loosely according to the size and sophistication of the institution. In those with pragmatic programs and a directive administrative tradition, the relation of department to dean and president may be quite linear. As in a business corporation, the chairman functions as an administrator in the line. His appointment and periodic evaluation may follow a procedural pattern with as much consultation sideways and downward as is consistent with the prevailing administrative style. Elwood Ehrle (1975) has described such a system in which department chairmen are appointed and evaluated according to uniform procedures and a published set of performance criteria. Departments led in that way know pretty much what to expect of their chairman, as he or she knows it of the top administrators. And up to a point the chairman knows what to expect of colleagues in the department. Where that point is depends on the level of collegiality that the chairman can maintain with the department members in an academic administration operated in line fashion. The loose style of department operation is found in colleges where for either of two reasons the degree of line accountability is low. One reason is that the college is small and communal enough so that in effect it is governed by the whole; the other reason is that the administration has delegated responsibilities to departments in the style of universities.

If the department has been given most of the reins by central administration, its own operation may likewise be loosely run or it may become a satrapy. The satrap chairman is a celebrated character in college literature. During times when colleges got along on their own without either great expectancy or great anxiety, departments that represented laws unto themselves were conventional features of the landscape. Now that survival needs are pulling college administrations up short, presidents are rediscovering a bit late that accountability once farmed out is hard to farm in again. One advantage of the college over the university is that its processes can be reversed if campus collegiality has been at all well preserved: more expressly, if administrators and faculty members are able to talk with each other about common aims for the institution.

The University Department

Turning to the department of the modern university, we find that it has become the main arena of controversy inside higher education. As was discussed earlier, it is the lineal descendent of the medieval scholars' guild; yet ecclesiastical and royal patrons today are few, and scholars increasingly must join the queues for public support. American scholarship enjoyed its greatest public acceptance from 1958 to 1967, after the National Defense Education Act reflected congressional fears that by teaching more mathematics, biochemistry, and, yes, foreign languages, the Soviets might beat us to the moon. In the decade after those years, universities still figured largely in federal support for research and training. In fiscal year 1974, for example, federal obligations to all colleges and universities totaled 4.462 billion dollars (National Science Foundation, 1975). But the aid programs themselves caused a build-up of the higher education establishment so vast and costly that in present days of inflation most institutions are undergoing unprecedented retrenchments in order to stay financially solvent. The result is that academic survival has become more competitive than ever. The focal unit in that battle for survival is the university department.

The strategic posture of the department has been underscored by many studies of the dynamics of campus power. Salancik and Pfeffer (1974) surveyed one Big Ten university to measure the ingredients of departmental strength. Among their findings: "Departmental power is found to be most highly correlated with the department's ability to obtain outside grants and contracts, with national prestige and the relative size of the graduate program following closely in importance. . . . the scarcer the resource [that is, the university-allocated resource] the more power is used to allocate it to the sub-unit [department]." The authors captioned their study, "The rich get richer." That hard-core fact is acknowledged by most university presidents, including those who have made efforts in opposite directions. Such realities led Cohen and March in *Leadership and Ambiguity* (1974, p. 102) to conclude, among other things, that a "strong research reputation in the faculty makes weak budget presidents. On the whole, that means that most of the better-known academic institutions will have 'weaker' presidents than the less-known institutions."

In their own defense, if indeed they feel need of it, university departments hold that their accomplishments are the university's stock in trade and the chief source of its support. Although legislatures relate more quickly to a strong department of surgery than to one in romance languages, any stellar department can help the university shine more brightly for some of its public. Presidents take their Roose-Andersen graduate ratings to state budget hearings. Knowing this, department chairmen can argue for funds and faculty positions either positively or negatively: that is, either by pointing to accomplishments or by warning of ruined prestige if the department loses any of its graduate fellowships or, worse yet, three key professors to another university. William Rainey Harper's plundering of almost half the faculty of Clark University early in the century set a pattern of interinstitutional conduct that has changed little. The principal change is that these maneuvers are now carried out by department heads with the connivance of deans, and a president may be confronted in any month by threats of a major defection from his staff if he does not come through with resource allocations to forestall it.

In the mid-seventies general austerity has led some governors and legislatures to call on state universities to curb Ph.D. production. In New York State a Regents Commission on Doctoral Education headed by President Fleming of the University of Michigan made the following its number-one recommendation: "The Regents should regard all the doctoral programs at both public and the private institutions as constituting together an interrelated system for doctoral education" and went on to urge "cooperation and coordination in doctoral education by the institutions within the State" (Regents Commission on Doctoral Education, 1973, p. 3). But everyone noted another Commission recommendation that "only programs of present or potential high quality and need should be offered," and the immediate response among departments within the twenty-eight doctorate-granting institutions of New York was to seek to increase their staff and resources unilaterally. Thus, the regents' effort exacerbated the very trends that their Commission had been charged to help reduce. University departments may be inclined to "coordinate and cooperate" when their own security is not threatened, but if their programs' survival is at stake, their single-minded motive is *sauve qui peut* and lifeboats for first-class passengers only.

The New York regents' experience with statewide doctoral reviews underscores a quantum difference between college and university departments as far as the dean or president is concerned. In the college, the power base is local. The administrator controls most of the reward structure and can include in it items reflecting the institution's welfare. Personal ties tend to be closer, tenure longer, and turnover less. In the university, departments which either are strong or which aim to grow stronger bargain from a national base. In good years for higher education the bargaining tends to be freer; both sides have time and options. When austerity and retrenchment arrive, as they have in the 1970s, the chairmen of strong departments have a bargaining edge on the administration. Universities in a defensive stance must work harder to preserve what academic assets they have, since stronger universities are ready to descend on the weaker ones and pick them clean.

In good times or bad, however, mobility always is available to professors of top reputation in publication and grantsmanship. As Dressel, Johnson, and Marcus (1970) have observed, the more advanced in research most universities become, the more their professors feel drawn to the discipline and away from the institution, even from the department (although some well-endowed small universities with top graduate reputations, such as Princeton, have retained collegiality and even community). When they are attracted by a more rewarding institution, the loser assumes that they will take with them research equipment, graduate assistants, and perhaps even tenured colleagues involved in whatever project grant may be under way. The university may feel lucky if it can salvage a hardware item no longer exclusively claimed by the departing scholar. While the decampment is going on, the president of the expropriating university may act blissfully unaware. If a sharp phone call comes from his counterpart at the campus about to lose the professor plus entourage, the expropriating president will voice surprise and regret in tones similar to those of the president whose athletic department has been caught offering illegal subsidies to high school seniors. Yet that analogy is not accepted in the university world. The mobility of professors, even whole departments, is an element of academic freedom. Unless it is carried off under unusually flagrant circumstances, institutional heads will live with the practice and work hard at mastering it themselves. State or regional coordination of increasingly scarce resources may in time phase out traditions of academic piracy, but that time is not yet. Meanwhile, the ability to bargain with administrators as a free agent is one mark of a university department's success.

In making decisions concerning academic tenure and promotion the university department has long since taken over the major role. The arrival of a no-growth condition has brought problems to tenure cases that departments had not bargained for. The buck is more readily passed upward now than it was in years of roomier decision making. Still, the department holds to its prime role in tenure review as a precondition of its strength. Caplow and McGee stated it in *The Academic Marketplace:* "The process by which a department replaces its members and maintains its immortality is as nearly central to an understanding of academic institutions as anything can be" (1958, p. 28).

What has changed in the nearly two decades since that was written is that tenure has become a matter of job security rather than recognition of merit. With generally younger faculties, with no-growth faculty projections, with retrenched faculty lines, and yet with graduate schools still pumping out Ph.D.s, the department confronts an unholy set of dilemmas. The strains have prompted numerous chairmen to trade in the prestige of office for life as a senior professor, still about the most untrammeled existence in the world of the professions. Chairmen who stick it out must face decisions on assistant professors that would never have occurred ten years earlier during the euphoric growth period. The young teacher in his sixth year at a competitive university now is judged by standards of scholarly recognition that thirty years ago might have been reserved for candidates for full professor. Collegiality fractures under such pressures; factions, charges, and grievances abound. Unanimous departmental judgment on any close case is rare. More often a split vote along with acerbic comments on both sides is forwarded to the dean. A decade ago Jencks and Riesman anticipated the current scenario: "Academicians are neither a tolerant nor an easy-going species; and their apparently congenital feelings of irritation and frustration require scapegoats. Administrators serve this purpose" (1968, p. 17).

The tenure battles land on the dean's desk and, increasingly, on the provost's or even the president's before they are done. The eventual decisions leave scars; the deepest scars appear in adminis-

trative-faculty relations. It is impossible for the academic fraternity
not to believe that somehow, somewhere, administrators must be
to blame for the times that have so hardened the edges of faculty
tenure decisions. In a decade when academic values seem at a low
ebb in the public mind the clamor over tenure troubles is not very
helpful. One departmental response may be to vacate its responsibilities for appraisal and cynically to hand up nothing but favorable
recommendations to an administration which then has the unlovely
task of making the discriminations the department should have
made. It takes an unusually stable chairman to extricate himself or
herself from such a deadfall. More often it hastens a resignation
from the chair.

The tightening lines of tenure have affected relationships
with another constituency thus far neglected in this discussion: students. As a general rule students seem to have had slight mention in
studies of the academic department, an omission that in itself may
tell us something. The protest years of the late 1960s made inroads
for students in university governance, including departments.
Recommendation 13 (out of 47) by the Keast Commission on Academic Tenure states, "The Commission recommends that institutional procedures for the assessment of teaching effectiveness include
an explicit and formal role for students. . . . If student evaluation
is to be useful, each institution must develop means to ensure that
student opinion of teaching effectiveness is in fact consistently given
serious weight in decisions about reappointment, the award of tenure, and subsequent personnel actions" (Commission . . . , 1973,
p. 38).

On many campuses students have not waited to be invited to
evaluate faculty teaching. Compendiums of ratings processed by
computer are published by student agencies and sold in the university bookstore (it is interesting to note how these data are filtering
into official departmental files on tenure candidates). Still, as decisions grow harder, the department leans more heavily on comparisons of published research; and as research looms larger in decision
making, teaching evaluations loom less. The current dynamics of
faculty appraisal thus are deemphasizing those qualities that most
students support. The faculty-student gap grows widest when the
quality of undergraduate teaching is given the least importance.

Department chairmen there are who honestly regret it; after all, no one could live from 1964 to 1970 and not take in some of the message. Yet when a department's competitive survival is threatened, they will say, and when no more faculty positions are to be funded by the administration, the department's recourse must be to retain the young scholars who will help win the only kind of reputation that keeps the university department alive. The students after a period of protest concede their inability to do anything about the basic academic realities. The rift such issues have widened cannot help but have a negative effect on campus morale.

Departmental Problems

This *Realprinizip* of academic status especially when budgets are shrinking makes the department in its own eyes incapable of correcting what is habitually called its worst abuse, the downgrading of undergraduate teaching. It was prophetic that on the cover of "The Muscatine Report" (*Education at Berkeley,* 1966) appeared the blurb, "the first major evaluation of higher education since the Harvard Report of 1945, *General Education in a Free Society.*" The Muscatine Report used the student crises of 1964 and 1965, as the Harvard Report had used a quiet, reflective campus during World War II, to recommit the university to liberal learning for the undergraduate as against the fragmenting of learning by overspecialization. Ten years after Harvard's Red Book appeared, the program of general education it had launched in the Yard was dead. Berkeley's 1965 Tussman Program, its first concrete effort in the spirit of the Muscatine Committee, lasted approximately half as long. Perhaps more attention should have been paid to the twenty-six page minority report by a staunch graduate professor at the end of *Education at Berkeley.* "After prolonged consideration of the criticisms that have been made of education at Berkeley," George C. Pimentel, professor of chemistry, averred (1968, pp. 195–196), "I remain convinced that the word 'reform' has no place in the deliberations. . . . Only with clear recognition that our students are presently offered magnificent and widely varied educational opportunities should we begin our investigation into ways to polish and identify them. . . . Only with full acknowledgment to the outstanding quality of the faculty and to their devotion to the University should we proceed to inquire into the optimum use of their creative talents." Perhaps more than Muscatine, Pimentel represented the Berkeley faculty's view of its role (p. 210):

> If a department aspires to recruit to its faculty the world's foremost authority on field theory, it may or may not be able to insist that he teach an introductory course in Physics for Non-scientists. It certainly will not be able to insist that he have a resonant lecturing voice and a captivating way with students. What it can expect is that when he is speaking about field theory, the lecture room will be well-filled and the attention will be intense no matter what the timbre of his voice. There is our clue to the optimum use of the faculty.

So long as they depend on department professionalism to advance university status, presidents and provosts are not in a position to greatly alter circumstances. The chairpersons remind them they cannot have it both ways. It is the undergraduate, especially the nonmajor, and the occasional broadly gauged graduate student who lose. The undergraduates are aware of their loss, as the past decade's protests showed, and occasionally in the present decade a campus battle over tenure for some challenging young teacher revives the fervor. But the issue appears too complex for outside public awareness. It is translated into a grumble over "professors who don't do enough teaching," which if it registers at all may lead to reductions in appropriations for faculty members, thus worsening teaching the more.

Robert Straus, himself a university department chairman, stated in *Science:* "Because I believe that the departmental power base of universities has been a major factor in resisting inevitable and continuing changes in the disciplinary boundaries of research and teaching, I predict that significant changes in the nature of departments are inevitable. Departments will either permit, or even seek, a realignment of their spheres of control over disciplinary activity or they will lose the power of control over basic academic decisions and rewards. . . . Society's current disenchantment with academics may make radical internal change seem vital to the maintenance of public support" (1973).

The correctness of such a prediction may depend on how accurately the dissatisfactions can be traced to a remediable cause. Social critics and policy scientists to date have not excelled in their abilities to analyze the dynamics of higher education. The vectors of force that make for a creative teaching and learning university are hard to grasp; they are also highly individualized among campuses. They do not promise yet to be readily responsive to systems management, whether it be via P.P.B.S., M.B.O., or the services of the National Center of Higher Education Management Systems in Colorado. NCHEMS has produced useful studies of how professors spend their working time, yet we still know little about the impact of individual differences on workload data (Yuker, 1974). And we have not begun to study how to equalize rewards for faculty productivity other than sponsored and published research.

Amitai Etzioni in *A Comparative Analysis of Complex Organizations* (1961) included universities among his R-(rank) structures as opposed to L-(line) structures (example, the Roman Catholic hierarchy) and T-(top) structures (example, Ford Motor Company under Henry Ford). For R-organizations the example given was "doctors in hospitals." Professors in a university department illustrate equally well the organization wherein the personal dynamics actually come neither from the top nor from down the line but from the members of the organization themselves. They are the ones who have what Etzioni terms charisma; with it, they practice their profession, drawing "from their special knowledge or skill and from their organizational rank." The head of the R-organization need not have charisma (except to charm money from people, perhaps); indeed the members may feel threatened if the top officer has it. There can be a department, to be sure, whose charismatic chairman has turned an R-organization into an L-organization. In that case, as a study by Oncken (1971) has demonstrated, the productivity of the department members tends to go down.

The leader of an effective department in a university or in a college should be the "first among equals" while allowing his equals to be the more visible ones. The tempting analogy is that of the cast of an opera; yet a prima donna is hardly a welcome model for an effective department head. The more it is studied, the more an academic department presents vexing leadership problems. It may seem odd that chairmanships so rarely carry extra compensation. Additional pay, however, makes the chairman more of an administrator and thereby more suspect to colleagues. The successful chairman typically carries on out of a professed grudging loyalty to the institution and more especially to the advancement of his discipline on the local campus. He makes plain to colleagues and dean that nothing would be more welcome than a return to full-time scholarship.

Maximum Use and Minimum Abuse

If the maximum use and minimum abuse of academic departments are to be achieved, the first route leads not to the department leadership but rather to the plenary faculty and to the public around the universities. This discussion has proceeded upon a given of our times: that faculties even in colleges have lost a sense of common purpose in their effort to keep up with specialized knowledge. No one can give a common purpose back to them; it is not, however, impossible to challenge a faculty to seek it for themselves. Outside their departmental settings professors readily will agree that their institution would be stronger for each and all concerned if it could make its public more clearly aware of what it is trying to achieve as a whole. Groups like the Muscatine Committee have shown repeatedly that professors are willing to discuss the problems and prospects of general education. But the prospects break down in the transition to process. When the members of the faculty, back in their departments again, take an objective look at the rewards for changing course and at those for pushing on with the pursuits they have been following, the latter wins every time.

Solutions that involve the elimination of departments based on the recognized disciplines have been effective on some smaller campuses where liberal education has been made communal and alive. However, for most of higher education the feeling of having one's feet in a known field of learning is somehow important, not only to faculty members but to students as well. The pea-green freshman feels better if he can introduce himself in the dorm as a "chem major" even before he has taken his first course. A similar sentiment buoys the mid-forties professor who finds his university department listed on the chemistry page of the latest A.C.E. *Rating of Graduate Programs.*

To persuade departments to place efforts such as nonmajor teaching and interdisciplinary seminars among their priorities will first require public understanding of why those efforts are important. They are important if American mass higher education is to be measured by quality as well as by numbers. To date, that kind of public communication has scarcely been discussed, let alone attempted. To the public mind, higher learning is still portrayed by images of a famous professor lecturing and a bespectacled student peering into a test tube. The picture of students and professor exchanging thoughts around a table is somehow vague, even unsettling. When we begin to make progress in communicating the broader requirements of higher learning in a democracy, we may hope for a greater public willingness to provide for universities the means to fulfill those broad requirements. It could help convince both the public and the academic departments if there were a better reporting of college teaching models around the country, together with more sensitive measures of their outcomes and their rewards.

If there is blame for self-serving departments, it might be shared by university administrators who have become too preoccupied with institutional stasis—currently no simple trick, to be sure—to spend time on the larger purposes of learning. That aim is part of the unwritten agenda in the Final Report of the Carnegie Commission on Higher Education (1973). Against the conclusions of Cohen and March that the presidency is negated by ambiguity and conflicting goals stand the findings of others (Gross and Grambsch, 1974) that academics and administrators share much the same goals for the university. It appears, moreover, that faculty members still believe presidents have power to do something. A few presidents in each era have managed to use power creatively for beneficial change. Change in education is not something at the end of a production order; it takes a faculty interested in the possible outcomes. Once the direction of the change is agreed on, knowledge must be arranged. Departments by disciplines over the years have supplied the elements of knowledge, some old, some new, out of which new programs come into being. The charge is not to break up the departments or optimistically to give them different names. It is to provide a setting in which departments have incentives to take on cooperatively the full range of our contemporary educational mission.

Coordinating Departments

One device used on complex campuses and occasionally among different continguous institutions offers the most hopeful example of such cooperation. It is variously known as the "coordinating department," the "all-university department," the "field committee," or the "interdepartmental committee." Environmental studies, urban studies, criminal justice, women's studies, and the various concentrations reflecting ethnic minorities in the United States are current illustrations of multidisciplinary and interdisciplinary programs originated by enterprising faculty members and, increasingly since 1965, student groups, programs that have led to the birth of new field departments and even to colleges with full faculties. Such coordinative units have a long tradition, however: field committees at the Claremont Colleges and School of Theology have been in existence for decades and now stretch over seven institutions, and the long-time Committees on Social Thought and on Human Development at the University of Chicago represent well-known efforts of professors to break free from the professional solipsism of restrictive university departments.

Minimally, the coordinating department aims at reducing the most glaring redundancies of course offerings within a university or among colleges of a geographic region. Maximally, such units can aim at multiplying resources in a field, thereby achieving new breadth and levels of strength in subject matter. The impetus to collaborate may come from some carrot like a large grant for combined research or conversely from a live threat of lost faculty positions. A provost may find it natural in these financially stringent times to enjoin colleagues from different ends of the campus to get together; and faculty members meeting together from different cell groups may find stimulation and collegiality to be useful ends in themselves.

Coordinating departments work best when all are beneath

one academic tent or at least one institution, and they are especially attractive when interfield or multifield developments are afoot. Even so, as with all recipes for academic omelets, the mixture of different departmental entities is never easy and sometimes next to impossible. For eight years, starting in the 1950s, the Ford Foundation funded interdisciplinary graduate seminars at Claremont Graduate School and cooperating regional colleges; but when the grant ran out, so did the seminars. Departments in the same or contiguous fields develop separately because that is the way modern scholarship works. Identities grow according to existing arrangements. Differences in intellectual approach to a field become important. If a merger is suggested, such as between mathematics and applied mathematics, psychology and educational psychology, or sociology and social work, the differences may become mountainous. Settling on a chairman for such a union, even if it be planned as temporary or experimental, can be extremely tricky and often contingent on a key departure or retirement.

A field committee comprising members of one discipline distributed among two or more contiguous colleges can seldom be ordered by an overall administrator, even if the colleges are part of the same administrative system. Professors themselves need to bring it about out of mutual interests, and sometimes such an effort has a serendipitous beginning. The most frequent incentive is a combining of colleagues in order to put on a scholarly seminar or institute. A joint graduate program if it is financially feasible and educationally appropriate will supply a more lasting binder. The question then of which among the professors of one discipline in several colleges will be asked to teach graduate courses for the consortium is one decision that is better postponed until the bonds have been well tied. In the Claremont Colleges, the Graduate School has provided such a bond for fifty years; but admission to the active graduate faculty (typically for one semester-course per year) is one of the touchiest issues.

In the interdisciplinary enterprise we see counterbalanced a spirit of enthusiasm for new subject matter and a pact of limited liability. Professors who are working on tenure or senior promotion have to be intrepid to spend significant time away from research in order to enter some teaching venture of wild surmise. I have known new programs that were doomed at the outset by the advice of chairmen in established departments to their junior colleagues not to risk their careers in such a foolhardy direction: for example, environmental studies at the State University at Albany. Beyond this, unless the administration is prepared to include interdisciplinary programs explicitly in the institutional reward structure, they will most often founder. A hopeful effort can sometimes be snuffed out in its infancy even by such a casual inquiry among the participants as, "Who's in charge here?" One way to bolster interdisciplinary work can come via the attractiveness of a new field to outside research sponsors who provide money for projects calling on the combined expertise of persons from established disciplines. Another Albany example, happier in this case, is the Department of Atmospheric Sciences and its accompanying Research Center, which in less than ten years became nationally known. They have brought together in fruitful collaboration physicists, chemists, meteorologists, ecologists and not infrequently economists and engineers.

Coordinating departments, in summary, offer in smaller dimension much the same prospects and the same limitations as the institutional consortia known as cluster colleges (see Gaff and Associates, 1970). At their weakest they may represent surface efforts toward intercollege diplomacy. At their best they can enrich both teaching and research while mitigating some of the symptoms of academic satrapies, small subkingdoms that duplicate resources or stunt new growth. Like the cluster colleges, they rarely develop actual savings in instructional dollars. What they can achieve, however, is better education for the same dollars.

4

Fred Harvey Harrington

Shortcomings of Conventional Departments

"Don't do it. Don't go into central administration. Stay in the department. That is where the important things are decided. That is where you can have the greatest influence and do the most good."

Such was the advice given to me when I was about to move into the academic vice-presidency at my university. The words came from a senior colleague, a wise professor who had devoted much of his own career to rebuilding what had been and what he had again made a distinguished department.

Why Departments Have Flourished

Though I chose another course, I concede that there is point to the advice. A great deal of the strength of American higher education comes from the strength of its academic departments. Through these units colleges and universities win or fail to win recognition for excellence. National assessments by scholars, rating groups like those of the American Council on Education, foundations, and government agencies are more apt to be by subject (that is, by department) than by institution. It is the same, really, with the informal judgments of undergraduate and graduate students, alumni, townspeople, and the interested public. College and university reputations rest on the reputations of their departments.

Further, the campus power structure is likely to be based in departments. Rarely are deans and presidents professional administrators. Normally they are scholars who learned how to handle situations when they were members of departments. Moving up, they tend to think of their institutions as clusters of departments and of academic goals as a sort of consensus of departmental positions. They can, of course, look to the total faculty, to the faculty senate, or to committees or individual professors for contrasting views. But here too the departmental voice is strong. Whether speaking for themselves or as committee or senate members or whatever, professors—most professors, most of the time—are inclined to reflect the attitudes and interests of their departments.

This situation is not surprising. The faculty member feels most at home in the department. There he or she builds a career, wins or tries to win promotion, develops lasting personal friendships (and animosities), obtains protection when it is needed. There most of the basic decisions are made about appointments and tenure. There the teaching and research strengths and weaknesses of individuals are weighed most carefully. There important curriculum questions are discussed and decided. For all these reasons, one survey showed, the most significant faculty participation in academic decision making is not in the senate, or in committees, or in the American Association of University Professors, but in the department (Dykes, 1965, pp. 29–30).

The literature on college and university governance supports the previous chapters of this book in emphasizing the power of departments. They are the "dominant agency," says Leon Epstein in *Governing The University* (1974, p. 126). They are the "major vehicle for faculty involvement," states John J. Corson in *The Governance of Colleges and Universities* (1960, p. 100). "The work for which the institution exists is carried out in principal part through the departments," he observes. Others say the same: "a potent force . . . in determining the stature of the university" (Dressel and Reichard, 1970, p. 387); "the major avenue through which faculty members in large universities influence decisions" (Ryan,

1972, p. 464); the sovereign power, "practically self-governing" (Duryea, 1973, p. 25); in "full control of appointments, promotions, degree requirements, new courses of study, and research arrangements" (Shils, 1970, p. 3); and, in combination with the course system, they form "the basic pattern of the American university" (Veysey, 1973, p. 33).

In short, as my colleague at Wisconsin suggested and as my associates in this volume agree, departments constitute the heart of most universities and many colleges. They are a key to some of the glories of American higher education—so much so that the American academic department is much admired by visitors from abroad.

Well, then, if departments are all that important in the post-secondary structure, why write about their shortcomings? Why not discuss their virtues?

For obvious reasons:

First, every successful institution needs to be reassessed regularly; and more can be learned by the examination of weaknesses than by cataloging past successes.

Second, departmental power has historically been bad as well as good. Associated with the glories of American higher education, the departmental structure has also been linked with its failures.

And third, beyond these long-standing problems, the department is less than totally successful in handling new problems of the present day.

Long-Standing Difficulties

Consider the long-term problems of departmentalism, several of which have been noted in more detail in earlier pages.

Useful in developing disciplines, departments have championed specialization at the expense of generalizations, broad learning, and interdisciplinary and multidisciplinary studies. They have been criticized since their beginnings in American higher education, mainly for what Dean Andrew F. West called "the break-up of knowledge into pieces" and for what Irving Babbitt put in stronger terms: the "maiming and mutilation of the mind that comes from over-absorption in one subject" (Veysey, 1965, p. 200). As the size of institutions increased, faculty members tended to live their lives inside their departments, to have less to do with members of other departments. And after helping to build institutions, by their insistence on autonomy departments have tended to pull these institutions apart, weakening the principle of college unity and the basic theory of the university. Strong departments have tended to build loyalty to the discipline rather than to the institution. Raises, promotions, and chances for better jobs have depended more on recognition in one's special field than on contributions to faculty committees or one's reputation as a teacher. Two examples impressed this point on me:

"My life is in the world of physics," one young professor told me. "I'm not much interested in campus questions. My future depends on what my colleagues around the nation think of me. If I don't like what's happening here, I'll move on to another university."

Again, when invited to speak at a first-rate southern liberal arts college, I asked the sponsors if they wanted me to talk about a problem in my discipline or a question of higher education policy. "Oh, the discipline," my host-to-be answered. "As for the rest of it, we'll leave that to the deans."

Student unrest at the end of the 1960s and faculty unemployment in the 1970s have changed such attitudes a little; but the department system still pulls professors toward concentration on their specialties and away from giving proper attention to the critical questions facing postsecondary education. In addition, although departments were launched to reorganize and improve teaching, they have contributed to the overemphasis on research in many prestige universities and to the teaching crisis in higher education. One can argue that the department system has often advanced the cause of good teaching, and on more than one occasion I have heard the question of teaching effectiveness discussed in university tenure and promotion cases more at the departmental level than in divisional committees; still, the dominance of departments has had adverse effects on the quality of teaching. By cutting knowledge into little pieces, the department system has made it difficult for students to get the broad view of learning. Departmental influence over degree requirements often has had more to do with protecting department enrollment than with educational theory. And as the home of the disciplines, departments have spearheaded the "publish or perish" movement to give research publication the top value rating on campuses. Teaching has not been the only casualty: public service is another. Educators are fond of saying that the tasks of higher education—especially in the public sector—are research, teaching, and public service. But most academic departments, with their links to disciplines, have been noticeably cool toward public service, problem solving, extension, adult education, and action programs. Though departments can be praised for their promotion of research, their praise would be greater if more of them had worked harder to see that teaching and public service retained as much respectability as research has acquired.

Moreover, departments were introduced to effect needed change—in particular, to replace tired clergymen with professional specialists—yet they have prevented further change. William Rainey Harper, after setting up many departments at Chicago, came to consider their division of knowledge as artificial and misleading yet as fixed as "sacred scriptures" (Veysey, 1965, p. 32); and R. M. Wenley compared them to one "Lilliputian grand-duchy" after another (p. 200). Now, they have become the major obstacle to change within American colleges and universities. Inside their own disciplines, departments may keep up with the forces of change; yet even here there is a tendency for them to fall under the control of a few ranking professors who have settled down and who are inclined to be conservative in their attitudes toward shifts in curriculum, the introduction of new subspecialties, and experimentation with new research methods. Young men who want to usher in the new day find it difficult to make headway. Until they have tenure, they may think it wise to avoid controversy. When they have jumped that hurdle, they may discover that it is not easy to overturn seasoned veterans with long experience in departmental politics. Early in their history, departments served to increase faculty power against administrators, governing boards, and forces beyond the campus. As Veysey says (1973, p. 33), they were an "ideal strategic device" by which "professors gained leverage of their own" and were able to erect "stout barricades against outside encroachment." Now that it is time to take other initiatives, departmentalism stands in the way.

But besides these weaknesses, which have already been noted

in this volume, another perennial one deserves recognition: that of the inability of most departments to revive themselves when they begin to deteriorate. When departments slip in quality, they tend to keep on slipping. Strong departments insist on making good appointments, but middling departments more commonly seek additions at their own mediocre level. They know that standout scholars will hesitate to join an inferior department, and their members feel more comfortable with weaker candidates. Deans and other departments can see the results of these selections, but under the department system they are reluctant to interfere. Given the right of departments to choose their own members, critics cannot easily insist that department members vote to add faculty members who are superior to those on hand. Steps may be taken without departmental consent in institutions in which administration retains a strong hand (in many community colleges, some state colleges and universities, and certain of the smaller private colleges); but elsewhere, as Jacques Barzun notes (1968, p. 7n), making an appointment without departmental approval "would blow a president sky-high." Only by careful use of the budget power—a reward and punishment device—can one overcome this insistence on remaining mediocre. Otherwise, a divisional, college, or all-faculty committee must be persuaded to declare the department bankrupt and in need of wholesale reorganization.

New Problems

The departmental system has been equally unsuccessful in dealing with such recent problems as size (the enrollment revolution), student unrest (the student revolution), and collective bargaining (the faculty revolution).

To handle the enrollment revolution, departments have increased in size from fewer than a dozen faculty members to more than thirty in many institutions. Some have handled this transition with reasonable efficiency, by subdividing most functions or even splitting off into new departments. Others, however, have suffered in the shift, and, confused by the complexity of the new age, members of many departments have surrendered their democratic privileges, turning authority over to managers or committees. Turn-of-the-century presidents, themselves a rather autocratic breed, built up their institutional strength by importing headliners as department heads and giving them appointing powers in their disciplines. Correctives to the heavy-handed headship—rotation in office, election of chairmen, increased participation of department members in policy making—were necessary, though they came very slowly in many institutions. Robert K. Murray (1964), who has developed a theory of departments, feels that they have now moved full cycle: from the dictatorial chairman of former years through the successful struggle for democratic participation to the present management by "almost nameless administrative assistants."*

Perhaps no one could have handled the student revolution of the 1960s. Departments bore much of the burden when classes and meetings were disrupted and the departments were charged with neglecting undergraduates and emphasizing research not relevant to the needs of the day. Adjustments were made—students were admitted to department councils, even to discussions of appointments and promotion. But in the process departments were split into younger and older members and in other ways; and student protests were handled, if that is the word, mainly outside department channels.

Departments have also been off center-stage in the matter of collective bargaining for faculty members. As with student problems, they have been painfully involved and divided; and again they have not provided the main proposals or the solutions. In fact, the main "department issue" in collective bargaining in the 1970s has threatened the cohesion of the department by posing two questions calculated to divide departments: Are chairmen administrative agents, chosen outside the department and responsible for enforcing rules on members of the department? Or are they full professorial colleagues, entitled to participation as such?

Having been both a head and a chairman at different times, I can appreciate the problem. (As head at the University of Ar-

---

* The old strong-chairman system is not without its defenders. "There were some great department chairmen in those days," Lawrence Kimpton observed, referring to the first decades of the century, "and, more important, there were some great departments." Later, he thought, departments suffered because of the introduction of "too much democratic razzle-dazzle" (Corson, 1960, p. 94).

kansas, I was appointed by President J. W. Fulbright and Dean Hemphill Hosford to "run the department"; as chairman at the University of Wisconsin, I was nominated—really elected—by my colleagues to represent them.) But whatever the structure, the head or chairman and the rest of the department belong together, as a unit. The National Labor Relations Board decision in the Long Island University collective bargaining case, ruling out the chairman's participation as a professor, tends to reduce departmental strength. (For more on the question of the chairman in collective bargaining, though not on precisely this point, see Carr and Van Eyck, 1973, pp. 100–112.)

Suggested Solutions

Granted that traditional departments have shortcomings, the next question is what to do about them. Should higher education get rid of departments altogether?

In their treatment of governance in their volume on *The Academic Revolution* (1969, p. 525), Jencks and Riesman refer (whether in jest or in earnest) to Thomas Jefferson's recommendation of a revolution every generation. Such a revolution might sweep away the traditional departments, but it would not necessarily provide a satisfactory alternative.

Some critics of the department system do have alternatives to propose. Faricy is one of these. "The department was invented, once," he writes (1974, p. 111); "perhaps it is now time to reconsider, and to ease it toward a resting place with Ptolemy's epicycles and alchemists' humors." To replace it, he suggests groupings by topic (health sciences or the standard divisions), or by function (the service people who help all disciplines to be together, such as those who teach beginning statistics), or by source of funding (say, those with off-campus financing).

It is easy to see that Faricy's new groupings would have problems at least as severe as those of existing departments. Divisional groupings are all right in small institutions; community colleges have them. But many departments are too large now; divisional groupings would be worse on most campuses and would tend to break into pieces, like departments. Service groupings, which have been tried in some places, are unpopular with the faculty members assigned to them ("second-class citizens" in the eyes of their colleagues). And funding is usually mixed—on-campus and off-campus—for most professors and groups of professors who can attract outside money. The big objection, though, is none of these. It is the difficulty of pulling down the existing department structure, whatever its shortcomings.

The easiest way to go about this dismantling is to do what is described in the next four chapters of this volume—start a new campus. This action avoids the long and tedious struggle against vested department interests, a fight that may be lost, or only partly won. As the examples here make clear, the key decision to depart from the traditional department framework is best made before the campus is established. More, too, is required: a favorable governing board for the new unit or the system of which it is a part; a good (and preferably also a beautiful) site for the campus; able leadership from the start, with a vigorous, imaginative, resourceful, and tough chief administrator who is given some backing and freedom of action; skill and luck with the initial faculty appointments.

Even so, difficulties arise when the first administrator departs or when some faculty members begin to feel that they will be losing their identity in their national disciplines if they serve long in nontraditional departments or other units outside the standard pattern of most of higher education. Yet the effort is worth the struggle. These institutions are leading the way toward reform of the traditional department structure.

To be sure, the reform is as yet limited to small and medium-size institutions. How well this approach will work in larger universities is not clear. Moreover, experimentation of this sort is not found on all or even many of the new campuses that have appeared in the past two decades. Most are striving mightily, almost hysterically, to be carbon copies of the older prestige colleges and universities, with traditional departments and much else to match.

Nor can we expect a great upsurge of new campus action in the immediate future. With the slowing down of enrollment increases, and with today's budget crisis, there will be fewer new campuses launched than in the recent past. There is also some decline in the enthusiasm and optimism of the 1960s, which produced the bulk of the successful experiments.

It is clear, therefore, that much of the effort to change the department system must come on the established campuses. One approach, often successful, as Benezet noted in the previous chapter, is to have a portion of the faculty and students set up a new program or interdepartmental committee outside the established departments. This was easier to do in the days of mounting enrollments and rising budgets than it is today; but it still can be done. Faculty members engaged in such an endeavor can cut loose from their old department ties or enter the new program while retaining membership in a traditional department in the traditional part of the institution.

There are other possibilities. Sikes and his coauthors (1974, p. 73) show how "change-oriented faculty" in conservative departments can bring innovation to established campuses by operating in concert outside department lines. Cincinnati uses institutional studies to make departments more efficient and also to make sure that innovation is not forgotten (Bolton and Boyer, 1973). Cooperation across department lines is achieved on many a campus by allowing faculty members to belong to more than one department and by departments' appointing faculty members from another discipline as full members of their own unit. These actions have had good results on the research side, with the general recognition of the need for combined approaches to complicated problems. And with something of a revival of interest in teaching, some progress is being made on the instructional side.

As educators move into this field and try to make traditional departments function a little better in our unity-of-knowledge day, one hopes they will give attention to what has been achieved on campuses like those chosen for study in the next chapters. Much of the success of these institutions is associated with their determination to change the traditional department system.

5

Edward W. Weidner

Problem-Based Departments at the University of Wisconsin— Green Bay

The University of Wisconsin–Green Bay was authorized by the legislature in September 1965. The regents of the University of Wisconsin, and in particular the president, as well as the state Coordinating Council for Higher Education, specified that the new university should be an innovative institution. Certainly, the circumstances surrounding its birth greatly influenced both the stated mission and the actual academic plan of the new university. At that time, higher education was being attacked from many quarters. Faculty members, students, authorities on higher education, parents, and other critics said that contact between professor and student was no longer close and was becoming ever more distant; that the liberal arts colleges were without theme or flavor; that universities tended to restrict themselves to the basic disciplines, even at a time of major knowledge explosion. Many persons accused colleges and universities of reproducing mainly their own kind—that is to say, professors were primarily interested in their basic disciplines and in students who would help preserve and extend the boundaries of those fields. At the same time, they castigated liberal arts education for being overly general, covering a little bit of everything and not much of anything. Certain humanities programs, American studies, and international studies were especially criticized on these grounds. Students were more restive than ever before, largely because college education had little or no relevance to the world in which they lived. Students wanted to be involved. Furthermore, the teaching, research, and public service activities of universities were carried on in isolation, if not actually in opposition to one another. Universities seemed to be run on the theory that the undergraduate student should not be concerned with research or with what goes on in the community outside the university. Finally, the critics asserted that the course content of a college education remained heavily culture-oriented or culture-conditioned, and students were not encouraged or required to compare cultures.

As the planners of Green Bay reflected on these and other criticisms, they came to feel that the crux of the difficulty was the nature of the traditional academic department: it was based on a discipline; its professors normally had great authority over programming, personnel, and budget decisions; and they had little incentive to relate their intellectual interests and programs to those of other departments. In some ways they existed in splendid isolation, turned inward on their own concerns and the concerns of their discipline. At most they paid minimal attention to the world outside the university or to the interface between subject matter and society. Thus, given the mission of innovation, the planners had to reconsider the traditional department.

The Educational Plan

The evolution of the plan for the new university was rather rapid. The site for the campus was selected in February 1966. The first employee, the chancellor, was appointed in October 1966. Within six months the planners had decided to develop a problem-based department as the major organizational unit to which both faculty members and students would relate, and within two years, the major aspects of this departmental form had been defined. The rationale for a series of problem-based departments was supported by, and in part flowed from, a previous decision to have a general organizing concept for the university as a whole. The mid-1960s were marked by the dawning of environmental awareness. Because of this growing public interest, the planners chose environmental concerns as the broad, unifying theme. This emphasis included not only the traditional biophysical characteristics of the environment, but also the social, cultural, and aesthetic dimensions. In a sense, an environmental focus was viewed as an approach to life. Anyone, regardless of societal role, would be a more effective citizen if he or she were fully sensitive to all these aspects. Thus, environment became a framework in which general education, as well as professional preparation, could become far more meaningful and integrated.

In defining problem-based departments, the planners had to choose between two quite different approaches. One possibility was a series of flexible departments, each focused narrowly on a specific problem that would change from time to time. For example, solar energy might be such an organizing topic. The pollution of the Great Lakes could be another. Environmental design in homes could be a third. Still another might be the recreational environment. Such impermanent departments could be mechanisms for faculty members and students, working together, to carry out specific investigations over a three- to six-year period. At the end of that time, the department could be disbanded and a new set of topics could be selected. The second approach was to create a limited number of departments with much broader bases. In effect, each would be concerned with a large problem area. Although the specific subjects on which it might focus could vary widely over the years, the organizational nature of the department would remain. For reasons of stability and simplicity, the latter choice was made.

Initially, eleven departments, called concentrations, were created and grouped into four theme colleges. The term *concentration* was chosen purposely to avoid association with the disciplinary characteristics of traditional "departments." Yet for convenience, I shall use the designation "problem-based department" here. Most of these departments had quite broad terms of reference. A theme college called Creative Communication was divided into two problem-oriented departments. One department was concerned primarily with aesthetic awareness and environmental design (Communication Action), the other with Humanism and Cultural Change. A theme college of Community Sciences had three units. The problem of modernity was thought to be an appropriate organizing concept (Modernization Processes). Regional problems (Regional Analysis) and urban problems (Urban Analysis) were the other foci. In the College of Human Biology, four problem-based departments were authorized. There were twin units concerned with population (Population Dynamics) and nutrition (Nutritional Sciences), to address the world hunger crisis. Human Adaptability to different environments and Human Growth and Development from infancy to death were the other two. A fourth theme college, Environmental Sciences, had two units. The attempt of human beings to control their environment was the focus of one (Environmental Control) and concern with ecosystems (Ecosystems Analysis), the other. The hope was that in both the short run and the long run, the departments would be devoted to the entire gamut of human environmental concerns, including such basic elements as conflict and cooperation, human rights, the human condition, empathy, understanding, and love.

With the problem-based departments defined in this manner, many of the other aspects of the academic plan of the university became clear. Each department would be headed by a chairperson who would report to the dean of his or her theme college. The departments would have to be interdisciplinary, since no broad group of problems could be approached through a single discipline or even through a combination of closely related disciplines. Thus, every department would have to be authorized to hire biological and physical scientists, social scientists, and humanists, as its members thought best. Alternatively, they could make arrangements to "borrow" staff from other departments on a part-time basis. Obviously, the course structure of the concentration needed to be interdisciplinary, too. Clusters of courses in a series of disciplines would not do. The department would have to give more attention to the future than to the past, except to the extent that the past presented a series of guideposts for the future. The curriculum clearly would be highly relevant. Students would be given opportunities to engage in many kinds of experiential or project learning. Getting off the campus and participating in community projects or problems and analyses would be a basic part of their education. If students were going to be prepared to identify and analyze a problem, develop alternative solutions, and help implement such solutions, the university would have to encourage students to take initiative in their own learning. They would, thereby, be prepared for taking similar action after graduation. Ideally, professor and student would work as co-learners, with the professor acting as group leader rather than as the traditional authority. Students would be able to pursue their education in a variety of ways, subject to the overall educational philosophy of the university. Among the choices would be lecture-discussion courses, seminars, laboratory and studio work, projects or practica, independent study, student-initiated courses, programmed instruction, cooperative education, and open education.

In sum, the context of the problem-based departments was to be egalitarian rather than elitist. Compared to the traditional department, it would be less cognitive and more involved with the instrumental abilities of students, their capacity to solve problems and implement programs. In addition, students would be challenged to participate actively in the world. They would be asked to identify a problem concerning which they wanted to develop their skills and insights and around which their educational experience would be organized. As a result, they would be better prepared for the responsibilities of active employment and citizenship.

The implications of a problem-based department for faculty members were many. The ideal faculty member would be future oriented and well grounded in at least one discipline, but willing to broaden his formal training by becoming a constant learner. After all, few potential faculty members would have genuinely interdisciplinary doctorates. Therefore, much on-the-job training would be necessary, and the planners recognized that this effort would be time consuming and demanding. Faculty members would have to demonstrate both a willingness and an ability to work in an unstructured and an open-ended manner. At the same time, shallowness would have to be avoided. Although many academics were beginning to consider "interdisciplinarity" an interesting experiment that should be tried from time to time, the academic plan of Green Bay required a much more basic commitment. The professor whose

formal training had been in biology might be working side by side
with a colleague trained in sociology, and a mathematician might
find himself laboring beside a music professor. The possibilities were
nearly limitless, and experimentation in many combinations was to
be encouraged. Clearly, problem-based teaching and research would
require faculty members with better than average communication
skills and the ability to work as a part of a team. Since most faculty
members would have to train themselves as interdisciplinarians,
initially many of the new courses would have to be taught by teams.
Later on, when the various professors became more familiar with
interdisciplinarity, most of the courses could be taught by single
faculty members.

In addition, the university obviously needed faculty members
who could develop good, long-term relationships with community
personnel and a wide familiarity with community resources. In
many instances, faculty members would serve as the liaison between
the students and the community. Clearly, then, sensitivity to both
students and community members would be an important attribute
of the staff of the new university. Perhaps youth would be a particular asset, since one would expect more flexibility in the more recent
products of the graduate schools. Still, the basic mind-set or attitudes
of a potential faculty member were more important than age. What
was essential was to identify those who were devoted to the kind of
educational philosophy and plan that the new institution was to
pursue. Commitments to such a plan and to the challenge it represented would be critical for its success.

For all faculty members, the problem-based department
would be home, the source of their voting powers and the possessor
of the authority to identify, recruit, and evaluate the work of the
faculty as well as to initiate curricular proposals. Under the supervision of its college, the department was to have full budget authority over such items as professional personnel, clerical personnel,
student help, supplies and expenses, and capital. Many services of
the university were to be available to faculty members through the
college, such as clerical help, telephone and mail service, office
space, meeting rooms, and so on.

One of the greatest difficulties in conceptualizing the operation of the new university was how to handle the traditional disciplines and professions. No problem-based department with its interdisciplinary courses could possibly serve as a complete substitute for work in mathematics, physics, biology, sociology, or literature. No problem involvement, no matter how complete, could remove the need for professional preparation courses in teacher education, in social work, or in business or public administration. Indeed, interdisciplinarity assumed or required appropriate work in basic fields of knowledge. The solution that was reached, after rather extensive debate, was to provide courses grouped by discipline and profession, but falling outside the problem-based department. In the case of the disciplines, all such courses would have to be sponsored by one or more of the departments. In other words, if at least one department did not consider a particular disciplinary course as important or essential, there was no basis for its being given. Without sponsorship, the course would have no personnel and no money available to teach it. The disciplines were called options, until recently, since work in them represented options or electives for students. The disciplines were, thus, an informal device for identifying courses that were essential for any university, but they would not provide a regular organizational basis for faculty members and would not have personnel, budgetary, or curricular authority. Of course, faculty members could teach disciplinary courses as well as courses in the problem-based department. In fact, it would be considered normal for them to have such divided teaching responsibilities.

Special professional courses were treated differently. Since most of these courses seemed to be largely independent of problem-based departments, they needed their own separate structure, and in this case a few faculty members were permitted to have professional units as their home. However, these particular units would remain small and supplementary to the problem-based departments. In keeping with this approach, a School of Professional Studies with its own dean was created. Several foci were chosen: business and public administration, social services, mass communication, and leisure sciences.

Like their teachers, the students would have their academic home in the problem-based department. Thus, their major would be identified in problem terms. For example, students might major in population problems, urban problems or the problems of modernization and change. The professors of the problem-based department would be their advisors, and students would be expected to take a substantial number of interdisciplinary problem-based courses in the concentration of their choice. The problem-based department could also be a central unit in student governance.

Beyond the department, a student would be able to co-major in a discipline. In this case, the student would be encouraged to relate the discipline to the problem on which he was focusing within the major department. Finally, the student could minor in any professional area and relate it, too, to the major. In this manner, the educational planners of the University of Wisconsin–Green Bay hoped that work in all disciplines and professions would be integrated with the problem base and thereby "come alive."

Obviously, this overall pattern was more complicated than the typical structure of a university. Yet the educational planners for Green Bay believed they had developed an exciting new concept in applied liberal education. Their intent was to make liberal education relevant to the world and applicable to the life of a college student after graduation. No doubt the planners were influenced by events in the mid- and late 1960s, as well as by the land-grant college idea. In many ways, the principles of Green Bay's academic plan were similar to the principles that had been a part of the best colleges of agriculture in the United States for some decades. Nevertheless, there were two major differences: first, the new university proposed to apply these principles to the liberal arts and sciences, and not just to a particular profession such as agriculture; second, the new university proposed to give students far more freedom of choice and a much greater degree of student-initiated education than had traditionally been true in colleges of agriculture.

After three years of planning, the University of Wisconsin–Green Bay opened its doors for students, from freshmen through seniors, in the fall of 1969. Five years later, in the fall of 1974, the university accepted candidates for the master's degree, with an innovative program very similar to that developed at the undergraduate level. Since its very opening, the university has relied on the problem-based departments as the central element in its program.

And these departments not only have withstood the difficulties arising from newness and innovation, but grown stronger with time.

Implementation

The accomplishments of the problem-based departments are
evident in the effects they have had on students, faculty, teaching,
and other aspects of the academic enterprise.

The Green Bay Student. For seven years the undergraduate
students have selected majors within these departments. As problem-
based courses have developed and strengthened, their majors have
become increasingly multidisciplinary as well as interdisciplinary. In
fact, a surprising proportion of students, 53 percent, have made
only a single choice—a problem-based interdisciplinary major. Only
about 35 to 40 percent have chosen a discipline in which to co-
major, and a third have chosen a special professional area in which
to minor (with or without a disciplinary co-major). There has been
an increase in the proportion of students seeking problem-based
interdisciplinary majors alone—from between 33 and 48 percent
during the first four years to more than 60 percent in the past three
years.

Since most of the problem-based departments have relatively
few requirements for a major, students wishing to develop their own
kind of major can usually do so, and many have taken advantage of
this flexibility. In the majority of departments, no two students have
graduated with exactly the same combination of courses; and widely
different kinds of programs within a single department are very
common. The flexibility in the regular problem-based departments
has been so great that very few students have made use of the personal major, which is also possible here. Although enrollment in
recent years has hovered around four thousand, the number of personal majors has been as low as six at any one time. Of course, the
departments vary in terms of how many alternatives they give to
students, but most in effect permit a student to have a personal
major within a problem framework that is quite broad.

For students who have selected a major, one of the rewards
can be a close student/professor relationship. This is a product of
the students' freedom to construct their majors, as well as the fact

that they are required to try to relate their major to a specific problem or problem area. To do this, students naturally turn to an appropriate professor. Many one-on-one informal relationships develop as a consequence. In fact, in the best situation, the relationship is not unlike that which occurs at the graduate level, when a student is preparing a thesis on a topic of great concern to his major professor. One difference flows from the problem-based and interdisciplinary character of the Green Bay program. A student normally has to identify professors whose formal preparation covered several fields of knowledge. To a considerable extent, juniors and seniors find they are branching out into a number of fields, rather than progressively specializing in narrower aspects of a single discipline. For example, in the College of Environmental Sciences, during the first two years students tended to confine their supplementary interests to biology, chemistry, mathematics, and teacher education. More recently, interest in other areas has increased—earth science, physics, environmental administration, and environmental health. In the College of Human Biology, Human Adaptability majors began immediately to emphasize biology, but other fields soon surfaced, as well—chemistry, medical technology, anthropology, psychology, sociology, teacher education, environmental administration, social services, and environmental health. Thus, students with problem-based majors may relate rather closely to a cluster of professors, rather than to only one. However, the same freedom of choice that permits these close relationships has permitted some students to isolate themselves. It is difficult to balance appropriately for all students between an advising freedom and an advising requirement.

Just as there is a mix of faculty members in each department, there is a substantial mix of students in terms of talents and vocational goals. What they have in common is a concern for and interest in a certain range of problems in society. Of course, instructional imperatives narrow the contacts of students in certain respects. In the laboratory sciences and in the studio arts, for instance, there is substantial evidence of the same kind of in-group feelings among students, and between students and professors, that is typical of universities more traditionally organized.

In other respects, the student social system seems to have substantial breadth. In the governance area, students have pro-

ceeded in a fairly nontraditional manner. Some years ago student leaders abolished student government, feeling that its organization was too traditional, and for some time, no student government existed. Then students gradually developed a system of governance that parallels in part the problem-based departments. They formed a series of student unions composed of those who are majoring in a particular department. Each union relates directly to the department through its chairman, executive committee, and members. In turn, in a somewhat federated manner, representatives of all the unions come together for institutionwide student government. This pattern has the great advantage of focusing attention on the academic plan. Rather than being concerned just with the typical student issues that have almost nothing to do with the substance of the university, the student leaders at Green Bay tend to be highly concerned with the day-to-day working out of the academic plan, as well as with long-range improvements.

Yet another effect of the problem-based department on students relates to the project orientation of the university. The original planners particularly wanted to strengthen students' abilities to identify, organize, and carry out individual and group efforts. And therefore each student undertakes a series of projects during his or her education. Participation in such projects, most of which occur off the campus, is designed to develop the skills associated with "getting a job done," whether it is a regular job after graduation or a nonvocational activity. The intent of the academic plan was to have seniors take a compulsory course devoted to the problems of program implementation. That course was never developed, and this is a shortcoming of the curriculum at this time. Still, the student gets substantial exposure to project experience, including considerable orientation in advance and an opportunity for reflection and discussion after carrying out a project.

Obviously, a full evaluation of the impact of problem-based departments on students cannot yet be made because graduates have been outside the halls of ivy for only a few years. Short of a generation—ten years at least—little can be concluded definitively. Nevertheless, the university has already begun a substantial program of evaluation, and its findings are encouraging. At a time of national job shortages for college graduates, Green Bay alumni have been virtually fully employed, and employed to a surprising degree in positions that have at least a general relationship to their undergraduate majors. Although universities tend not to keep comparable statistics on their graduates, it would appear that this new branch of the University of Wisconsin would not suffer if comparisons could be made.

The Faculty Member. The problem-based department has changed the environment for teachers as well; it offers the prospective faculty member a job, regularly evaluates his work, and makes initial recommendations concerning merit increases as well as promotion and the possibility of ultimate tenure. It differs from the traditional department in that a Green Bay professor is evaluated by people who have their doctorates in a variety of fields. Frequently, this variety even encompasses the divisions of knowledge, such as the humanities, fine arts, and the social, biological, mathematical, and physical sciences. Faculty members are evaluated on criteria that outwardly seem similar to criteria used at other colleges and universities. The evaluation has four elements: teaching, research, community outreach, and institutional development. This last element refers particularly to contributions to the development of a new and innovative institution. The other three criteria are to be found at most major universities throughout the country. Still, even here there are substantial differences. For example, teaching a disciplinary course based on one narrow field or speciality and teaching an interdisciplinary and problem-based course, which draws heavily on a variety of disciplines and a variety of community roles and experiences, are not the same thing and need to be evaluated from different perspectives. Normally, the teaching of an interdisciplinary, problem-oriented course is a much more time-consuming and demanding kind of enterprise. Consequently, a number of departments give special recognition for excellence in this area, in contrast to teaching traditional disciplinary courses, although unfortunately not all do. Happily, team teaching is an aid in the assessment of teaching; in many cases several people have taught in a team situation with an individual to be evaluated.

The social system of professors is obviously greatly influenced by concentrations. Originally, the university had a policy of mixing faculty members' office assignments so that those from different departments as well as those with different kinds of formal backgrounds had offices side by side. However, this arrangement proved disadvantageous in limiting the capacity of departments to serve as true intellectual centers, and now office assignments are by department. Obviously, this interdisciplinary system affects faculty members' gatherings, such as lunches and coffee breaks, and their social entertaining at home. For instance, political science professors, or those from any other one discipline, rarely get together for a social evening.

Faculty members get most of their services from departmental offices, especially since the college and school deanships have been abolished. Included are access to various pieces of equipment, supplies, reimbursement for travel, and, of course, secretarial services. Because the departments have budget and curricular authority, any faculty member who wants to get something substantial done or changed, must seek the cooperation of an interdisciplinary group of peers.

Over the years, the University of Wisconsin–Green Bay has tried to recruit faculty members who were highly sympathetic to the academic plan of the institution. Thus, in many ways, the faculty is not a representative cross-section of the national members of the disciplines. Rather, it is a group of individuals interested in innovation in higher education, especially in the kind that is being attempted at Green Bay. Overall, the faculty is a youthful group. Young faculty members were chosen partly because they were less expensive to hire but primarily because, as graduate students in the late sixties or early seventies, they were particularly interested in a problem-based and interdisciplinary approach. They have been among the most enthusiastic and creative members of the faculty. They, and their older colleagues as well, have found that the problem-based department gives flexibility for professors as well as for students. Professors can pursue their intellectual interests on a wide front very easily, within and among the departments. As a consequence, they find themselves developing interdisciplinary habits of mind simply because of the professional and social systems in which they find themselves. They also find that there is a considerable stimulus to become project oriented. Community projects represent opportunities for both students and professors, and the staff is thus active in identifying projects and then in participating in them or relating to them.

For the faculty, the problem-based department has probably had its greatest impact on teaching and the general intellectual environment of the university. Sooner or later, interdisciplinarity and problem-based thinking become a way of life. Both intellectual interests and companionship are influenced by it. An experience of one of the senior professors is illustrative. He had a leave of absence to teach engineering at one of the better known large state universities in the country. After a semester he returned to Green Bay and was very happy to do so. He explained that although it was a commonplace experience at Green Bay to talk to people from a variety of disciplines throughout the course of the day, about a variety of topics, at the other institution this simply was not so. It was not that his social contacts were limited to just other engineers, or even to other civil engineers—the situation was narrower than that. During coffee breaks or lunch breaks or informal conversation, almost the only people he talked to were civil engineers interested in water problems. This kind of narrow experience is simply not possible at Green Bay.

Of course, not all faculty members are equally problem oriented and interdisciplinary. Perhaps a quarter of them teach in disciplinary areas only or are reluctant to sponsor practica or to teach interdisciplinary courses. Their influence is not facultywide, however, and their numbers are not increasing.

The problem-based departments have not perfectly followed a problem-based interdisciplinary format in all their courses. Still, the majority of such courses may be characterized in this manner. In recent years, specific problem foci have multiplied in the several departments.

The forms of teaching in the problem-based departments have been similar to what was planned. For example, a number of courses, especially new ones, are team taught. Eventually, they tend to be taken over by individual professors, because many faculty members now feel comfortable about handling an interdisciplinary course alone. Of course, some courses began and have remained team taught. The difficulty with team-taught courses is primarily their cost. In the long run, if team teaching is to remain, some other instructional economies must be found in order to support the heavier costs involved. Other characteristics of teaching that were anticipated are the emphases on practica or projects and on independent study.

Research. After seven years of university operation, the impact of the problem-based departments on research is not yet clear, for several reasons. First, in developing a new university with an innovative teaching pattern, the faculty concentrated their energies on that activity. Second, the early formulation of the academic plan and its appeal to those who were interested in an innovative approach to higher education tended to attract professors who were more interested in teaching than in research. Third, the relatively young average age of the faculty members means that their best years for research lie well ahead of many of them, even at this point. Fourth, the national decrease in funds available for research has had a deleterious effect.

Whatever the reason, the quantity of research has not been large. Still, there have been about a dozen substantial interdisciplinary, team-oriented research efforts, as well as many smaller ones. These efforts have often involved undergraduate students as well as faculty members, and most of them have been assisted by outside funding. Some of the concentrations, such as the College of Environmental Sciences, have been much more active in research than others. Nevertheless, the major research efforts so far have more often crossed the lines of the problem-based departments than been confined to a single department. This trend may be a particularly good omen for the future. It would indeed be frustrating to develop an organizational pattern that avoided the barriers of the traditional discipline-based departments, only to develop a new problem-based departmental structure that erected similar kinds of obstacles. At least in research, barriers are not evident around the problem-based department. Symbolizing the faculty's concern for research on an institutionwide basis, a formal research institute was organized in 1975. This institute is designed to help faculty members secure funds for their projects as well as to promote cross-departmental research.

Supporting Services. A widespread policy of support for the problem-based department exists at Green Bay. One aspect of this support is the physical planning of the campus. For example, the connection of all buildings promotes the flow of students and professors among different parts of the campus, as does the distance of some classrooms from the professors' offices. Building interconnections and patterns of layout help prevent the kind of isolation that exists in a more traditional setting, where a chemistry building, for example, is an independent structure and becomes, in effect, the property of the chemists—both faculty members and students. The chemists or members of other disciplines at Green Bay have no similar kind of isolated facility. Of course, isolation is an ever present danger, and continual alertness is required to avoid it. It is very easy for persons concerned with music or art to encounter only those who frequent the fine arts studios. It is equally easy for biologists to communicate mainly with those who frequent the biology labs. In the latter case, the labs are divided between two buildings that are distant from one another, and professors and students therefore have to walk through most of the buildings of the campus if they work in both locations.

Aside from building interconnection, several other physical characteristics are supportive. For instance, the offices of senior administrators are distributed around the campus, rather than being located in a single administrative building. Currently, the chancellor, the vice-chancellor, and the dean for academic affairs are housed in widely separated buildings. This arrangement permits a communication flow between faculty and administration that would not otherwise be possible.

Administrative support for the problem-based department is substantial: budget reviews consider priorities associated with problem-based departments; academic support services are geared particularly to problem-based studies; and the business office, working with the Central Administration of the University of Wisconsin System, has developed distinctive accounting codes that reflect the needs of problem-based departments. (For example, the original computer code that provided only for disciplinary and professional courses was adjusted.) Senior administrative officers, as well as faculty members, speak widely, both within and outside the university, about a problem-based university and the significant potential contribution of the problem-based department. This kind of public remark or public paper has a very beneficial effect on those who are working to achieve problem-based innovations. For example, each year at a September breakfast the chancellor addresses the faculty on the academic plan. His remarks are mimeographed and made available to all staff members. Similarly, many papers delivered at national and international conferences or prepared for professional journals by several professors and/or administrators have been circulated to the faculty.

Opportunities for faculty members to visit other institutions and to participate in discussions on the future of higher education are also an important way of giving support for innovation. So is the encouragement of visitors from around the United States and from around the world, particularly those who want to experiment with their own university and are seeking ideas they may adapt to their situation.

Problems and Challenges

Although the first ten years of the University of Wisconsin–Green Bay have been pleasing ones in the main, three major sets of problems have arisen: (1) the changing attitudes and characteristics of students; (2) the definition of problem-based departments and their relations with other parts of the university; (3) and the amount of faculty time required by the curriculum.

Changing Student Body. Green Bay's academic plan had considerable appeal to those students who wished to be involved in the world, and a decade ago, many prospective students demanded this kind of education. Yet today, in the latter part of the 1970s, students tend to shy away from this or any other kind of innovation in higher education. They want to play it safe. It is astonishing how few students are committed to making the world a better place in which to live if that commitment involves any risks on their part. Considering the severe economic problems that have faced recent college graduates, more young students today want only to prepare for a job in as direct and traditional a manner as possible. They resist innovation whether it is related to preparation for employment or more generally to liberal education.

Ten years ago, many educators thought all students were

demanding changes. Obviously, that was never true. Relatively few students, faculty members, and members of the general community were actually seeking such changes. Those who did demand them came largely from privileged families, educationally speaking.

In particular, students who are the first members of their families to go to college demand overwhelmingly a traditional credential, a conservative approach to higher education. The normal and expected thing has more standing, seems far safer. Such students do not want to take chances. Yet the academic plan of the University of Wisconsin–Green Bay was deliberately designed to give equal opportunity to students from less privileged backgrounds, because they are the ones who suffer the most from a lack of instrumental abilities—abilities related to getting a job done by applying knowledge while working with others. So, despite its original intent, Green Bay finds today that the academic plan appeals primarily to those students who come from the more well-to-do families and from families where higher education has been the tradition for some generations. The university has yet to discover how the importance of applied liberal education can be effectively communicated to those from less advantageous backgrounds.

An academic plan based on a problem-based department tends to develop its own terminology. And because that terminology is unfamiliar to them, some students who are uncertain about whether they want to go to the university no doubt decide against it. Green Bay is currently trying to simplify the explanation of its unusual and rather complicated academic plan, both to prospective students and to students currently enrolled. Nevertheless, the university is what it is and cannot respond equally well to all needs. The freedom of choice that is so effective for some students in certain stages of their educational development is exactly counterproductive and confusing to others. Certainly many students blossom when they have alternatives among which to choose, but there are other students who flourish with a set plan. Such set plans have not been available at Green Bay. Their unavailability may make the institution both less attractive and less effective for those who need a tight structure, and rightly so. The university must not make the mistake of trying to be all things to all people. It must content itself with appealing to those students who wish to be challenged by problem-based learning and by a wide array of choices.

Students entering an innovative institution such as Green Bay must have an appropriate briefing on what sorts of opportunities are available and on how these opportunities differ from those they might find elsewhere. This orientation has not been provided as well as it should be. Among the solutions being considered is an addition to the freshman curriculum that would help students learn how to take advantage of the academic plan. Yet even with the most extensive orientation program, certain practices will be advantageous for some students and disadvantageous for others. For example, a new student can register without ever seeing an adviser; the choices are up to him. However, many freshmen and even many sophomores are probably not ready for this kind of independence. They may be reluctant to see a faculty member, even though it is a rather simple thing to do here. As a result, they may never have a close human contact with a professor, simply because such a contact was not mandated by the registration procedure. Other students flourish with such leeway. Again, the faculty is currently considering a change, making the signature of an adviser compulsory, in order to register, at least until a major is selected.

Departmental Problems: Internal and External. A second set of problems has developed relative to the definition of the problem-based departments and their relations with other parts of the university. Originally, as I mentioned earlier, the eleven departments were divided into four theme colleges, and a school of Professional Studies handled specialized professional courses. But during the first year of actual operation, these college and school units proved to be dysfunctional, particularly since barriers tended to develop around them. One evidence of this problem was the development of special regulations and restrictions concerning those students who "crossed over" and took courses in more than one college. As a result, these five units, while formally retained, were in fact eliminated as important organizational elements before the second year of operation began. The five deans were phased out, and department chairpersons reported to a single dean of the colleges (since styled the dean for academic affairs). Of course, the possibility remained that the problem-based departments would still develop barriers among them, but great effort was exerted to prevent this eventuality, and on the whole, that effort has succeeded.

Somewhat more serious, although still not to be classified as a major difficulty, has been the tendency to restrict the number of disciplines represented by faculty members in typical problem-based departments. Such restriction has been in part the result of the budget crisis and the shortage of funds for higher education in Wisconsin and elsewhere during the past three years. Another explanation is the fact that it is easy to "borrow" faculty members from other departments. This exchange reduces the need always to have the complete sample of disciplines that would be relevant to any particular cluster of problems. Moreover, faculty members who have had formal training in one of the major divisions of knowledge naturally feel most at ease with colleagues who have had similar training. One could easily criticize the distribution of faculty members in the principal problem-based departments from this point of view. For example, in one (Communication Action) department, more than three-quarters of its professors were trained in the visual and performing arts. Another (Humanism and Cultural Change) is heavily represented by professors who had formal training in the humanities. Three others have heavy concentrations in the social sciences, and still others emphasize backgrounds in the mathematical, biological, and physical sciences. Despite this tendency, there is considerable give and take among faculty members in the different departments and a considerable mixing of the curriculum. And in a number of cases, the staff is not distributed in these narrow ways. As long as departmental groupings remain fluid and open to the contributions of others, as they are today, we have little cause for concern. Even if departments come to be more rigid than they are today, Green Bay still would be fostering a kind of interdisciplinarity that is not often found elsewhere. For example, the social sciences are completely melded in each of three different concentrations—Regional Analysis, Urban Analysis, and Modernization Processes. And the biological, physical, and mathematical sciences are similarly integrated in the College of Environmental Sciences. Such blends are seldom found in traditionally organized departments elsewhere. Still, the University of Wisconsin–Green Bay aims at loftier goals, and whether those goals will be fully obtainable in the long run remains to be seen.

Another problem arising from the nature of the problem-based departments has been their size and the specificity with which they address problems. Initially, some of them were exceedingly small and had only a handful of regular faculty members. At the same time, however, the concentrations were rather broadly conceived and had a cluster of concerns; and they have tended to merge and become still broader in concept. For instance, the four problem-based departments in the College of Human Biology merged in 1976, following the pattern set by the two in the College of Environmental Sciences, which merged in 1974. This joining should give students and faculty members much greater freedom in focusing on issues of major concern and encourage larger groups of professors with more diverse backgrounds. A minimum module for a department of at least ten or fifteen faculty members seems desirable.

The problem of a lack of specificity has been exacerbated by the mergers. Obviously, a large problem-based department runs the risk of becoming overly diffuse, without focus. Both faculty members and students have suggested that it might be possible for departments to identify a few specific problems on which they will concentrate for a certain period of time—perhaps the next five years or so. The departments might then want to move on to other problems or continue along the same path from time to time. At one point early in the history of Green Bay, the departments were asked to list the three or four specific problems to which they intended to give most attention during the next four to six years. This task proved to be difficult, and the attempt was abandoned for the most part. Currently, some student leaders are suggesting specific problems as the basis for informal seminars of students and faculty members that might stay together for three to five years. They could form either within problem-based departments or across their boundaries. To some extent, such a process has been carried out ad hoc by a few faculty members. The proposal suggests that such a practice be institutionalized and that twenty to thirty such groups be identified among which students might pick and choose if they wished to do so. Many informal, noncredit activities might characterize such groups, as well as certain kinds of credit activities. One effect of such groups or seminars would be to encourage projects that lasted for more than a semester.

Although most people are generally satisfied with the problem-based departments currently, no single definition of these units would appeal to everyone under all conditions. We expect that the problem-based departments will continue to grow and change from time to time, the opportunities for change being influenced greatly by the interests of the students, the interests of the faculty members, the resources that are available, and the emerging needs of the times.

Demands on Faculty Time. A third very evident problem has been the large amount of time required of faculty members to make this problem-based curriculum work. Interdisciplinarity obviously takes time and energy away from a professor's research or concern with his or her discipline. And it is also true that a project approach to education is exceedingly time consuming and demanding. Although a faculty member may not have more hours to teach than a comparable colleague in a more traditional institution, the preparation needed is far greater. The factors in the situation are multiple—the individual approach to education, the project or practicum element, the interdisciplinarity, the innovation.

One possible way to deal with this extra time demand is to give an innovating institution having a problem-based orientation somewhat more money than its sister institutions. In fact, the University of Wisconsin System tried that approach, but the experiment lasted only a short time because supporting intrasystem institutions at different levels seems politically impossible. Many constituents demand equity, and the tendency to define equity in terms of sameness is ever present. It is the least common denominator. The University of Wisconsin–Green Bay has been treated fairly by the state of Wisconsin, by the regents, and by the president's office, given the political pressures in the state. Still, it now appears doubtful at best that the system can ever allocate more funds to Green Bay just because its mission is to continue innovation throughout the breadth of its curriculum.

The initial 16:1 student/faculty ratio at the undergraduate level has now become 18:1 and may be on its way to 22:1 or even 24:1. Thus, in the future, the university may well have to find even better techniques of instruction so that there can be time for inter-disciplinarity, problem-based and project-oriented studies, continued innovation, and research and publication. The result may be a greater reliance on large classes in selected instances, or programmed instruction, or a drastic reduction of instructional support and administrative services at the university.

Conclusion

When the University of Wisconsin began its planning in 1966, many persons suggested that the development of a problem-based and interdisciplinary academic plan was an exercise in futility. Even the most sympathetic observers believed that the experiment might last as long as three or four years, but that the university would then be forced to go back to the traditional departments. Yet if anything, the dynamics at Green Bay currently are in the opposite direction. The problem-based departments are becoming stronger, and the faculty is deeply committed to the plan of the institution. Enthusiasm runs high, even in the midst of severe budget constraints. So there is no evidence that the university is headed away from its original purpose.

The full benefits of this form of organization will only be evident in the long run. However, we can conclude now that the problem-based department does give students both more freedom and more breadth in their education. It gives faculty members equal freedom and breadth. An atmosphere of interdisciplinarity has been developed and is thriving.

The academic approach of the University of Wisconsin–Green Bay may not serve the needs of all potential students. It was not designed to do so. However, in the short space of seven years, it has proven to be a desirable alternative for students who want an instrumental, real-world education as a step to their future employment experiences and life satisfaction.

6

Dean E. McHenry

Academic Organizational Matrix at the University of California, Santa Cruz

The Santa Cruz campus of the University of California was planned from the beginning with bifurcated aspirations: to make a notable contribution to undergraduate education, with built-in safeguards against later dilution; and to lay a firm foundation for graduate and professional endeavors. The consequences of implementing these twin objectives are not yet fully seen after a dozen years, but an account of the setting, the structure, and the results so far may be instructive to others who wish to consider departing from forms that are conventional in American higher education.

Genesis

The Santa Cruz campus was launched in response to rapid growth in California. The census reported the state's population at 6,907,387 in 1940; 10,586,223 in 1950, and 15,717,204 in 1960. (The 1970 figure was 19,953,134.) The need for additional campuses of the University of California and of other public colleges was indicated in a report by a liaison group in 1957. Projections of the

State Department of Finance showed that, without new campuses, the Berkeley campus might be called upon to enroll 35,200 students by 1970 and the Los Angeles campus 39,900 (Liaison Committee . . . , 1957, p. 85). On the same day in October 1957 that the regents elected Clark Kerr as president of the university they authorized three new campuses: one in Northern California, one in the Los Angeles–Orange area, and one in San Diego. Little progress was made on the new campus program until Kerr took office in July 1958.

After receiving a careful study of criteria and a thorough survey of possible sites, the regents narrowed the choice for Northern California to two possibilities: the Almaden Valley of Santa Clara County and the Cowell Ranch of Santa Cruz County. In March 1961 the Cowell site was chosen; I was appointed chancellor the following July and the campus received a general allocation of functions in a universitywide academic plan (University of California, 1961, p. 52).

Academic planning commenced under the direction of the chancellor, during 1961–1962 in Berkeley and after July 1962 in Santa Cruz, while a master-planning team composed of leading architects began work on physical design.

Like Green Bay, Santa Cruz was born into a state university family that already had a governing board, established procedures, fixed standards, and several active siblings. We were handed the chalk and invited to write on the blackboard, but the slate was not unmarked. It had a frame composed of provisions of the Constitution of California, standing orders of The Regents, regulations of the Academic Senate, the Master Plan for Higher Education, and other authorities. The task of the campus planner was to fit desired innovations into the frame, occasionally asking for waivers when the frame proved too confining. The university system proved to be a great boon to Santa Cruz. Presidents Kerr and Hitch well understood what we were trying to do and were consistent in their support. The system and the older campuses contributed advice, personnel, and technical services. The UC connection did require, however, that the new campus accept the system's salary scale, tenure rules, and admission standards—none of which we found oppressive.

During 1961–1962 substantial agreement was reached between President Kerr and the campus administration that: (1) a
series of liberal arts colleges was to be the basic unit of planning and
of student and faculty identification; (2) undergraduate education
would receive initial emphasis; (3) residential facilities would be
provided for more than the usual proportion of students; (4) early
distinction would be sought in the arts and sciences; (5) a restricted
curriculum would serve student needs; and (6) tutorials, seminars,
and independent study would be stressed. The Regents approved a
provisional academic plan containing these features in 1962 (University of California, Santa Cruz, 1962), and a more comprehensive plan in early 1965 (UCSC, 1965).

The latter fleshed out some skeletal parts of the 1962 plan.
The colleges were defined as educational units, each headed by a
"provost," a tenured member of the faculty. The provost would
have aides, called "preceptors," who would deal with academic,
student, and other problems. Faculty "fellows," the academic staff
members attached to a particular college, were to be joint appointees
of the college and the disciplinary group to which they belonged.
Santa Cruz staked out its distinctive goals, including the use of its
residential accommodations, in such a way as to combine living and
learning and to foster a sense of belonging that would, as President
Kerr put it, "make the campus seem small as it grows larger."

Students were to be admitted under university systemwide
standards but through campuswide (rather than college) procedures. After admission to the campus, admittees would be asked to
express preferences among the colleges and would be assigned—
insofar as space was available—according to those preferences.

Why a Collegiate University?

The decision to plan Santa Cruz on the basis of residential
colleges was influenced by several factors. One was our observation
that university undergraduates, particularly lowerclassmen, were
often begrudgingly and poorly taught by specialized faculty members whose interest was advanced study and research. If we could
establish firmly a series of colleges primarily devoted to undergraduate teaching that could command respect and status, collegiate
values might endure after the campus became quite large and the

graduate component became substantial. Although graduate education may have benefited, undergraduate education has been affected adversely by extreme specialization by faculty members and extreme particularization by departments. The American pattern of public secondary education leaves a heavy responsibility of general education to be assumed by the colleges and universities. The postsecondary teacher cannot proceed with assurance that his freshmen or sophomore students have a background of reading in depth in any sector of knowledge; indeed, some cannot even read effectively. To get this work of general education done, higher institutions have adopted a variety of organizational forms and methods.

Many universities have turned the general education function over largely to a few skilled lecturers, assisted by armies of teaching assistants. This method leaves intact the emphasis on graduate and research functions, which serve as giant magnets drawing senior faculty members away from undergraduate teaching. Yet some of the Ivy League institutions have clung tenaciously to the tradition that part of the teaching time of even the most distinguished faculty members should be reserved for undergraduates.

We thought that the most effective way to establish such a tradition in a new institution would be through the college plan and we rejected at the outset the notion of separate undergraduate and graduate faculties. Such an arrangement invites a double standard, sets an unfortunate pecking order. We thought we could find a teaching staff that would be both interested in undergraduate teaching and capable of doing first-rate graduate and research work.

A second factor in the decision to have minicolleges was the selection of the Santa Cruz site over one in the San Jose area. The San Jose location was in the outskirts of a city that in 1960 had 204,196 people, in a county of 642,315. Santa Cruz had 25,596 in the city and 84,219 in the county. A San Jose campus would have large numbers of students within commuting range; a Santa Cruz campus would be largely residential. If extensive student housing were to be built anyway, we asked, why not consider a collegiate system?

A third reason for the collegiate plan was the hope that it might alleviate the impersonality that often afflicts large, monolithic universities. In too many of them the web of acquaintanceship is inadequate both between student and student and between teacher and student. We coveted a living and learning arrangement that would make contacts close and frequent. An important proviso, however, was that the individual colleges would be small enough for a normally gregarious student to know many, if not most of his college mates and a fair proportion of the faculty fellows of his college.

Mode of growth was a fourth consideration in adopting the college plan. The necessity of growth was widely accepted; the young people who would populate our colleges in the early years were already born and soon would be college-bound in record numbers. In the past, with few exceptions, American universities generally absorbed enrollment growth by letting each unit grow larger. The result often was schools, colleges, and departments stretched to the breaking point, amid increasing depersonalization. If the size of a college could approximate annual growth, we reasoned, then a new college each year—on the average—would provide the least disruptive way to grow. (Indeed, eight colleges were launched in the first eight years;* the typical size, originally 600 students, is now overcrowded at 700.)

There were potent arguments against undertaking the college plan. Cost was the one most frequently mentioned by state officials and university regents. In the course of securing approvals for the academic plan, I made the commitment that the campus would not ask for state funds in excess of those made available for comparable campuses that were noncollegiate. I had in mind raising substantial amounts of money from foundations and other private sources.† In sum, to get the plan approved, I made a commitment

---

* The colleges, with year of opening to students are: Cowell, 1965; Stevenson, 1966; Crown, 1967; Merrill, 1968; Five, 1969; Kresge, 1970; Oakes, 1972; Eight, 1972.

† For each college we sought a donor-sponsor who was willing to finance the capital items not available from state sources and not feasible from loan funds. In fact, the first seven colleges did receive, by 1976, around $5,000,000 for capital outlay in grants and gifts. On the operating budget side, however, our parsimonious approach soon made Santa Cruz the lowest in per-student operating costs in the university system. Although UCSC has the smallest contingent of graduate students (in 1975–1976, 328 out of a head-count total of 6,098), we maintain that some freshmen need more faculty attention than some graduate students. By 1975–1976 the faculty/student ratio had deteriorated to 1/18.

on costs and subsequently practiced economies that still plague the campus in its second decade.

Another objection was that we could not recruit a first-rate faculty with a heavy obligation to teach undergraduates. In practice, however, we were able to bring in a faculty of distinction, most members of which were enthusiastic about teaching undergraduates. (Faculty characteristics will be covered in a subsequent section.)

Critics of the college plan often charged that it is outmoded and inefficient. The one-to-one tutorial, hallmark of traditional Oxford, was assumed by opponents to be an inevitable feature of any such college. Actually Cambridge for some time had been moving to group "supervisions," and one-to-one tutorials were increasingly less common at Oxford. Tutorial instruction certainly is one of the most expensive forms of teaching ever invented. We replied that the tutorial need not be the only method; indeed, we thought there could be colleges without tutorials. We suggested that the modes of instruction be quite varied, employing small group tutorials, seminars, independent study, and lectures. The time had now come to examine the literature and the practice of collegiate universities, and to that we next turned our attention.

Some American Cluster Plan Models

One of the first things I did after being appointed chancellor was to read and reread works on higher education and to visit and revisit colleges and universities. Daniel Coit Gilman, who left the presidency of the University of California to found Johns Hopkins University, was of special interest. Although his greatest contribution was building a research-oriented institution on the German model, occasionally he turned to the English model, as he did when he declared: "One experiment remains to be tried: the establishment of a hall of residence which shall be what a college is to Oxford or Cambridge, a hotel with a scholar and his staff at the head of it; with privacy, comfort, oversight, and intellectual guidance; where visitors may be received and entertainments given, but where the dominant pursuit is study, the society restricted to men of intellectual pursuits" (1898, p. 305).

As a lifelong admirer of Woodrow Wilson, I returned to my

books by and about him. Soon after his inaugural as president of Princeton University be began his advocacy of the "preceptorial system": He proposed to add fifty tutors to the faculty who would give close instruction resembling that at Oxford, but better than Oxford's (Myers, 1946, p. 13). Then he went to work to raise the money to launch the plan. By 1905 there was enough in hand to begin recruiting preceptors, and that autumn the fifty launched the new program. They were among the finest young scholars in the country, and they instituted a system of teaching undergraduates that is still one of Princeton's hallmarks.

Wilson in 1906 launched his campaign for a "quadrangle plan" of housing students (Baker, 1927, pp. 213–274). He had in mind housing all four classes together, rather than separating lowerclassmen and upperclassmen. This arrangement would open up social and other advantages to all students, not just those who were members of the exclusive upperclass clubs. He proposed to divide the university into residential colleges, each headed by a master and some resident preceptors; each college was to have its own dining facilities. His colleges would not teach, but would be residential and social. The faculty voted its support of the plan by a large margin, but opposition rose from the clubs, especially among their alumni. The board of trustees approved the plan in June 1907, then rescinded its action in October. By 1908, says Yale's Pierson, "the first bold attempt to graft the English collegiate system into an American university had failed" (1955, p. 224). Wilson carried on the struggle until 1910, when he was elected governor of New Jersey.

Wilson's lost cause first became a reality at Harvard. The gift that made possible the Harvard houses came quickly and the houses were launched without long preplanning. Edward Harkness, Yale '97 and heir to an oil fortune, was persuaded by his alma mater to take an interest in solving its student housing and social problems imposed by growth. Once convinced of the collegiate solution, Harkness set a deadline of mid-1928 for presentation of an approved Yale plan. When none came, he went to Harvard, where President Lowell received the idea with enthusiasm. Lowell had admired Wilson's valiant effort to establish the "quadrangle plan" at Princeton and had himself been concerned about student social life that segregated the wealthy. The climate at Harvard was also more welcoming because the Harvard Student Council in 1926 had published a proposal for a residential college system. Thus, when Harkness offered about $11,400,000, Harvard accepted with alacrity.

Harvard then proceeded to design its house plan. Architecturally, it was a skillful combination of existing structures and new buildings. Organizationally, it called for seven houses (now eight) with sophomores, juniors, and seniors numbering around 250 (now 350) per house. Freshmen were separately housed in the Yard. Each house was presided over by a master, chosen from the faculty and aided by tutors. The houses had no particular educational function; the departments continued to offer the courses. At Harvard today there is general satisfaction that a small-college atmosphere has been preserved by the house plan as student bodies have grown larger. The small units have served as bases for a wide variety of activities and athletic programs. In 1936, Morrison (p. 479) was able to report: "For the great majority in the College the houses mean a vast improvement in living conditions and social opportunities."

Yale got its plan to Harkness soon after the Harvard gift was announced. Before long he relented, and the Yale residential colleges were under way as well. My first visit to New Haven was in the summer of 1932 while the residential colleges were being readied for their 1933 opening. During the 1960s I revisited repeatedly both to recruit for the Santa Cruz faculty and to see the nine original colleges and especially the new ones: Morse and Stiles. I found them physically attractive and liked very much the clubby atmosphere fostered by their small size. By talking with fellows and reading, mainly in Pierson, I learned that the educational mission of the colleges had not been made clear at their beginning and that the original Harkness gift made no allowance for teaching in them. The $15,725,000 Harkness benefaction included an endowment to pay the masters' salaries and expenses, but nothing for teaching spaces, libraries, or tutorials. Later Yale found some money for college libraries, Harkness funded a group of advisers (divided between the colleges and the freshman year), and Paul Mellon gave $5,000,000 for sophomore discussion courses (Pierson, 1955, p. 270). Although the Yale colleges were judged by Pierson as a "resource Yale could not do without" and the "right size," and they served to "promote civilization," they did not emerge at first as major educational forces. Almost the whole of academic responsibility continued to rest in the departments, but in recent years the colleges have gone well beyond their early academic mission of helping to prepare undergraduates for their comprehensive examinations.

In planning the colleges at Santa Cruz, I was influenced also by two groups within California: the Claremont Colleges and the cluster colleges of the University of the Pacific.

The Claremont story has been well told by Clary (1970) and others. I had long been an admirer of Pomona College (founded in 1887) and a close observer of the founding and flourishing of its associates: Scripps College (1926), Claremont Graduate School (1927), Claremont Men's College (1946), Harvey Mudd College (1955), and Pitzer College (1963). This cluster of academically self-contained colleges shares a common library, some science facilities, and numerous nonacademic services. Its founding father, James A. Blaisdell, had expected the component parts to retain their own foundations and trustees but to be closely linked through shared academic programs and facilities. Instead, each college has instructional autonomy, although they do provide for cross-enrollments—17 percent in 1971–1972.

My aspiration for Santa Cruz was similar to some aspects of the original Blaisdell proposal: separate residences and a distinctive flavor for each college, but extensive sharing of course offerings and instructional space. Blaisdell's notion of a separate corporate status for each college, however, was not suited to a state university campus, which is part of a public corporation, The Regents of the University of California.

The Santa Cruz plan sought to avoid one of the weaknesses of the Claremont structure, which has not enjoyed across-the-board success in getting the parallel departments of the constituent colleges to work together on common problems. The device of "field committees" (for undergraduate fields of study) composed of all the faculty members in a particular discipline from all colleges appears to have worked well only in a few areas (mathematics and classics are often commended). The 1972 report called the subdivided

character of the Claremont faculties a weakness that should be cor-
rected "within the framework of college autonomy and individuality" (p. 98). Clary (1970, p. 246) quoted the 1968 annual report
of President Benezet, "Intercollegiate academic exchange and academic planning remain the least developed front of our cooperative
mechanisms," and pressed for integration of the teaching force,
saying, "this is the most important problem that confronts us, and
its solution is the key to the future of the Claremont Colleges, both
separately and collectively—and, I would add, financially" (p. 281).

On the other hand, the Claremont group has been quite
successful in putting together and operating a tricollege science program for Scripps, Claremont Men's, and Pitzer. (Pomona and
Mudd have their own.) Claremont Men's and Mudd have a joint
physical education program; Pomona and Claremont Men's have
a common ROTC unit. There is extensive cooperation among these
later colleges in drama, choral, and forensics.

Thus, today the Claremont group might be described as a
consortium that shares heavily on the business side and lightly on
the academic side. In short, it is more a confederation than a federation. It characterizes itself as "the pioneer and principal exponent
in the United States of the 'cluster' or 'group' plan of organizing
higher education. This form of organization—small independent
colleges located contiguously and sharing certain joint facilities—
allows the best of two worlds: collegial communities of personal,
human scale and the outlook and facilities of a major center of
learning" (Claremont . . . , 1972, p. 5).

The other cluster college arrangement that interested me
was the University of the Pacific in Stockton, which was launched
in the early 1960s while Santa Cruz was being planned. Its chief
craftsman was Robert E. Burns, president of UOP. He saw the
addition of a series of quite small cluster colleges (about 250 students in each) as the logical way for Pacific to grow; he also recognized that funds could be raised on behalf of the collegiate units
that might not be available for older, established units of the university. Three cluster colleges were started: Raymond (1962),
Covell (1963), and Callison (1967). Although their finances were
interwoven with those of the university, their academic and curricular arrangements were quite separate. Each cluster college main-

tained such a rich faculty-student ratio that their operating costs in
the early 1970s compared unfavorably with those of the College of
the Pacific, the older arts and science college. From close observation
of the Pacific experiment, I learned that funds could be raised for
a distinctive enterprise and that good students could be attracted to
novel and exacting programs.

As the three cluster colleges developed, the University of the
Pacific was slow about adapting its departmental structure, which
was based on the College of the Pacific, to the new situation. From
my reading in the early 1970s, it appeared that the "graduate faculty" concept did not adequately take into account the potential
contributions of cluster college faculty members.

British Models

Oxford and Cambridge constituted other models, but my
contacts were rather remote when we began planning Santa Cruz.
Although I was in Britain during my dissertation year, 1935–1936,
I visited Oxford only once and then saw little except Balliol College.
In 1950, I had the opportunity to look at Oxford again. In 1963
and 1965 I had fuller visits and was able to see Braesnose, Corpus
Christi, Exeter, New, Oriel, Queens, St. Catherine's, and other col-
leges at closer range.

The merits of the Oxford colleges I had long viewed rather
overcredulously, in part because the Oxford graduates I had known
as colleagues and as graduate students seemed to me to be extra-
ordinarily well educated. So I hoped to include some features of the
college plan in what we were projecting at Santa Cruz. From the
beginning, however, we realized that teaching mainly by the tutorial
method could not be adopted because of its high cost. Neither could
we follow Oxford's example in separating the teaching from the
examining function; there is a long American tradition of combining the two and we could see little prospect of finding a way to
finance a corps of examiners.

Nevertheless, Oxford practice did offer some guidance on
how to organize the disciplines in a collegiate university. Its "boards
of faculties," composed of professors and readers in the subjects of
the faculty, gave us the direction if not the precise name for our
"boards of studies." As initially proposed in 1965, our boards would

have been representative bodies, as at Oxford, but in the end the Academic Senate pressed for inclusion of all faculty members connected with the discipline, and that view prevailed.

In the early 1960s I felt the shift of Oxford from an earlier confederation of independent colleges toward a federation of university and colleges. This was confirmed in the report of the commission on inquiry (Oxford, 1966, vol. I, p. 27) : "By 1966 it can be seen that a federal community, the 'collegiate university,' has been developing: it is inhabited by a new type of academic, the 'fellow-lecturer,' who has double loyalties, joint functions, and composite remuneration." The report went on to argue that despite difficulties, the "great benefits" of the federal form included "experiment and initiative."

At Cambridge University, my wife and I had an insight into the beginnings of Churchill College. Actually, we found that Cambridge had more features that seemed suitable to Santa Cruz than did Oxford, including: a better balance between science and non-science, "supervisions" that more frequently broke the 1/1 tutorial syndrome, the "dual employment" of teaching staff members with split salaries, and the urge to tie the teaching efforts of college and university closer together. We were there not long after publication of the "Bridges report" on the relationship between the university and the colleges (Cambridge, 1962). I liked its case for integrating excluded university teachers with the college system and for providing faculty lectureships for college fellows. It stressed the importance of good lecturing for "presenting information and argument to students in the mass" (p. 1087).

The British universities that were launched in the 1960s also influenced my thinking about internal organizational forms. A month in the British Isles during May–June 1963 afforded the opportunity to visit the planners of the seven "plate glass" universities—East Anglia, Essex, Kent, Lancaster, Sussex, Warwick, and York—and to have a look at Keele, which was founded in the 1950s. In 1969 my wife and I were able, thanks to the Danforth Foundation, to revisit the seven and to add Stirling in Scotland and Ulster in Northern Ireland.

On the first occasion I was much concerned with physical planning, particularly with the design of the residential colleges at Kent, Lancaster, and York. On the second, after all were in operation, I inquired more closely about the academic programs and structure of the colleges, schools, and departments of each institution. The three collegiate universities left teaching almost wholly to the university; the colleges were mainly for social, residential, and extracurricular purposes. The educational task of the three universities was entrusted to academic departments of a conventional sort. The noncollegiate four chose "school of studies" as their principal academic units. Sussex, the earliest, originated the plan, and its spread to other institutions is described by Willson in Chapter Nine.

Outside of Oxford and Cambridge, the typical older "red brick" British university administers its academic programs through a series of "faculties," concerned with a group of related subjects. Within each faculty the unit for teaching and research was the "single-subject department," usually headed permanently by the one professor, although sometimes two or more professors were authorized.

The University Grants Committee stated in more than one report its interest in broadening the undergraduate curriculum, breaking down the rigidities of departmental organization, and strengthening the relationship between teacher and taught. H. J. Perkin (n.d., pp. 145–146) in his study of new British universities said: "Departmentalism, in fact, is the besetting sin of the academic profession, whether in the old or the New Universities. It is easy to see why it should be so: a university teacher has invested an enormous intellectual and educational capital in his specialized subject, and to allow changes or encroachment upon it by other specialties represents a threat to "property" which could render the investment obsolete and the specialist redundant if not intellectually destitute." The danger, says Perkin, arises when the grouping of specialists becomes so introverted "they can no longer cooperate with other specialists beyond their boundaries, use the tools and insights provided by them, or explore the borderlands" (p. 146).

Representation of Subject-Matter Fields

With such a background of reading, visiting, and experience, I faced up to the critical choice of how to organize the disciplines in such a way that the colleges at Santa Cruz would not be inhibited. From the beginning of planning, I had assumed that there would be some kind of grouping by discipline. Most students would choose single disciplinary majors. Requirements would have to be set, courses offered and manned, comprehensive examinations prepared and evaluated, and senior theses supervised. Nearly all faculty members would have been trained in a single subject, and most would wish to maintain contacts with others in their subject, both on the campus and in national and regional learned societies. Graduate work and research were to be important considerations, and in many fields these require a critical minimum of colleagues who associate frequently and have access to facilities—laboratory, library, and other. I argued that groupings by discipline would be needed to fix responsibility for judging professional competence, for determining the quality of research and other creative work, and for guiding graduate students. They would also be helpful in placing our graduates in appropriate graduate and professional schools and in employment.

I was fairly certain that the initial groups, outside of the colleges, should comprise a limited number of related disciplines. In the 1962 plan I therefore proposed three groups, the humanities, social sciences, and natural sciences, initially to be called "faculties," and perhaps later "schools." I expressed hope that unique results in teaching and research might come from the interdisciplinary cooperation fostered by such an alignment. In the 1965 plan the same groupings were suggested, but the terminology of "divisions" was employed; that arrangement was implemented and has persisted.

The possibility of ultimately developing campuswide departments was not foreclosed in the 1962 provisional academic plan (UCSC, 1962, p. 9), but they were relegated to the remote future:

> The school or faculty might ultimately be further subdivided into campus-wide departments for convenience of administration. In the initial years, however, formation of departments will be deferred for policy and pedagogical reasons. Until the colleges are firmly rooted and the character of the undergraduate instructional function is established, it appears ill-advised to set up conventional departments. The early years should be a period of ferment and cross-pollinating among the disciplines.

Particularism at that stage might lead to deemphasis on undergraduate education. If this took place, the colleges might end
up being little more than dormitories with occasional tutorials.

By 1964, however, Clark Kerr and I were inclined to defer the coming of departments indefinitely, perhaps permanently. Departments
were not mentioned in the 1965 plan, with the exception of a limita-
tion on the colleges: "To encourage interdisciplinary cooperation
and to minimize particularism, there will be no formal departmental
organization within the colleges" (UCSC, 1965, p. 6).

The notion of joint appointments for all, or virtually all,
faculty members was spelled out. Typically, the 1965 plan said, an
academic position would appear in the budget as a combination
item: for example, "assistant professor of history and faculty fellow
of Cowell College." The provost and fellows of Cowell, on one
hand, and the vice chancellor or dean of the division, on the other,
would have mutual responsibility for finding and recommending the
appropriate candidate for the post. "Who takes the initiative and
which recommendation to follow in case of disagreement will be
determined by the Chancellor, advised by the appropriate committee of the Academic Senate" (pp. 15–16). In practice, about 98
percent of regular faculty appointments, exclusive of administrators,
have been divided equally between college and division. To give the
colleges bargaining power, we allocated to them the funds to pay
half of each faculty member's salary.

The reasons for our decision to forego departments have
been suggested in earlier chapters of this book, yet they deserve further discussion here. The particularism that is fostered by the disciplinary departmental system often tends to elevate orthodoxy and
makes of chairmen and others "boundary riders" who both keep colleagues from reaching out beyond the agreed-upon jurisdiction and
keep outsiders from poaching on departmental territory. This particularism has been exacerbated by the explosion of knowledge in
the twentieth century. At least in the areas I know something about,
no individual today can read and assimilate all of the published
work in one discipline, and many find it impossible to keep up even
in their special field or subdiscipline. The situation has encouraged
academic people to specialize even more, to read less widely, to

teach only in their special field, and to write within the narrow bounds of their extra competence.

As a consequence of this explosion, as well as the great expansion in enrollments, social and intellectual contacts tend to be limited to the department or even to a particular field. For example, physical anthropologists may keep to themselves and mix little with cultural anthropologists. The international relations people find they have less and less in common with their political science colleagues in the department. To keep some semblance of departmental viability, splits take place and further specialization is bolstered. At Berkeley, for example, there are at least eleven departments in the biological sciences.‡ Excluding the medical schools, Harvard and Stanford have consolidated nearly all biological sciences into one department of biology, but both have major problems of management, with more than fifty members. With these considerations in mind, we then turned to the practical task of devising a plan to give the disciplines representation without dominance.

Emergence of Boards of Studies

The Santa Cruz campus received its first students in the autumn of 1965. Although a few faculty members had been available for planning some months, most arrived shortly before the opening. The initial complement of students, numbering 650, included about 150 junior transfers who urgently needed clarification of how to proceed with their majors. Meetings of the humanities and social science faculties were held in mid-quarter, with the chief item on the agenda the establishment of a "board of studies" in each discipline to set requirements for the major, provide for a comprehensive examination, consult on disciplinary affairs, and—when ready—formulate a graduate program. Soon afterward the newly established Academic Senate set up a special committee on boards of studies, whose report was received and accepted by the senate in December 1965. In the report the board's functions were to be those sketched above, but instead of being a small appointive body

‡ Bacteriology and immunology, biochemistry, botany, cell physiology, entomological sciences, genetics, molecular biology, physiology-anatomy, plant pathology, soils and plant nutrition, zoology.

of three to five members, it would comprise all members of the Academic Senate in the discipline as ex officio members; the latter structure was designed to permit the younger members of the faculty to participate. The chancellor would appoint the "convenor." A second senate committee report in 1967 called for the allocation of funds for expenses, changing the convenor's title to chairman, annual appointments of the board chairman and reappointments up to a normal term of three years, consultation with college provosts on appointments and promotions, and office space and appropriate secretarial help. These recommendations were adopted. A motion to rename boards of studies departments was defeated overwhelmingly.

The administration took several precautions to prevent these boards from emerging as departments. Budgetary responsibility was vested in the divisions. Stenographic services were provided to faculty members through a campuswide stenographic pool that had branches in each college, where humanities and social sciences faculty members had their offices, and in the laboratories, where the natural science professors had theirs. Nevertheless, there were inevitable pressures to add functions and services that made the boards of studies semidepartments. Most of the majors (fields of concentration) were disciplinary; both the setting of requirements and their implementation were tasks of the disciplinary group. Both the division heads and college provosts looked to the boards for nominations when new faculty positions were authorized. As these burdens grew, all boards were assigned half-time or full-time secretaries, depending on the workload involved.

The emergence of the boards modified somewhat the planned function of the division heads. The latter became, in part, "brokers" who negotiated on behalf of "their" boards with the central administration and with the college provosts. They continued to control instructional support funds for courses offered in the division, but one or more began allocating funds in advance and allowing the boards to have considerable discretion over fiscal decisions.

The joint appointment arrangement means that both college and division play a real part in the appointment and advancement of a faculty member. In theory, at least, each unit looks at an individual from a different angle. The college is expected to judge the candidate's potential or actual relations with students, collegial colleagueship, and contributions to the college. The division looks hardest at research promise or achievement, professional standing, and graduate teaching, if any. Both usually have something to say about undergraduate teaching.

The disadvantages of this double structure are that the appointment and promotion processes are more complicated than those normally found under the conventional departmental system. The Santa Cruz Academic Senate interpreted the rule governing consultation on personnel transactions as requiring full participation by board and college faculty members. The faculty time taken for this dual review is excessive. Junior faculty members complain often about the hardship of "serving two masters."

The Santa Cruz boards of studies in fact look and act like departments, although rather incomplete ones. They offer about 80 percent of all courses. They had, in 1975–1976, twenty-six of the thirty-four undergraduate majors offered:

Humanities: *Art History, Art, History, Linguistics, Literature, Music, Philosophy, Religious Studies, Theater Arts.*
Social Sciences: *Anthropology, Community Studies, Economics, Environmental Planning, Environmental Studies, Politics, Psychology, Sociology.*
Natural Sciences: *Astronomy, Biology, Chemistry, Earth Science, Information Science, Mathematics, Physics.*

The colleges offered six: Cowell, *Arts, Crafts and Their History* and *Western Civilization;* Stevenson, *Modern Society and Social Thought;* Merrill, *Latin American Studies;* Five, *Aesthetic Studies;* and Kresge, *Women's Studies.* Two were campuswide interdisciplinary majors: *Psychology-Biology,* and *East Asian Studies.* In terms of numbers of students, there were 3860 with board majors and 110 with college-sponsored majors; the remainder were interdisciplinary, individual, or undeclared.

What has evolved at Santa Cruz is a two-dimensional organizational matrix that works reasonably well but sometimes causes its proponents to wonder whether the extra effort is justified by the results. On the one hand, there are the colleges, charged with giving the student a sense of belonging, providing cultural and social opportunities on a human scale, contributing intellectual stimulus by close association of student and faculty member. On the other are the boards, fronted by the divisions, who represent the traditional interests of the disciplines; they do most of the teaching, set most of the standards, carry out most of the examining function.

Yet the two factors, both warp and woof, are part of the same tapestry. Some 300 (in 1976) men and women, as fellows of their colleges, make judgments concerning academic personnel and programs, judgments that they may make and review again as members of boards of studies. Sometimes the verdicts are contradictory, because only a portion of the total is eligible to participate in a particular decision. For an example of a somewhat typical problem, assume that a position has been allocated to be shared by the board of studies in Information Sciences and Oakes College. The board has half of a position for an assistant professor and the college the other half for a fellow. No appointment will be made unless they can reach agreement. The board usually has in mind getting someone with a particular specialty needed for its teaching or research program. Oakes College may want most a person able and willing to counsel and tutor minority students in science. In the great majority of cases, agreement is reached and an offer is made. In case of disagreement, the dean of the division and the provost may try to find a different combination: a young chemist for Oakes, and for Kresge College an information scientist who has an abiding interest in women's studies. In a few cases, disagreement is so complete and flexibility so limited, it is not possible to make an appointment during that recruiting season.

One might assume that these complexities in faculty recruiting would frighten away leading prospects. Actually, we found we could recruit both mature scholars from leading universities and young people out of the best graduate schools. Most were enthusiastic about the collegiate plan and welcomed the opportunity for close instruction of undergraduates. The inflow of top faculty members was aided by the evidence, made quite clear from 1966 on, that the incoming students were—according to their grades in secondary school and their scores on the Scholastic Aptitude Test—among the most select in the nation. Scientists were attracted by such factors as the excellent new laboratories and the opportunity to have as

colleagues leading astronomers of the Lick Observatory, which became a part of UC in 1888 and moved to the Santa Cruz campus in
1966. Other scholars were impressed that the university could provide on opening day a library with a carefully chosen collection of
75,000 volumes. The 500,000th volume was added in August 1976.

The self-study that preceded the accreditation of 1976
(UCSC, 1975) recommended that a joint committee arrangement
be used to simplify both the process of recruiting new faculty members and that for considering faculty promotions. Such joint committees would have representatives from both college and board,
and the senate rule requiring faculty consultation would apply to the
joint consideration. This seems to me a sensible solution *if* it can be
implemented in such a way that it does not add an extra step, rather
than—as intended—reduce two steps to one. In other words, the
full reviews of college and board faculties must yield to the new plan.

Figure 1 depicts the entire organizational structure of Santa
Cruz during the final year of my administration. The crucial matrix
interrelationships involved the divisions (and their boards of studies)
shown in the left column, and the colleges, shown in the adjoining
column. After 1974 an academic vice-chancellor was assigned much
of the oversight of divisions and colleges; and from 1976 each division head was given the title of dean.

One proposal to change the relationships between the colleges and the divisions and boards was made by my successor, Mark
Christensen, who took seriously the discordance he heard in college
and division-board disagreements. The reorganization plan he put
forward in November 1975 called for abolishing the humanities and
social science divisions and relating, in some unexplained way, their
boards of studies to the colleges. The natural sciences division would
become a school, with jurisdiction over both undergraduate and
graduate work. A Council of Colleges would govern and regulate
intercollege coordination, cooperation, and liaison. The Academic
Senate declined to consider the proposal. If it had been examined
on its merits, I think it would have been found wanting. Budgetary
authority that is now in the divisions would have to be assigned
somewhere if the two divisions were abolished. If given to the
boards, each would require additional assistance to the extent that
the board staffs would turn out to be larger than the modest ones

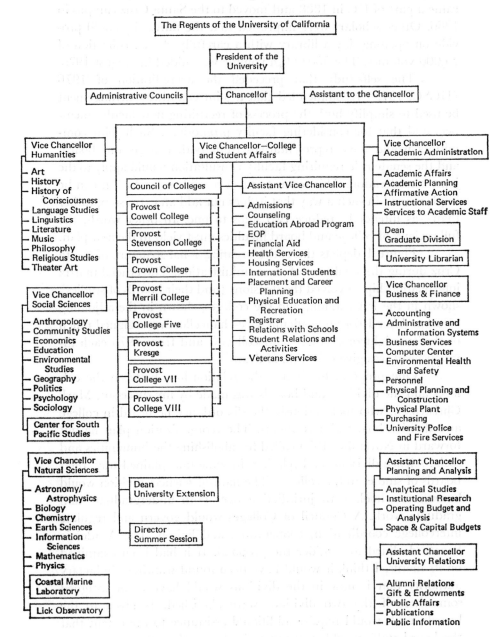

Figure 1. University of California, Santa Cruz,
Administrative Organization, 1973–74

The Regents of the University of California

President of the University

Administrative Councils — Chancellor — Assistant to the Chancellor

Vice Chancellor Humanities
- Art
- History
- History of Consciousness
- Language Studies
- Linguistics
- Literature
- Music
- Philosophy
- Religious Studies
- Theater Art

Vice Chancellor Social Sciences
- Anthropology
- Community Studies
- Economics
- Education
- Environmental Studies
- Geography
- Politics
- Psychology
- Sociology

Center for South Pacific Studies

Vice Chancellor Natural Sciences
- Astronomy/ Astrophysics
- Biology
- Chemistry
- Earth Sciences
- Information Sciences
- Mathematics
- Physics

Coastal Marine Laboratory

Lick Observatory

Vice Chancellor—College and Student Affairs

Council of Colleges
- Provost Cowell College
- Provost Stevenson College
- Provost Crown College
- Provost Merrill College
- Provost College Five
- Provost Kresge
- Provost College VII
- Provost College VIII

Dean University Extension

Director Summer Session

Assistant Vice Chancellor
- Admissions
- Counseling
- Education Abroad Program
- EOP
- Financial Aid
- Health Services
- Housing Services
- International Students
- Placement and Career Planning
- Physical Education and Recreation
- Registrar
- Relations with Schools
- Student Relations and Activities
- Veterans Services

Vice Chancellor Academic Administration
- Academic Affairs
- Academic Planning
- Affirmative Action
- Instructional Services
- Services to Academic Staff

Dean Graduate Division

University Librarian

Vice Chancellor Business & Finance
- Accounting
- Administrative and Information Systems
- Business Services
- Computer Center
- Environmental Health and Safety
- Personnel
- Physical Planning and Construction
- Physical Plant
- Purchasing
- University Police and Fire Services

Assistant Chancellor Planning and Analysis
- Analytical Studies
- Institutional Research
- Operating Budget and Analysis
- Space & Capital Budgets

Assistant Chancellor University Relations
- Alumni Relations
- Gift & Endowments
- Public Affairs
- Publications
- Public Information

presently in the divisions. If teaching-support funds were allocated through the colleges, unequal treatment of colleagues in the same discipline but different colleges would almost certainly occur. Without a dean to represent a group of boards, each board would have to maintain a network of separate contacts with every college. Instead of simplifying the administration, I suspect that such a change would have made it immensely more complicated and time consuming.

The College Quest for an Academic Role

Although the preplanning spelled out a good deal about the colleges, the actual division of academic functions between colleges and disciplinary groups was left vague. This lack of definiteness was born in part of humility on my part: I simply did not know enough, despite my reading and visits. It also stemmed from my long indoctrination in the University of California system. The regents decades earlier firmly delegated academic affairs to the Academic Senate. I wanted to wait to see how faculty members felt and to judge the competence of those who would bear responsibility. One of my co-planners in 1962, Karl A. Lamb, now feels that if we had started two colleges at the beginning we might have worked out a clearer assignment of responsibilities both between the colleges and the divisions and between the colleges and the campuswide administration. As it happened, we launched Cowell College alone in 1965, and the first year few other faculty members were teaching outside Cowell, so the rubric under which courses were offered seemed unimportant.

The first phase of collegiate academic endeavor was characterized by an interdisciplinary thrust. When Cowell College got underway in 1965, its freshmen were required to take a college "core" course, World Civilization, that continued for six quarters and constituted one-third of their instructional program in the freshman and sophomore years. Almost all the faculty fellows participated: a few as lecturers, the others as seminar leaders. It survived as a required course on that basis for three years, when the sophomore level was dropped; the freshman requirement continued until 1971. Now freshmen must take Western Civilization for one quarter only. Stevenson College, launched in 1966, had a freshman-year core course, Culture and Society (reduced to a single quarter in 1970), and a series of sophomore seminars. Crown followed in 1967; its core course was Science, Culture, and Man and seniors were required to take one college seminar; the core course was dropped in 1969 and college offerings became fragmented. Merrill started in 1968 with a one-year core course called The Third World and a fieldwork program for advanced undergraduates.

Before we were out of the 1960s, the trend was clear: the colleges were truncating core courses, making them voluntary, or abandoning them. This trend was the result of two predictable pressures: the faculty grew tired of teaching them, and the students' complaints about compulsion were telling. The colleges then began expanding their lists of courses, many of which were offered only occasionally, and some only once. Some could be classified as courses that elaborated or supported the core course or college theme (Examples: Merrill's Southeast Asia–Indonesia, Black America, Hispanic Culture). Others were team taught and clearly interdisciplinary (Examples: Crown's Pollution of Air and Water, Stevenson's Enology). Still others covered subjects that were not among the board offerings: College Five's The Art of Jazz and Photographing the American Landscape.

Without any official sanction, administrative or senate, the notion emerged that a faculty person each year should teach four courses for the board and one for the college. Later colleges, particularly Oakes, have tried to change this to two for the college and three for the board. Of course, the important thing is to apply teaching resources where they are most needed, so the validity of the demand for more teaching time varies with the program of each college.

Around 1970 the colleges turned their attention to developing their own majors, supplementing the campuswide majors that continued to exist. By 1975–1976 there were six college majors. Cowell had two: Arts and Crafts and Their History and Western Civilization; Stevenson: Modern Society and Social Thought; Merrill: Latin American Studies; Five: Aesthetic Studies; Kresge: Women's Studies. The Cowell and Five majors were confined to their own students; the others were available to outsiders on petition.

Coming after the initial allocation of support funds and after the availability of funds from state sources was increasingly restricted, the colleges were hard pressed to finance the additional courses deemed necessary to back some of the majors. They used their shares of the Ford Foundation Venture Grant to cover the most essential expenses, but this grant ended in 1974. Without steady sources of funds, advanced work in fields as expensive as arts and crafts and some aspects of aesthetic studies was quite difficult to provide.

Thus, it is evident that the educational functions of the colleges were inadequately defined and supported in the original academic plans. The core courses of the early colleges, particularly of Cowell, seemed to fulfill the rather vague aspirations that the colleges would provide (1) their own distinctive ways of meeting campuswide breadth requirements, (2) common ground for faculty and students related to the college theme, (3) close contact of students with fellows of their own colleges. The decline, and in some cases demise, of core courses was accompanied to some extent by the proliferation of other college courses, usually unrelated to a general plan and too often the grudging response of a fellow to a provost who asked, "What are you going to do for the college next year?" To this muddled situation were added the college majors, precariously financed but genuinely interdisciplinary. Looking ahead, one can see bright promise in programs of groups of colleges, such as the Cowell-Stevenson joint science program. Less promising, it seems to me, are proposals to link particular colleges to particular graduate programs. In original conception, and by definition in the University of California, colleges are for undergraduate education; graduate work belongs to the Graduate Division and professional schools.

A recent tendency to encourage faculty shifts among colleges seems to me equally fraught with danger. A senate-initiated scheme of faculty intercollege transfers is called "reaggregation." Its avowed purpose was to ease shifts in college affiliation so that a critical minimum of faculty fellows with common interests in a problem or a specialty could be together. But its effect was unsettling to colleges that were still attempting to carry out meaningful academic programs; a fellow who wished to avoid the commitment could put in for transfer to a college with a minimal program ("a noncollege").

There had been quiet shifts before, perhaps thirty to thirty-five between 1965 and 1973, but now the musical chairs game tempted many more to play. In self-defense, a college losing fellows was induced to recruit others to replace them, and the competitive show was on, amid rumors that transferring fellows had been promised various forms of relief from college duties. The net result was a realignment that left some colleges with a more adverse faculty/student ratio than others and with a roster of fellows that was unbalanced by discipline. These effects bode ill for the college that conscientiously tries to provide academic counseling to its student members. Now some colleges have good grounds to complain that they are so short of faculty manpower they cannot take additional students. And students can validly ask to transfer because their college has no fellow in their field of interest.

Students and Academic Programs

Students came to Santa Cruz for a variety of reasons. One, which has been experienced by several promising new institutions, was the attraction of newness. A fresh beginning often draws adventurous young people. When it is coupled with an innovative or challenging program, exceptionally able students may be attracted. Certainly that was true of the "pioneer" classes of such colleges as New (Florida), Raymond (California), and Hampshire (Massachusetts). Santa Cruz's popularity in the early years came as a pleasant surprise to its planners.

Originally the new campuses were expected by some to serve as overflow receptacles for applicants the older and larger campuses could not accommodate. Actually, in its first six years, Santa Cruz redirected thousands of qualified applicants to the older campuses. At the height of its popularity, UCSC had four times as many qualified applicants as it could admit. Opening just after the so-called Free Speech movement erupted at Berkeley, its announced intentions—smallness of scale, personalized approach, closeness of instruction—seemed just the corrective to the alleged ills of the large, monolithic university.

As the campus became known, the list of attractions expanded. It was located in an area of exceptional natural beauty: on a plateau amid redwood forests and meadows, overlooking Monterey Bay and the Pacific Ocean. The design of the buildings was sensitive to the surroundings and gave first consideration to the trees and terrain. Although the town was, in some ways, an old-fashioned beach resort that time had passed by, most students came to like it. Indeed, it proved difficult to get them to go home during vacation time, and many graduates sought employment in the area rather than return to the "hassle" and smog of urban life.

Surveys of graduates have shown conclusively that the evaluation system adopted by UCSC was the most frequently mentioned asset of the institution. The academic plan (UCSC, 1965, p. 12) had promised reform in this sector: "To reduce student anxieties and to focus attention on learning rather than memorizing, steps will be taken to modify the grading system. Much can be accomplished under existing Senate regulations. Fuller use can be made of "pass/fail" grades, which were authorized long ago and are little used. Another possibility for securing more meaningful evaluation would be to ask faculty members to write for each student at the end of each course a brief summary of the student's capabilities and achievements."

Soon after the Academic Senate was organized at Santa Cruz, the Cowell faculty sought approval of the Universitywide Senate for an exception to the basic requirement that letter grades (ABCDF) be awarded. The proposal was for an across-the-board use of Pass/Fail; this was modified to allow letter grades in a few science courses if requested by the student. (In fact, .003 percent of all grades recorded in a recent quarter were letter grades.) The Pass/Fail grade (now Pass/No Report) was to be augmented, however, by a narrative evaluation in all except the largest lecture courses. Most of the students liked the Pass/Fail with written evaluation plan; they argued that highly competitive letter grading deters wide reading and broad understanding and that good written evaluations give a better index to their potentialities than grade-point averages. The Academic Senate, statewide, voted a five-year waiver on letter grading, renewed it for another five, and then made it permanent in 1974.

Of course any deviation from the norm brings problems. We had a job getting graduate and professional schools to look at our graduates rather than push aside their applications because they lacked a given GPA. We stressed reliance on the Graduate Record Examination (GRE), the Law School Admission Test (LSAT), the Medical College Admission Test, and other scores. Most effective in the early years, we phoned and wrote key educators to call attention to the applications of our graduates. The problems are not over, but we are reasonably satisfied that most of our graduates who apply get into postbaccalaureate programs that are commensurate with their abilities.

To deemphasize further the mechanistic ways of computing a student's academic progress, we abandoned the variable "unit" or "credit" values assigned to courses and gave each an identical value. A "course" at Santa Cruz has an "outside" value, on transfer elsewhere, of five quarter units. Its inside value is 1/36th of the total course requirement for a bachelor's degree. The typical four-year student takes three courses per quarter (nine per year) for four years. In addition, however, one must either write a senior thesis or take a comprehensive examination in the major field.

A student may earn distinction, beyond all passes and securing praiseworthy written evaluations, through the award of honors with his degree. The outstanding graduates in a particular major may be awarded highest honors or honors by the board or committee that administers their curriculum. In addition, the college awards the graduates it regards as outstanding something called general honors, signifying academic achievement and special contribution to college life. A third type, less well known because it appears only on student records and not on the diploma, is honors on the senior thesis or comprehensive examination.

Some find it curious that Santa Cruz does not separate the teaching and examining functions, as does Oxford. This separation would be difficult, in view of the small amount of formal teaching done by our colleges and their relatively modest role in sponsoring majors. In fact, the boards of studies do most of the teaching and examining. The examining function, except for comprehensive exams, is tied to course offerings, so whichever unit teaches a course also assesses. The comprehensive examination (and whatever defense of thesis there is) is administered by the sponsoring unit.

Undergraduate students in 1976 could choose from among

twenty-six majors offered by the boards of studies and eight offered by the colleges and interdisciplinary committees. In addition, they may formulate an individual major or put together a joint or double major. Biology attracts the largest number, followed by psychology, literature, and politics. In terms of numbers of majors, the social sciences have the most, natural sciences the next, and humanities the fewest. There are eleven graduate degree programs (M.A., M.S., and Ph.D.), covering all fields of science, as well as literature, history, psychology, and the history of consciousness. The largest numbers are in biology, history of consciousness, and chemistry. There is a small teacher internship program.

We took great satisfaction in the academic qualifications of the students who came to UCSC. Although many institutions prefer not to share scores with others, we soon became aware the Scholastic Aptitude Test (SAT) scores of our freshmen were relatively high.*

We also kept an eye on the ACE Freshman Survey, particularly the responses of our incoming students to the question about average grades in high school. In the eight years 1966 through 1973, the proportion reporting averages of A+, A, or A− ran from a low of 53.6 percent in 1969 to a high of 67.9 percent in 1972. After looking at these figures, Harold L. Hodgkinson wrote: "Given students of this level of ability and proven performance, almost any campus would look good" (UC, 1972, p. 2). By the mid-1970s, however, the honeymoon was over, and the UCSC freshman scores, both on the SAT and in the ACE survey, went down. In 1974 the ACE survey A averages dropped to 47.4 and in 1975 to 45.6. Among the more plausible explanations were: the admission of in-

---

* One of the few bases of comparison was the SAT scores of enrolled freshmen reported in the latest *American Universities and Colleges* issued by the American Council on Education (1973). For 1970–1971, this edition showed Caltech leading the California institutions at 1429 for the average combined verbal and mathematical scores. The next in line were Occidental, 1269; Santa Cruz, 1257; and Pomona 1252. (Stanford and Harvey Mudd were not reported.) Among American state universities, UCSC's 1257 appears to have been highest. It was followed by Virginia, 1206; Michigan, Ann Arbor, 1203. (SUNY, Albany, reported 1264, and SUNY, Binghamton, 1239, but these were extrapolated figures and excluded some students.) Compared with top-rank private institutions across the country, UCSC was outscored by at least two dozen, but was ahead of Sarah Lawrence, 1250, tied with Brandeis at 1257, and just outranked by Grinnell, which had 1260.

creased numbers of disadvantaged students, the lack of professional and career-oriented curricula, due concern lest the evaluation scheme handicap entry into graduate school or employment, and the nationwide decline in SAT scores. Three years after the campus was surfeited with applicants, it was out recruiting students and accepting redirected applicants from Berkeley and Davis.

Another change in the characteristics of incoming students is the shift from freshmen to students with advanced standing, primarily juniors. In fact, in recent years the transfer students have outnumbered the freshmen. This shift helps to carry out one of the goals of the Master Plan for Higher Education, which was to encourage freshmen and sophomores to attend community colleges rather than four-year institutions (Liaison Committee . . . , 1960, p. 59). For Santa Cruz the change requires a good deal of rethinking concerning general education and breadth requirements, as well as college programs.

Summary and Conclusion

Those of us who had the responsibility for planning Santa Cruz, and for implementing those plans, chose to make the residential college a basic unit of student and faculty identification. We also provided for groups of disciplines to be represented through "divisions" and disciplines through "boards of studies."

To keep the college/division-board balance, faculty members were given joint appointments, with half of their compensation coming from each source. In practice, the division-board side tends to speak more authoritatively in academic personnel matters. This voice can be attributed in part to its larger role in teaching (about 4/1) and in part to its use of norms developed in the particular field of study. The colleges continue to search for a more meaningful role in academic affairs. They are unlikely to achieve it by offering more scattered courses or marginal majors. A more hopeful line might be for the colleges to assume responsibility for general education and provide all the ways to meet breadth requirements. They might also set up batteries of group tutorials or seminars at various levels and make them compulsory.

The highest priority, it seems to me, is for the colleges to establish and maintain an efficient academic advising system that would put every new student in close touch with a fellow of his college during the first year at Santa Cruz, preferably in the first quarter. In some cases this advisory function could be carried out largely through small seminars, the students in which would be all of a fellow's new advisees. After an initial period on the campus, advising can be less structured: the more advanced student has a major and often will prefer to seek counsel from a specialist in his field, whether within his college or elsewhere.

To what extent has the organizational matrix contributed to the relative success of Santa Cruz? The differential diagnosis is extremely difficult. My impression is that the existence of the matrix has helped substantially to attract a faculty that is good both at undergraduate teaching and advanced inquiry. By the conventional criteria—memberships in the National Academy of Science, Guggenheims, Fulbrights, distinguished-teaching awards—the academic staff is outstanding. Not only do they spend extraordinary amounts of time at teaching, but they also are unusually productive in creative work. I have a five-foot shelf of books and monographs produced by the faculty since the campus opened. Some chose Santa Cruz over older and more prestigious institutions because it offered the prospect of a balanced career. Far from being repelled by the notion of close relations with students, most faculty members we approached were attracted by it.

What difference does the matrix make to students? Again the weighing of various factors is a hard task. Undoubtedly such features as the natural beauty of the area, the prestige of the University of California, and an evaluation plan that assures freedom from memorizing are often elements in the decision to choose Santa Cruz. But involved in many, perhaps most, acceptances is the reputation of the campus for having a faculty interested in both teaching and research. The matrix assures institutional attention to both.

After students arrive and settle in, many experience unusual intellectual growth. For some this is evidenced by the research that goes into a senior thesis. (In the early 1970s, about 40 percent of the seniors chose the thesis plan; 60 percent took comprehensive examinations.) When Woodrow Wilson Fellowships were in full swing, Santa Cruz graduates repeatedly scored in the top brackets. In 1976

UCSC seniors won two of the sixty-five Danforth Fellowships awarded nationally, four Fulbrights, six National Science Foundation Fellowships, and four of the fifty-seven Ford Foundation Graduate Fellowships. In proportion to the size of graduating classes, such records—repeated year after year for a decade—put the number of awards to Santa Cruz seniors among the highest in the nation.

If one accepts our argument that the particularism fostered by the conventional department tends to divert faculty time to advanced study and research and away from undergraduates and to erect barriers to experimentation with different approaches to learning and solving academic problems, then having avoided full-blown departments at Santa Cruz is a negative achievement of value. Whether setting up the colleges and the boards of studies in juxtapositional relationship is a positive achievement remains to be seen. Tensions exist, but they seem to me largely healthy ones. As J. Douglas Brown says in another essay in this volume, tensions can be turned to constructive ends if the antagonists have mutual respect and are willing to make reasonable concessions to one another.

The two points of view represented in the matrix ought to be present in any multipurpose university: the needs of undergraduates, on the one hand, and scholarly work and advanced teaching on the other. What is new at UCSC is that they have been institutionalized in such a way that neither is likely to be overlooked.

7 Charles R. Longsworth

Academic Organization by Schools at Hampshire College

"Instead of organizing the curriculum by departments, each of which attempts to provide a course offering which it regards as adequate to cover its subject, New College will aim to fit its students to master subjects, chiefly on their own initiative, by providing them with the necessary skills, resources, and intellectual stimulation." These words, and the antecedents of Hampshire College, may be found in *The New College Plan* (Barber and others, 1958, pp. 8–9), written at the request of the presidents of Amherst, Mount Holyoke, and Smith colleges, and the University of Massachusetts by a committee of faculty members from these four institutions. The committee had been asked how the four neighboring colleges might "extend their own programs and make better use of their resources" and was invited to "rethink the assumptions underlying education in the liberal arts and to reevaluate accepted practices and techniques in order to draw up plans for a college which would provide education of the highest quality at a minimum cost per student and with as small a faculty relative to the student body as new methods of instruction and new administrative procedures can make possible" (p. 3).

The impetus for such planning in 1958 was the large college-bound population, pressuring the four colleges to expand to accept an increased number of qualified applicants. The three private colleges were reluctant to change size in any significant way in the belief that becoming larger would risk modification of the values of the small residential college that they so prized and that were their strength. Amherst, for example, felt it would be self-defeating to grow from twelve hundred to two thousand students, thus risking a change in the character of the college. Thus, the New College planning was a way of responding to a social responsibility and the need to protect institutional identity and character.

The New College Committee members, Caesar L. Barber, Amherst; Donald C. Sheehan, Smith; Stewart M. Stoke, Mount Holyoke; and Shannon McCune, University of Massachusetts, were cast initially into a planning framework that assumed the new institution would have severe financial constraints. Their planning therefore had to make possible the construction of a college of high quality that could function in the competitive environment of the other four colleges without the benefit of a large and relatively assured budget, as in the case of the University of Massachusetts, or without the substantial endowments and derivative income that undergirded the operations of Amherst, Mount Holyoke, and Smith Colleges.

However, the final paragraph of the letter of charge to the committee (by Sidney R. Packard, coordinator of the four colleges in 1956–1958), continued redeeming language that enabled the New College planners to devise an ingenious educational plan, one that had profound financial implications and appeared to be feasible. This paragraph said, "Finally, whether or not your study arrives at a conclusion that such a project is feasible, the four presidents feel strongly that great benefit will come to our respective institutions by the freshness and daring of your approach, by your challenging of long-held assumptions, and by your exploration of new techniques and practices in higher education."

The Plan

The New College Plan laid down the lines for a new institution whose academic organization grew out of and strengthened the educational ideas that were to be the basis of the college. Very briefly, those ideas were that the main goal of a college education is to help students acquire the skills and maturation to continue to learn after formal education ends; that most college programs are too structured and too restrictive of the capacity for independent thought of which many students are capable; that faculty and students should be freed from the artificial constraints of an educational system which relies on taking and giving courses and the coverage of subjects. (Barber and others, 1958, pp. 3–4).

A retrospective look at those ideas leads me to believe that they are as fresh and important today as they were eighteen years ago. Even the best of our undergraduate liberal arts colleges struggle still, or worse, don't yet struggle, with narrow specialization and departmental tyranny. Subject matter covered, courses completed, and term examinations are still the principle and still a very inadequate way to define education.

More than ten thousand copies of *The New College Plan* were distributed and the document was widely read by educators. It is in demand today. The impact of the *Plan*'s ideas is difficult to measure fully and accurately, but it undoubtedly affected educational thinking in the United States. Few credits are given; yet an examination of the literature of higher education and the programs of many institutions reflect *The New College Plan* thinking. For example, the *Plan* first proposed the January Term calendar, now known popularly as a 4-1-4 calendar, and adopted by hundreds of institutions, and Harvard College's widely touted freshman seminars were inspired directly by the *Plan* and so acknowledged.

The New College Plan did stimulate an effort to begin the college in earnest, and efforts were made through early 1960 to fund the organizing effort and initial construction of the campus in the four-college area. An approach to the Ford Foundation, which had backed the New College planning through the Fund for the Advancement of Education, resulted in a promise to grant six million dollars if an equal amount of matching funds could be found. However, by 1960 important changes were occurring in the leadership of the four colleges. The *Plan* had been sponsored by presidents Cole of Amherst, Gettell of Mount Holyoke, Mather of the University of Massachusetts, and Wright of Smith College. President Cole, who had led the effort to obtain Ford Foundation funding, and President Mather resigned their positions in June of 1960; President Wright of Smith had resigned in 1959; so only President Gettell survived. Understandably, the agenda of their successors did not include the creation of the New College as first priority. The effort to match the $6 million was abandoned, and the planning for the New College went into eclipse.

Nevertheless, the ideas of the New College stayed very much alive in the minds of some of its advocates. In 1965 Harold F. Johnson, an Amherst College alumnus, inquired of Henry Heald, president of the Ford Foundation, and Charles Cole about the possibility of picking up the loose threads from 1960. Subsequently, working with Calvin H. Plimpton, Charles Cole's successor at Amherst, an agreement was reached in 1965 whereby Harold Johnson pledged $6 million and the Ford Foundation pledged $3.5 million on a one-to-one matching basis. A search for leadership began, and Franklin Patterson was appointed first president of the new institution, called Hampshire College, in June 1966.

"The Making of a College"

Patterson began immediately to write a planning document to make current *The New College Plan* and to elaborate in a much more expansive and detailed way the organization of Hampshire College. The resultant book, *The Making of a College* (Patterson and Longsworth, 1966), and *The New College Plan* are the basic documents with which Hampshire College has been created. This book portrays the organic relationship between Hampshire's academic organization and its educational ideas:

> The ultimately controlling factor in Hampshire College's academic program is the view of liberal education which the college has chosen to take. This view is that the college exists not alone to prepare students for the high level of technical competence demanded by preparation for graduate school, nor to prepare them in skills of inquiry, nor to give them an opportunity to explore the development of themselves through art and experience. All of these things are subsumed under Hampshire College's view of liberal education, that the college has a larger and higher aim than any of these taken separately.

Hampshire . . . is deliberately designed to equip the student as best we know how to learn how to make his own way as a whole person in the emerging age [p. 71].

In constructing a program, the New College planners "dethroned the course as the basic unit of knowledge" to encourage attention to larger questions than those that may be derived from courses, to deemphasize specialization and narrowness, and to stress alternatives to course work (independent and field study) as the means to organize a successful, high-quality college with a relatively small faculty. They focused on the ways in which scholars worked, regarding these as the key to gaining a capacity for learning, as opposed to an accumulation of factual data, much of it transitory in nature and the rest likely to be soon forgotten.

Fundamental to the foregoing statements, as manifested in the academic organization, is that the college had to enable both students and faculty members to achieve breadth, to maintain flexibility, to seek and achieve perspective, and to synthesize and integrate. These aims required the faculty to have broad rather than narrow views and interests, to have a capacity to continue to learn both within and outside their own fields, to be able to advise and examine students successfully on a range of ideas and subjects broader than the faculty members' training had prepared them for, and to have sympathetic attitudes toward the comprehensive and universal questions raised by students with high expectations and aspirations. To achieve even a modicum of success with such educational goals, students could not be trapped in a structure.

The ways in which scholars work, or the methods of conceptual inquiry, became, and still are, the touchstone of Hampshire College, the basis for rejecting the course as the basic unit of knowledge, subjects as the building blocks of an undergraduate education, and subject coverage as the definition of education. Daniel Bell's *The Reforming of General Education* (1966) was a convenient and articulate expression of educational reform at the time *The Making of a College* was written, and it provided important insights into the implications of conceptual inquiry as the heart of the apparently permanent revolutions in knowledge in which we now live. Bell said, "Conceptual inquiry is at the heart of the apparently permanent revolution in knowledge in which we now live. Currently the rate of revision of theoretical knowledge in the sciences may be twenty to a hundred times higher than it was less than 100 years ago. In such a state of flux in all the fields of knowledge, the centrality of method becomes clear. Inquiry; ways of discovering and knowing; of analyzing; of going from hunch to hypothesis to test to reconsideration, with conceptual tools to help you—these make up a reasonable keystone for general education now" (in Patterson and Longsworth, 1966, p. 87).

The thinking of the New College planners was not as fully developed as Bell's, but they did stress conceptual inquiry as the basis for the New College curriculum. They said, "At New College, subjects will be covered, not by providing complete programs of courses, but by training the student to master recognized fields of knowledge. A systematic and sustained effort will be made to train students to educate themselves" (Barber and others, 1958, p. 4). These comments certainly refer to the essence of conceptual inquiry and reveal a beginning sense of the need to free students from the bonds of subject coverage and course definitions so that they may competently employ those intellectual skills that are not outmoded by the evolution of knowledge.

The discussion of Hampshire's academic program that follows will make clear that its curriculum "is not committed to a wholly elective or individualized approach to studies while allowing room for choice; is determined not to allow narrow specialization to dominate its character; regards its central task . . . as requiring certain common studies for all students; accepts conceptual inquiry as its pervasive, pedagogical style, and training for self-use as a principal obligation of the college" (Patterson and Longsworth, p. 91).

Academic Organization

Both *The New College Plan* and *The Making of a College* concluded that organizing the college faculty by departments was unlikely to achieve the stated goals of the respective documents. The New College Committee aimed at the heart of the traditional departmentalized organization, reasoning that departments' self-protective qualities and unquestioned belief in subject matter coverage stimulate wasteful course proliferation. Each departmentally based professor furthers his own interests and those of the department by attracting undergraduate majors and thus enlarging the departments' claims for more faculty positions, programs, and courses. The alternative, the committee stated, was to help students master subjects on their own by teaching them the necessary skills and providing useful resources and intellectual stimulation.

The assumption of increased independence on the part of students, made possible a plan whereby the faculty was approximately half the size, relative to the student body, of the faculties of the sponsoring private colleges; the proposed student/faculty ratio was 20/1. The small faculty helped satisfy the Committee's charge to develop an economical plan and its own good sense that economy was vital if the plan were to have a chance of becoming a living institution. But economy and efficiency were the result, not the priority considerations.

The Committee did think fundamentally, and it proposed a divisional organization—a collection of related disciplines organized according to the usual divisions of social science, natural science, and humanities and arts—as the basis for an integrated departure from the usual in higher education.

The opportunity to think fresh and start anew without the impediments of a real institution with a history and a present existence is rare, of course, and few who are concerned with changes in academic organization and its implications have the opportunity to design a new college or to build one. Yet it is instructive to be reminded by the New College planners that a clear statement of the problems and issues, a recognition that the aims and means of education are the starting point for academic organization, and a sure sense of how the relationships among disciplines, subjects, curricula, teachers, and students may be affected by alternatives in academic organization are all vital to design or redesign. Sometimes, unfortunately, organizational thinking is an exercise only distantly related to problems or solutions.

Beginning with a clean slate, Hampshire had the opportunity to design an academic organization which expressed and was calculated to best serve its assumptions and plans about teaching and

learning, without the inhibitions or limitations of an existing inherited structure or the prior appointment of persons with contrary
ideas. The concept of a divisional organization had been broached
eight years earlier in *The New College Plan,* had the support of the
founding group of Hampshire trustees and supporters, and was the
choice of Franklin Patterson, who, with myself and two secretaries,
composed the entire staff of the college in 1966.

Schools, Hampshire Model

The Making of a College retained an emphasis on disciplinary training. Such training was considered fundamentally important in determining the capabilities of an individual faculty
person and the quality of the faculty as a whole, and the discipline
is the pedagogical and epistemological basis for course and independent study work. The book nevertheless proposed that the faculty be organized not in discipline-based units but in four schools—
humanities and arts, natural science and mathematics (subsequently
changed to natural science), social science, and language studies
(subsequently changed to language and communication). The
schools as currently constituted have a high degree of autonomy
and flexibility in curricular, administrative, organizational, and
budgetary affairs, subject to certain overriding college policy guidelines, which are administered by the dean of the college and the
vice-president in counsel with the school administrators.

Membership in a school, which is distinguished by the right
to vote on school matters, is a necessary condition of service for
faculty members and is open to a limited number of students and
staff members. Faculty members usually outnumber nonfaculty
members and predominate on committees making recommendations on curriculum, evaluation, and faculty appointment and reappointment. In the spring of 1976 the membership of the schools
varied from thirty-three to sixty-six persons. The number of faculty
members ranged from forty-two in humanities and arts (which
also had eight students and six staff members) to twenty-eight in
social science (along with twenty-two students and seven staff
members).

The leadership form of the schools is evolving and varies

among them. The initial plan was to appoint persons who would be "permanent" school deans, serving for five to ten years and then, most likely, joining the faculty on a full-time basis. Each of the initial appointees had faculty and administrative contracts specifying that he or she would spend one-third time on faculty matters and two-thirds on administrative concerns; and each was chosen to foster the multidisciplinary and broad-based educational plan Hampshire favored. Since then, pressures from within the college have pushed toward a model of school leadership that was felt by the faculty to be more responsive to their concerns and their control. Moreover, it became clear that, as the college reached maturity, filling the deans' positions every three to five years (the average turnover period) with outside replacements, and then giving them full-time faculty status when their terms were up, meant absorbing more senior faculty members than would be possible.

In 1972, the language studies program was converted to the School of Language and Communication. At the same time it proposed and received a coordinator instead of a dean as its leader. The school's faculty choose the coordinator, who spends a year as coordinator-elect, obtaining on-the-job training. Then the coordinator is nominated to the president for a one-year appointment. The coordinator remains an active faculty member two-thirds time. He or she is more of a general secretary, helping to organize the school to allow it to express its will and conveying that result to the dean of the college or other authority. The coordinator is seen as having little or no independent authority or responsibility, a status that ultimately puts the school at a disadvantage in its dealings with other schools, such as when the coordinator and school deans meet to resolve issues of resource allocation. It seems to me unlikely that the coordinatorship will be adopted as a general model.

The most promising school leadership form is the deanship of the School of Social Science. After two conventional appointments were made, both from outside the college, the school and the president negotiated an agreement whereby a school dean, with enough power to ensure an independent and often decisive role in school affairs, would be recommended to the president for appointment from within the faculty for a period of two years. As in lan-

guage and communication, an assistant trains for a year. The dean
teaches one-third time and the assistant two-thirds time. Although
the deanship of social science is highly consultative, it differs from
the coordinatorship in the exercise of independent and determina-
tive action and judgment.

In time, I would not be surprised to see the social science
model become universal at Hampshire. It seems to satisfy the participatory needs of the school membership, carries appropriate
weight in the power balance between school and college, and maintains a desirable level of continuity, trust, and familiarity among
school leaders, qualities essential to the intraschool relationships so
vital to the Hampshire system.

A reader more accustomed to organizational uniformity and
neatness might wonder why Hampshire administrators and trustees
are so tolerant of a variety of faculty-initiated leadership models
and so patient with the slow and sometimes painful shift to a form
that looks remarkably like the standard small-college departmental
organization but with substantially more influence in budget formation, expenditure content, educational policy, and faculty appointments. Because its academic program and the structure that has
evolved from it are based on the assumption of high levels of
faculty and student freedom and responsibility, it has seemed important, therefore, to wait for the faculty to experience enough
variety of leadership models to settle on one that they favor and
that seems to work, rather than to construct and impress on them
one designed by the senior administrators, which may not work as
well. Although at this point the school organization and leadership
may look like the usual department expanded, there are important
differences.

The principal quality and key advantage of the school organization is that it is multidisciplinary and produces a high level of
colleagueship. The Hampshire schools are discipline based; that is,
each member of the faculty is trained in a discipline and is expected
to teach primarily in that discipline. However, there is not a rigid
discipline-subject relationship in appointing faculty members, nor
are the disciplines that are represented in a school at any one time
designated and fixed. Rather, in choosing new members the schools
mix the variables of discipline, subject, the candidate's qualities of

mind, and the existing fabric of the school. The faculty blend that results need not fit a curriculum, of course, because the Hampshire College curriculum is determined by the aggregated individual choices of the students, each of whom has a different program.

Therefore, no school is the exclusive province of a given discipline. Psychologists may be found in two schools, mathematicians in two, historians in three, and so forth. This arrangement has the advantage of freeing schools from the Procrustean bed of a rigid or single definition of disciplinary expertness. Obviously social and clinical psychologists differ very much in their approach to psychology, just as metaphysicians and analytic philosophers, who differ greatly, may yet properly call themselves philosophers. Therefore a social psychologist might be comfortable in the School of Language and Communication and find colleagueship there that is stimulating and productive, whereas the clinical psychologist might find a better fit in the School of Social Science.

In addition, of course, this lesson is not lost on students, who have often been led to believe that there is such a thing as an historian with a capital "H." Now, suddenly faced with historians in three schools, the students have an opportunity to understand that the rigidity, narrow definitions, and prescribed content and outlook sometimes manifested by teachers according to their disciplines are only representative of a convenient middle-road approach to the infinite variety and complexity of ways of knowing, teaching, understanding, and describing the world.

Physical Facilities

Hampshire College was planned, constructed, and is now operating as a residential college, and it assumes it is providing the values that research has ascribed to residential life—the enhanced opportunity for social growth, higher levels of aspiration, and greater intellectual stimulation. Both to encourage a sense of integration in the lives of students and to avoid the excess expense of constructing duplicate facilities, Hampshire's houses were conceived as places where students could live, eat, have their social life, and do their academic "work." It followed, given Hampshire's earlier base points, that the houses were not to be specialized. That is, they were not to devote themselves to a theme, a subject, or a discipline. Once again, the overriding goal of integration, comprehensiveness, and breadth prevailed.

In the original campus design, faculty offices and general class and seminar rooms, small branches of the main college library, and crafts and recreational spaces were also to be located in the houses. Although each of the four schools was to have a central physical headquarters, the planners assumed that many of the faculty members from each of the schools would have offices in houses. The idea was that if Hampshire professors were located physically without regard to school membership, they would be encouraged to become acquainted across disciplinary and school lines.

So the house was seen very much as a place for decentralized academic work, a place for student and faculty interchange to occur in an unremarkable way—the presumption being that such encounters often stimulate discussion of fundamental questions that may not occur in a structured learning situation—and the place where faculty members of differing disciplines have an opportunity to interact. This concept once again reinforced the wholeness of the academic enterprise and the multidisciplinary approach necessary to the consideration of questions of universal import.

Hampshire now has five houses, all funded in whole or in major part by loans from the College Housing Loan Program of the Department of Housing and Urban Development, and in three cases planned and constructed in tandem with educational facilities funded by loans or grants from the Office of Education through the Department of Health, Education, and Welfare. As might be expected, we encountered considerable difficulties in coordinating the planning and building of facilities funded by two separate federal agencies, and those problems, combined with the financial restraints inherent in the federal programs and in the financing and construction of a new college, resulted in our falling far short of our ideals in house construction. Only one of the houses, Prescott House—the fifth—has fully integrated faculty offices, seminar rooms, and classrooms. Rooms in one of the others (Greenwich House, number three) are used at times for instruction, and some student rooms have been converted to faculty offices. The other three (Merrill, Dakin, and Enfield) have a few integral offices, but rely primarily on closely related and architecturally similar classroom and faculty office facilities. Unfortunately, the difference between having a faculty office in a house and having one located nearby seems to be significant. The opportunity for informal interchange is reduced substantially when students go into one building and the faculty goes into another.

Branch libraries and craft facilities could not be afforded in any of the houses, but odd spaces in each of them have been appropriated and converted through student initiative and with some college support, so that now such things as darkrooms, woodworking shops, weaving and pottery facilities, and galleries exist among the houses.

Most important to the original design, however, is the disposition of the faculty members to accept and use offices that are not clustered with their schools or with their disciplines but are located in or near houses. Of the 128 individual faculty offices, 23 are located physically in the houses, nine in Dakin House, one in Merrill, ten in Prescott, one in Enfield, and two in Greenwich. The rest of the faculty is located in Franklin Patterson Hall (associated with Dakin and Merrill) or Emily Dickinson Hall (associated with Enfield and Greenwich), Charles W. Cole Science Center, the Harold F. Johnson Library Center, or Warner or Kermensky houses, two former residences on campus that are being utilized as faculty office space.

Functions of the Schools

The schools are responsible for performing the educational functions of the college, for curricular and program planning within the general framework of the educational policies established by the faculty, for developing budgets and controlling the expenses of those functions for which they are responsible, and for the maintenance of an appropriate faculty of high quality to carry on the work of the school. In addition, each school has the following principal responsibilities: it examines the progress of individual students through Divisions I, II, and III; maintains an Advising

Center and makes sure there are enough faculty advisors to carry that school's proportion of the Collegewide advising responsibility; and provides for faculty development.

Examinations. Progress at Hampshire College is not based on time, credit-hour accumulations, or satisfaction of course requirements. The college is structured to measure progress by the passage of examinations or the completion of projects, which in either case depend on the planning and initiative of the individual student. The divisional structure, as it is called, has three parts, each of which prescribes a set of tasks that the student must complete in order to move to the next. Graduation follows completion of Division III. Although the college does not assume that students shall be present or enrolled for any prescribed length of time, Hampshire does follow a 4-1-4 calendar in order to coordinate itself with the five colleges. Students spend on an average of three and a half years in residence at the college, and of that time an average of three semesters is spent in Division I, two in Division II, and two in Division III.

Passage of Division I follows the successful completion of four examinations, one in each of the four schools. The examinations are designed and initiated by students, and their form and content must receive approval from a member of the faculty in the school in which the examination is being taken. The examination, then, is an individual experience for the student conducted by a committee, at least one member of which must be a member of the faculty of the school in which the examination is being taken.

Division II is a period of concentration most closely akin to a major in other colleges, but with the important difference that it is best created from a combination of courses, independent study, and field-study experiences. Verification of the student's depth of understanding of the subject area he or she has pursued is undertaken by a committee of at least two Hampshire faculty members.

Finally, Division III, advanced studies, is the culmination of the student's work and most closely resembles an honors project in other colleges. The Division III examination committee comprises three persons, at least two of whom must be members of the Hampshire College faculty; its evaluation follows completion of an intense independent study or project and participation in an integrative seminar.

The examining role is a key one for Hampshire College faculty members, and at each level the school has the responsibility to make certain that there are well-trained, well-motivated teachers who are available to respond to interests.

Recall that the student is not obliged to satisfy the requirements by choosing Hampshire College courses or by accommodating him or herself to the established and declared interests of the faculty. The student may decide to pursue an area of study which is only peripheral to the expertise of any member of the faculty, and provided the student successfully negotiates approval of an examination topic and enlists the help of a committee, a number of interesting things may result. One is that the committee may be augmented by a student, a member of the staff, a faculty person from one of the other institutions, or a person in the local community who is expert in the student's subject. As a result, a faculty participant in a student examination, even at the Division I level, frequently finds himself scrambling to refresh his knowledge of graduate school subjects, long since put aside, to brush up on an area in which he is rusty, or to expand his understanding of a subject or range in his discipline in order to be responsibly judgmental about the examination to be undertaken.

An additional effect of the examination system is that it often brings together two faculty persons who would not normally be engaged in close intellectual interchange. They may or may not be from the same school or even both from Hampshire College. The result benefits both the faculty and students. Examinations sometimes include lively exchanges between the faculty participants, which probably result in more education for them and for the student than anything else that occurs at the college; further, the faculty members develop a fuller appreciation for each other and for the possibilities of their collaborating in some productive ways in future examinations, in shared courses, or in research.

In academic year 1975–1976, 114 persons from outside the Hampshire College faculty, including fifty-nine from the other four colleges, participated in Hampshire College Division III examinations. Since exams at this level have the greatest depth and range, these experiences provide the faculty with the finest quality of colleagueship and expose them most fully to the variety and expertness available on the faculty, thus, again, stimulating outgoing, collaborative, and challenging relations of a kind not available to most faculty members within a departmental structure. Such interactions are particularly valued by Hampshire's younger professors, for whom a departmental structure may define status and responsibilities in such a way as to proscribe senior colleagueship.

Illustrations from the records of the graduating class in January 1976 make the point:

Division III Project Title	*Faculty Committee*
"Children's Play in Bali"	Two anthropologists and a psychologist
"Determining the Health Care Needs of Urban Elderly: Problems and Proposals"	An anthropologist, a biologist, and a member of the Aging Conservation Committee of Hampshire County
"Hippocampus: Structure, Function, and Pathology"	Two biologists, a neurophysiologist, and a psychologist
"ESAAP's Foibles: The History and Development of Interdisciplinary Programs at Hampshire College with Particular Attention to Environmental Studies"	Professors of literature, English, and mass communications

Advising. Each student at Hampshire College is pursuing a different course of study determined by the student's interests and the advice the student receives. Each school maintains an Advising Center manned by faculty members and students to provide advice particularly oriented to the interests of the school's faculty, the possibilities for examination projects, and other pertinent matters that reflect the peculiarities of the school, which differs somewhat from the others. New students are assigned to an Advising Center for a period of thirty days before they are assigned, on the basis of the priorities they suggest, a faculty adviser. The faculty advising loads are apportioned by school, and there is some opportunity for differentiated staffing, determined within the schools, to provide the most effective combination of advising, examining, and teaching, depending on the strengths and proficiencies of individual professors. No faculty persons are without advisees, but some of them have more than others (the average is sixteen).

The school is responsible for seeing that student advising is conducted effectively and considerately according to collegewide standards. The adviser is responsible for the educational well-being of his or her advisees. That means that the adviser helps the student understand his or her interests, the structure of the college, the nature of the examination system and how progress is measured, the opportunities in five-college cooperation, the progress the student should be making, and the quality of the student's work. Because of the individualized nature of the Hampshire program, an adviser cannot simply sign forms. The students must be known individually, their differences appreciated and understood, and advice determined for each of them, depending on the circumstances. The schools take seriously the advising function; they discuss it regularly, and take pains to see that faculty members are advising responsibly and that the school's advising load has been handled satisfactorily.

Once again, the structure reinforces Hampshire's interest in faculty breadth and growth. Advising bright, motivated students demands that faculty members be aware of the activities, ideas, and interests of the Hampshire faculty and the five-college faculty and helps preclude faculty isolation and institutional inwardness.

Curricular Development. Although the program of Hampshire College is derived from the judgments and preferences of each student, and although the college is faithful to the call in *The New College Plan* to "dethrone the course as the basic unit of knowledge," the college does have a course structure and academic programs. Still, the schools' curricula are evolutionary and fluid since they result from student choices, faculty/student negotiations, and faculty combinations and recombinations that develop as both of their interests evolve and change. The organic quality of the subject areas and course offerings of each school is best revealed in their curriculum statements, which are found in the college catalog or in the course guides. Some excerpts are illustrative.

From the School of Humanities and Arts:

> The courses in Basic Studies are not intended to serve as intro-
> ductions to this or that subject matter, but as *introductions to
> modes of inquiry*. The difference is . . . critical. . . . each of
> the great, traditional disciplines of study (English, history, phi-
> losophy, music, etc.), rather than being treated as a closed sys-
> tem of knowledge in itself, is treated as a perspective on the
> whole phenomenon of Man. These are observably different ways
> in which the artist and the humanist (as contrasted, say, with
> the scientist) approach their subjects of study, conceive of their
> problems, attack them, resolve them, report them, or express
> them, and that is the main matter of concern in any Division I
> course. If you take a course with a literary scholar, for example,
> . . . [it] might come down to library methods, the mechanics of
> analysis, the selection and validation of documentary data or
> the techniques of argument, but the overriding concern will
> be to show you a working humanist in action up close. In the
> arts there is a much greater emphasis necessary on perception
> and expressive form, but the model should operate the same
> way. . . . we in this School . . . share the sense of Erich
> Fromm about the good that "flows from the blending of rational
> thought and feeling. If the two functions are torn apart, think-
> ing deteriorates into schizoid intellectual activity, and feeling
> deteriorates into neurotic life-damaging passions."

From the School of Language and Communication:

> Symbols are the foundation of all human activity. Perception
> is coding the physical world into a symbolic representation,
> thought is manipulating symbols, communication is transmitting
> symbols. The study of symbolic processes is one of the keys to
> human nature. The School of Language and Communication
> is an experiment which brings together the disciplines that study
> the forms and nature of symbolic activity. Although these are
> among the most vital disciplines in current intellectual life,
> they are taught as a central part of liberal arts education only
> at Hampshire. The listing by disciplines . . . is convenient,

but it should not obscure the interdisciplinary character of the school. Most of the school's faculty have studied more than one discipline, and many of the school's courses are substantially interdisciplinary.

From the School of Natural Science:

The major thrust of the School of Natural Science has been to break down barriers. There is no clear division here between those who teach and those who learn. Students are school members, attending meetings and participating in decisions, voting on faculty candidates and playing an active role in the ongoing evaluation of faculty, programs and projects, as well as of themselves and their educations. The sciences are not separated into departments; nor is science separated from nonscience. Animal behavior collaborates with anthropology; a physicist works on electronic music with a composer and holography with an artist, and so on. Our college is not an ivory tower which protects us from our surroundings, but a resource center which provides the impetus for us to look carefully at what is around us. We learn, discover, and use a variety of techniques to consider whether we wish to preserve certain features—as in the case of the Holyoke Range—or change them—as in the case of a local school system or sewage treatment plant—and then how to go about the job. We do not maintain the old science-technology split which has enabled scientists to disclaim responsibility for the uses to which their discoveries have been put; nor the science-politics split which led us further in the same direction. "Pure science," the self-vindicating cry of the scientific elite, has brought many problems as well as promises, and for the most part has failed to educate citizens in how to cope with them, or even to make informed decisions. At Hampshire we are attempting to put science back into its place—its real place—which is everywhere and everyone's.

From the School of Social Science:

The School of Social Science includes faculty representing many disciplines: history, sociology, economics, political science, psychology, anthropology, education, and folklore. Can such a diverse assemblage become a school? Do they share principles,

premises, and methods that can be communicated to students
who care more about problems than about disciplines? We
think so, and we are trying to demonstrate it: by developing
an increasing number of cooperatively taught courses, by exchanging openly our ideas about what constitutes a vital and
valid social science, and by moving toward a school identity
that will transcend differences rooted in narrowly defined views
of social reality.

One of the most significant consequences of the organic,
holistic, and comprehensive approach suggested by each of the
school curriculum statements is the frequency of multidisciplinary
teaching at Hampshire College. The faculty members regularly
teach together in the schools and to some extent with persons from
other schools in the college. By way of illustration, Richard Lyon, a
philosopher and professor of American Studies appointed jointly to
the Schools of Language and Communication and Humanities and
Arts, and Lester Mazor, a professor of law in the School of Social
Science, have taught The United States in the 1890s. Merle Bruno,
a biologist, and Nancy Frishberg, a linguist, have together presented Left and Right Bilateral (A)symmetry, a study of the physi-
ological, symbolic, and behavioral duality in human behavior. A
Critical Analysis and Interpretation of the Research on Inequality
in Educational Opportunities was given by Gloria Joseph, a professor of education, and Michael Sutherland, a statistician.

There are many other examples, but these give some flavor
of the way in which the organic quality of Hampshire College
schools is manifested in teaching interests and collegial relationships. It seems clear that removing barriers of physical segregation,
organizational and structural isolation, hierarchical structure, and
prescribed curricular forms frees faculty for multidisciplinary work
and a high and stimulating level of intellectual colleagueship.

Further, and more important, the collegial qualities of
Hampshire have led to new thinking about the justification for a
new college in a time of enrollment scarcity and budget crises.
Hampshire no longer is fueled solely by allegiance to changes in the
ways students learn and teachers teach. It is on the verge of insti-
tutionalizing redefinitions of scholarly concerns that are postdisci-
plinary, evolving out of disciplines and student demands of course,

but emerging with a focus on social problems and new approaches to old subject matters, a kind of synthesis, which has yet to be stated, although its characteristics may be perceived in practice. The Capitalism and Empire course taught at ten social institutes is an illustration. The thinking is policy-disciplinary and organic, the curricular implications of which are not yet available.

Faculty Development and Colleagueship

The schools are responsible for developing faculty members who suit the purpose of the college. Faculty development, in this case, encompasses identification of need, search, recommendation for appointment, training, evaluation, reappointment or discontinuation, and assistance in relocation if reappointment does not occur.

Hampshire has distinctive policies with regard to faculty employment which must be reviewed briefly in order to understand the full implications of the responsibilities recited above. The college decided in 1968, two years before it opened, to try out a renewable contract system as an alternative to tenure, aiming, at the same time, to protect the academic freedom of the faculty. The experiment was to demonstrate whether or not it might present to the institution and to the individual faculty members advantages not found in tenure systems. The college has now completed six years under the contract system, and it seems likely that the faculty will continue to endorse the system in spite of some structural and procedural flaws that have arisen and that are now being examined for rectification.

The principal features of the contract system are the annual evaluation process, which helps the individual faculty person understand how he or she is performing, and the periodic evaluations, whose consequence is either reappointment or nonretention. As an educative procedure, the contract system assumes, idealistically, that well-trained, able, and well-motivated persons have been appointed to the faculty and that the effect of evaluations will be to elucidate deficiencies and enable faculty members, through understanding and additional training, to overcome their weaknesses.

The contract arrangement is particularly appropriate at Hampshire, because it has no prescribed "slots" and therefore flexibility is valuable. The faculty's composition varies as persons come and go and as the needs of students change. If a faculty person is not reappointed or resigns, the instructional money supporting that person reverts to the dean of the college for reassignment, possibly to the same school for the same subject or discipline, but as likely to another school to satisfy a more urgent need.

The periodic reappointment process begins in the usual way. The school assembles a file of pertinent data on the criteria by which faculty are judged: teaching, advising, colleagueship, scholarship, and service to the community. The file may be reviewed by all members of the school or a representative committee of the school. In all schools, a vote of all school members decides whether or not the person is recommended for reappointment. The school dean is then permitted an independent judgment of the candidate's qualifications, and that judgment is passed to a collegewide committee of five faculty members and two students, known as the College Committee on Faculty Reappointments and Promotions. It examines the file, may gather more information, and, in turn, makes a recommendation to the president, who—with the materials in hand, more material if he needs it, and the evaluations he has received—makes a final recommendation to the board of trustees.

I want to emphasize the wide participation and extraordinary responsibility of the faculty members in making judgments about their colleagues, more often than not in areas in which they themselves are not expert. To gain reappointment in this multidisciplinary evaluation system, the candidate must exhibit a range of intellectual colleagueship, particularly an interest in and capacity for joint planning and shared teaching. Because there are no "slots" or prescribed curricula, candidates for appointment and reappointment are examined in terms of such colleagueship and the likelihood that they will, by their particular expertness, bring additional insights and contributions to the school's program that will enlarge, diversify, and enrich the wholeness of the school's intellectual enterprise.

As one can see, an extraordinary level of colleagueship is one of the great benefits of the differences between a school organization of the kind described and a conventional academic departmental organization. These differences may be summarized as follows: Junior faculty members are not assigned teaching responsibilities prescribed by the senior faculty; they are free to teach (reflecting their own interests) and co-teach, sit on committees, serve on examinations, and fill all other capacities in the school in the same ways and with the same responsibility as their senior colleagues. The commitment to individualized education places the initiative for what is learned and taught largely in the hands of students, forcing faculty members to be responsive and increasing greatly their incentive to continue to learn, to share, to co-plan, and to co-teach. The examination structure and advising system serve further to stimulate faculty to venture outside the security of their disciplinary expertise and to engage their colleagues, both within and without the college, and students in challenging and stimulating discussions of ideas.

There is little doubt in my mind that the most important feature of the Hampshire College academic organization is the colleagueship it stimulates. A junior historian, for example, works daily with senior and junior colleagues from the range of disciplines, such as (in the School of Social Science) urban studies, political science, psychology, sociology, law, anthropology, education studies, economics, statistics, and folklore. In a large or even small department in another university or college, his daily working, and to a great extent his social life, would be with and among historians, and the incentives would strongly favor increased, narrow specialization, precisely what *The New College Plan* and *The Making of a College* defined as antithetical to the goals of undergraduate education.

Five-College Cooperation

The second major feature of the academic organization of Hampshire College is its relationship with the four institutions that helped found it. Hampshire's academic structure is determined by and consonant with the fact that Hampshire was created in a cooperative framework with four nearby, supportive, high-quality institutions. "Implicit in the general statement is that the new institution would be located in close proximity to the present four colleges. It would draw upon the resources of the four colleges for its program. In turn, the four colleges could draw upon it for new ideas and techniques which they could adopt. It would be dependent at its origin upon the academic reputation of the four colleges, and it is expected that it would enhance that reputation by its subsequent pattern and action. This is to be no makeshift institution but one in which we all will take great pride" (Barber and others, 1958, p. 46).

The Making of a College says:

> The advent of Hampshire College provides a unique moment when the long-standing tradition of informal and formal cooperation among institutions of the Valley could be dramatically reasserted and usefully extended. If it were not for this tradition of friendly association, it might appear presumptuous for Hampshire, as the newest college in the group, to come out strongly for increased cooperative endeavor. It might simply seem that Hampshire, as the newest and neediest of the colleges, is making a case for sharing with others their hard-won resources. This is not Hampshire College's view of itself, nor is it believed to be the view taken by the older institutions of the Valley. Hampshire is the result of an act of cooperation; it represents and will seek actively to express a view of cooperation as creative collaboration, in which all concerned can find advantage.
>
> Straight sharing can be a successful short-term solution for a problem of scarcity, stretching resources that are already normally used. But this can tend to threaten faculty, and it does not contribute to creative expansion of the aggregate educational resources of cooperating institutions. Creative collaboration is not a piece of fancy terminology designed to cloak the impositions of one college on another. The ground on which creative collaboration stands is, by definition, mutuality. The structure that can be built on this ground can enrich programs, enlarge opportunities, and extend resources for all of the partners in the collaborative endeavor. Genuine collaboration cannot be a voluntary or involuntary act of charity whose chief end is to provide a makeshift answer for conditions of scarcity. Instead, it is a new departure for higher education which can materially increase academic abundance by collective action, while maintaining institutional autonomy, integrity, physical organization, and size among its individual partners [Patterson and Longsworth, 1966, pp. 220–221].

The expectations and assumptions on which Hampshire College are based are markedly different from those which govern the creation of most four-year colleges and which, even today, govern the curricular thinking of new and old institutions. Theirs is a sense of inclusiveness and completeness, a sense that a college must strive to cover the basic fields of knowledge to provide as full a range as possible of subject coverage, a long since futile effort to approximate the curriculum of major universities at a time when even the major universities recognize the impossibility of completeness. Hampshire's readiness and willingness to abandon such pretentions was outlined in *The Making of a College:*

> The small independent college now faces [difficulty] in providing sufficient faculty strength and quality, and sufficient research facilities and opportunities, to insure advanced undergraduate preparation in science, commensurate with the requirements for entrance into the better graduate schools. *It is manifest that Hampshire cannot expect to provide such advanced preparation on its own.* The current approximation of Hampshire's science program shows a realistic recognition of this limitation. The science program of the College is based on the assumption that adequate strength in advanced science preparation for Hampshire students can be assured *only through interinstitutional collaboration in the Valley.* In the foreseeable future, the latter assumption is very likely to be true for science students of *all* of the Valley institutions, considered singly [Patterson and Longsworth, 1966, p. 119].

In exchange, of course, Hampshire expected to tailor its curriculum and the subsequent appointment of faculty members to complement the curricular strengths of the other Valley institutions and to create special opportunities for students that would otherwise be unavailable. The most notable examples of Hampshire's contributions have been in electronic music and film and photography, fields in which none of the other colleges was active at the time Hampshire began and in which there is still a very modest effort in the Valley relative to that made by Hampshire.

Thus, it became an early tenet of Hampshire's planning that the college would not presume completeness. Hampshire is quite comfortable with the idea of integrating its academic program with the program of its four sponsoring and cooperating partners. In fact, it has found in that relationship corroboration and reinforcement of its disinclination to adopt or accept a pattern of development that might lead to or reinforce any predisposition on the part of the faculty or administration to departmental organization, specialization, excess structure, or adherence to a false belief in the possibility of inclusiveness or completeness.

Other major factors in the cooperative relationship among the colleges are powerful stimulants to openness, flexibility, and change, all of which strongly inhibit an inclination to take the sort of parochial view of institutional self-importance that could easily characterize a new small and aspiring institution. The most important of these factors is the agreement whereby students from any one of the five colleges can enroll in courses at any of the others. In the fall of 1975, Hampshire College had 812 student enrollments at the other campuses. On the average, about 20 percent of the course enrollments each term occur off campus. This interchange has a number of effects. It requires Hampshire College faculty members in their counseling and advising roles to be aware of and sensitive to the range of course offerings in their own fields and other fields at the other colleges if they are to successfully advise Hampshire students in constructing individualized academic programs. It also provides variety and stimulates independence of view among students who are free to engage in intellectual and personal exchanges with faculty members on five campuses rather than one.

The second factor important to the maintenance of openness and receptivity on the part of individual teachers is the ongoing departmental/faculty colloquia sponsored by Five Colleges, Inc. In 1975–1976 there were twenty colloquia, in which an estimated 450 Five College faculty members participated. Hampshire College faculty members participate not as departmental members, of course, but according to their disciplines. These colloquia have several important benefits. They expose the faculty of each of the participating institutions to a range of intellectual stimulation and points of view not otherwise available within the home institution, promote some exchange of teaching ideas and methods, and occasionally inspire a cooperative educational venture by two or more of the colleges. Examples that have been formulated but not yet made real are an urban studies center and a public policy center. The colloquia also result from time to time in various kinds of faculty-initiated educational exchange. For instance, two faculty members from different institutions will plan a joint course; two or more professors from different institutions will plan an informal exchange whereby each moves in turn for one semester to the neighboring institution, playing a kind of institutional musical chairs; faculty members will agree to maintain a certain number of places in their courses for Five College students, hoping that the mixture will produce educational vitality; or they will consider and give impetus to a Five College department.

This last example is one of the most interesting phenomena among the Five Colleges, the ultimate manifestation of sharing and cooperation. The resultant organizational form serves the needs of the individual members well, but because of their dispersed locations, institutional affiliations, interests, and loyalties, it does not have the same parochial and narrowing effects of a department in a single institution.

The first Five College department was astronomy, which was organized as a Four College department in 1959 and has functioned successfully for seventeen years. The department has sixteen members distributed as follows: the University of Massachusetts, ten; Amherst College, one; Hampshire College, two; Mount Holyoke College, one; Smith College, two. (The sixteen people represent 14.25 full-time-equivalent faculty members.) The contributions of each of the participants to his or her respective home institution and to the shared enterprise are determined by formula. Each faculty member teaches Five College courses as well as courses that are originated by the home institution. The department has both graduate and undergraduate students, operates the most powerful short wave-length radio telescope in the world, has a prolific research output, and teaches a range of students from beginning undergraduates to doctoral candidates enthusiastically and effectively.

In addition to the astronomy department, there is a Five College black studies department with twenty-nine members distributed as follows: the University of Massachusetts, fifteen; Amherst College, five; Hampshire College, one; Mount Holyoke College, five; and Smith College, three. Planning is now under way for a Five College dance department, and serious thought has been given to other joint organizations.

Finally, a new program, begun in academic year 1974–1975, makes short-term appointments of a few junior and senior faculty members on a Five College basis. These appointments are in fields that are of interest to all the institutions but not of sufficient interest to a single institution to warrant its sole support. The idea originated among the deputies of the Five Colleges, senior faculty or administrative persons who represent the president and carry the burden of day-to-day Five College cooperative planning and administration. Under this program, each institution contributes an agreed on portion of its instructional budget, which is matched by a grant from the Fund for the Improvement for Postsecondary Education. Appointments to date have been in the fields of pre-Colombian art, Irish studies, technology assessment, women's studies, and Judaic studies.

The nominations of the fields in which search is to be conducted in all the colleges are made by the several faculties. The opportunity to so participate, the realization of the value of shared appointments, and the additional colleagueship that results from new people and new ideas all tend to reinforce the openness of the Five College relationship and to reduce the closed and introverted inclinations that departmental organization can bring.

Cooperation encourages Hampshire College faculty members to be outer-oriented, to have interinstitutional as well as intra-institutional matters very much on their minds, and to be relaxed about the necessity to create new courses and programs and to hire new teachers to fill gaps in the college's curriculum as new student needs are manifested. By Five College agreement, each time a new course or program is proposed at Hampshire, the existing resources in the Valley are examined by the principal administrators of the five institutions before the proposal is given further consideration. Each college has agreed to include as a regular item in its faculty meetings a report from the Five College deputy on the status and progress of Five College relationships. This frequent and necessary reminder keeps the faculty members attuned to the opportunities and responsibilities they have outside their own colleges.

Conclusions

The Hampshire College faculty has no inclination to seek a different form of academic organization. As I see it, their satisfaction with the school organization is very high, because they find that growth results from the many opportunities for colleagueship and from the challenge of able, independent students. Two explanatory or cautionary notes must be sounded, however. The first and most obvious is that the multidisciplinary school form would probably fail if it had to be relied on to develop a structured curriculum. Collaboration would be insufficient and the politics inherent in creating structure would demand clustering and organizing around more closely shared interests and concerns. Thus, the success of Hampshire's school organization and the program it allows are probably contingent on attracting students (and faculty members)˙ who have enough intellectual ability and intellectual and emotional maturity to deal with ambiguity and to accept the responsibility for self-definition and self-direction. Second, the school structure does not afford a very useful political base for pursuing faculty interests, and the Hampshire faculty has still to find a corporate identity that enables it to speak as one entity.

Concommitantly, the school may not offer an individual faculty person who is threatened, demoralized, or uncertain in professional terms as much emotional, intellectual, and political support as a department of more like-minded colleagues might, but the degree of that support may depend as much on the department and the relationships within it as on the form of organization.

In summary, then, the academic organization of Hampshire College is determined by a view of education that is founded on the importance of individual students, who determine what they will study and, to a great extent, when their work is ready to be evaluated and what shall be evaluated. This view is comfortably reconciled to the ideas that education is not just courses completed, that all education does not occur in the classroom or even in faculty-student exchanges, and that students are capable of far more independence than they are allowed in most colleges.

Hampshire is organized to accommodate and enhance that educational view, recognizing that a lively faculty with wide-ranging interests and the advantages of cooperation with its founding neighboring colleges—Amherst, Mount Holyoke, Smith, and the University of Massachusetts (Amherst)—are the two factors vital to its success. Therefore, the faculty is organized in four schools—humanities and arts, language and communication, natural science, and social science—all multidisciplinary and the basis of student examining and advising and of the subject concentrations. The college's program is designed to take advantage, through cooperation, of a variety and range of learning opportunities far beyond the capacity of Hampshire, or any other small college.

The goals are to give students maximum choice, to advise and guide them in evaluating alternatives, to stimulate independent judgment, initiative, and intellectual colleagueship among and between students and faculty members. The result might be described as an undergraduate graduate school.

Most important, the faculty of Hampshire College like and believe in the organization of the college by schools. And it is the growth and well-being of the faculty in Hampshire's scheme of things that determine the success of our plan for undergraduate education.

8 Charles J. McCann

Academic Administration Without Departments at The Evergreen State College

We at Evergreen have never pretended that we are doing anything new in our modes of study, even though, I believe, we have carried interdisciplinary coordinated studies beyond the Tussman "experiment" at Berkeley and work-study beyond either the Northeastern or Antioch pioneering forms. We have been quite public about the fact that the youngest of our modes of study is at least 125 years old, with some others going back to the Middle Ages. Our only new accomplishment is in allowing a student to put together these modes in any combination that he or she sees fit and to have them all go on concurrently at the same place; for this arrangement we had to devise an administrative organization, which will be the central topic of this chapter.

Many of my fellow Evergreeners are surprised when I do not view their particular favorite study mode as our distinguishing characteristic. A student might say: "Where else can I do a full-time internship for a year, for credit?"; and a faculty member:

"When a year-long coordinated studies program has been planned well, when its faculty works at keeping its faculty seminar alive, my mind teems with ideas—even about my own discipline—in a way I never thought possible. Where else would that happen to me? It never did before." Both responses have truth in them, but the truth speaks to differences in degree; Evergreen's difference in kind is the flexibility made possible by our academic organization, a flexibility that in turn makes possible the differences in degree.

This chapter will consider why a departmentless academic organization was necessary to achieve that flexibility, what problems the organization solved—and caused—and what problems remain. To carry out this task in any detail, I have had to leave out answers to questions like: How did so "radical" a place as Evergreen grow out of so conservative a state? How can a college be "different" and still do business with state and federal bureaucracies? What's the intellectual and emotional effect on a student after his/her years at Evergreen? What's the student body profile? How does it feel to be a faculty member at a place so self-conscious about excellence in teaching? Interesting as gossip, political history, and the substance of academic life in a particular place may be, I must, for purposes of this chapter, keep my pen to this particular grindstone if I am to strike off any sparks helpful to readers contemplating a departmentless college. Yet academic administration does not exist for its own sake. Ours took its original form, and has since been modified, only to serve a certain way of going about teaching and learning. It may be useful, then, to recapitulate briefly the experiences and ideas that shaped our new way.

Origins

My ideas for Evergreen were composed of a list of negatives (no departments, no ranks, no requirements, no grades) accompanied by a vaguer list of positives (we should have cooperative education [internship] options for students, we should be interdisciplinary, there should be as little red tape as possible among the faculty members and students and what's there to be learned, freshmen—everyone—should have the opportunities and obligations presented by seminars, evaluation should be in narrative form, library and computing services should have disproportionally large shares of the budget, students should be able to study on their own when they're capable of it).

These proscriptions and urgings came mostly from my checkered experience. As an undergraduate at Yale, I took a hodgepodge of scientific and engineering courses required by the NROTC for a B.A. that Yale might blush to award these days. But the further I get from that experience, the more convinced I am of its having been a liberalizing undergraduate education, not because of the subject matter, but because of Yale's atmosphere; thus, my conviction that almost no matter what course of study an undergraduate pursues, his being surrounded by serious workers, in circumstances both esthetically pleasing and reflective of the serious work, has more positive effect on later attitudes toward learning than curricula approved by a thousand committees. After I got out of the navy, I took a master's degree in retailing from New York University, where I discovered the value of what we now call internships, as well as some of the pitfalls to watch out for. In my first job after receiving the Ph.D., I found what a tremendous teaching job can be done when you don't have a lot of administrative stuff to bother with, for it was a good urban liberal arts college run by a religious order whose administration "needed no help, thank you." I yearned for a voice in running some place, so I moved to one of the institutions Dunham called, perhaps not entirely inaccurately, but no less snobbishly, "colleges of the forgotten Americans." As a faculty member there, I plunged into committee work with a vengeance and came to see the costs to the intellectual life of a campus when "contributions to the college" are allowed to substitute for contributions to its intellectual life. I learned from the juxtaposition of those two teaching experiences that there had to be a middle way. Later, as a dean, I awoke to the effects of set curricula and some other departmental habits.

As for formative books, I'm sure I have Dewey and Whitehead in me, but it's a long time since I've read them. Newman, of course (John Henry, that is). I've always tried to follow his adjuration to avoid the treadmill and his ideas about students supporting and educating each other; these ideas are integral with my conviction about atmosphere. My notions about some foolishnesses of departmental economics stem, if they didn't stare me in the face as a dean, from Ruml's book. More recently, when thinking about Evergreen (just before I was named president), I remembered *The Making of a College* and was reminded that if everybody pulls his/her weight, one can do seminars for all students with a faculty-student ratio of about the sort one can expect with state funding.

To document the history of ideas at Evergreen would be to document other people's experience and reading, too, which goes beyond the scope of this chapter. Take the three original deans, for example: Merv Cadwallader, an exponent of the "moral curriculum," was hired because he had experience with interdisciplinary study at San Jose and SUNY Old Westbury. Charles Teske had had experience administering independent study in the winter term at Oberlin. And Don Humphrey had built a reputation for imaginative interdisciplinary work in the sciences at Oregon State. The books formative of their Evergreen experience, as well as that of David Barry, the founding provost, can be found in the bibliography (Arnest, 1970; Ashby, 1958; Conant, 1964; DeTocqueville, 1966; Dewey, 1966; Glass, 1959; Keats, 1959; Meiklejohn, 1972; Plato, 1914 and 1943; Russell, 1926; Ruml, 1959; Tussman, 1960; Whitehead, 1929).

The planning faculty shared our intentions about departments at Evergreen, and the faculty as a whole has worked for the five years since our opening without benefit of departments, out of agreement that departments would hinder rather than help the kinds of work they've been doing. Having undergone one minor and two substantive modifications, the academic organization behind the faculty has, compared to one based on the departmental unit, administered most functions as well; some, better. In a critical area, maintenance of high faculty quality, the outcome remains to be seen. Meanwhile, the faculty has achieved results that I believe very improbable, if not impossible, under a departmental scheme.

The Assumptions

I had an overriding assumption arising out of the fact that, for me, the state as funding source is the commonwealth. When that noble source pays for something, there is absolutely no reason in the world why that something shouldn't be a model of what is *good,* as opposed to what, out of lazy supposition, merely is expected.

Our academic intentions and operating assumptions had three crucial attributes together with an economic corollary. First, we were committed to exploring interdisciplinary study as far as it could be taken with undergraduates. The counsel of perfection we set for ourselves: to study phenomena from as many angles simultaneously as the expertness of the faculty would supply. We expected a side effect, in that as an expert becomes occasionally a learner in interdisciplinary study, a student benefits from the powerful example of a faculty member in the art of learning. When interdisciplinary—our term is *coordinated*—studies work at their best, faculty members begin to uncover new ways of knowing, new angles of pursuing and widening their own areas of study. For advanced undergraduates, this process, too, becomes a powerful example. Faculty members create ideas for coordinated studies, interest their colleagues, and jointly plan; we could not see them doing these things if the department were our basic unit of organization.

Second, many of us believed that learning occurs best when the learner takes responsibility for the program of study. Put in a more extreme way: with the infinite variousness of human minds and personalities, who shall say what their programs of study should be, who chop up the world they perceive into "X" compartments? The reality turns out to be not so extreme because of the students' own needs, self-perceived or pointed out; the demands of the next segment of life ahead; the fact that, while there are more ways of knowing the world than the number of disciplines and the possible number may match the infinity of minds, the number in practice at a given time is far closer to the zero end of the spectrum than to the infinite. With guidance and some negotiation, the student can perceive his or her responsibility, undertake it or not, and take the consequences. For the price of a few blinkered souls on the one hand and dilettantes on the other, we have mostly committed, responsible learners. And these without a set curriculum and requirements. The latter, of course, are not concomitants of departments, but they often form the counters of a favorite departmental pastime.

Third, to help students learn how to learn, to engage them with the act of learning rather than simply subject them to information transfer, to help them become articulate orally and in writing, to make interdisciplinary connections, to solve problems, to become competent enough in at least one discipline so that they can work on solving problems with others—all these require certain modes of study: seminars from the very beginning, in some subjects much field work in the third or fourth year, and the experience of working alone under the guidance of a faculty member.

The corollary of the foregoing attributes was the economic imperative of flexibility if we were to afford these modes of study. In a college funded for a 20:1 student/faculty ratio, every faculty member would have to share the student load. That would be far more likely if faculty assigning were more centralized than left to departments. Further, it was apparent that the flexibility gained from having faculty assignments made by a few deans, rather than by many department chairmen, would make for more effective deployment of the faculty as funds became tighter in the future.

Modes of Study

We developed three ways by which students and teachers can get together.

Coordinated Studies. A group of students and faculty members, usually in a ratio of 20:1, choose an area of study broad enough so that separate disciplines may be represented by the members of the faculty, yet not so broad as to be incoherent. These groups can be organized around historical eras; great and inclusive concepts, whether philosophical, social, or scientific; perennial human issues; or particularly demanding and complicated issues of the times. Examples: a group on the ecosystems of Western Washington, working in the field—sound, delta, and beach—with a marine biologist and a plant ecologist; a group on human behavior, with an applied behavioral scientist, a literary scholar, a mathematician, an ecologist, a social anthropologist; a group on political ecology, with a lawyer, two different kinds of biologists, a political scientist, a chemist, and a computer expert.

Group Contracts. A group of students and a faculty member agree to accomplish "X" in a certain time; for example, a group of students acquired a "major" in economics in one year.

Individual Contracts. These are self-explanatory, with the exception of an important subgroup, *internships,* wherein students work full time for credit, under certain conditions.

Two modes have been added since 1971:

Modules. Courses are offered in the late afternoon and evening to accommodate residents of the area and full-time day students who have found no other way to acquire certain tools they need, such as accounting or the calculus.

External Credit. Credit is awarded not for experience or for skills in themselves, but rather for written demonstration and communication of the experience and skills.

A student usually works in one study mode at a time for a period ranging from an academic quarter to a year. A student *graduates* upon receiving forty-five Evergreen units, one unit of Evergreen credit being equivalent to four quarter hours.

In the first two years, each dean was responsible for one of the principal modes of study, owing to his prior experience with that mode, and hence for the faculty working in the respective mode. Beginning with the third year, deans' groups became homogeneous with respect to distribution of modes of study, and in other respects as well. Before each academic year, the deans meet to assign faculty members to the deans' groups so that the groups are roughly similar with regard to distribution of modes of study; representation from humanities, natural sciences, social sciences; sex and race. They also take care to avoid assigning a faculty member to the same dean for more than two years. Assignment to a coordinated study program or to a group contract is usually a faculty member's entire teaching responsibility.

Sharing Administrative Chores: The "Desk" Principle

Our strategy for exploring the unknown (or forgotten) territory of academic administration without the department has proven basically sound. Credit belongs to then Provost Barry, in concert with deans Cadwallader, Humphrey, and Teske. Very briefly, the concept assigned a proportional segment of the faculty to each dean, who would be responsible for guidance, evaluation, and doing the scut work that faculty members require. The deans' other responsibilities were to the whole faculty; we called them "desks," in the state department sense. For example, the responsibility for orienting new faculty, instead of being duplicated by all three deans, would be centralized in one dean, and so on with regard to budget, curriculum, leaves of absence, faculty handbook, public events, and the like.

At the risk of inundating the reader with what may seem unnecessary detail, I shall chronicle the changes in the deanship year by year. The illustrations will shorten my narration; insofar as they include discarded versions, they also may be helpful to a faculty considering such a model.

When we opened in 1971, with a faculty of sixty, academic administration looked like this:

Dean A	*Dean B*	*Dean C*
Alpha faculty group	Beta faculty group	Gamma faculty group
All individual contracts	All coordinated (interdisciplinary) studies	All group contracts
Desks (collegewide responsibilities) :	Desks:	Desks:
Budget	Curriculum	Equipment
Foreign language study	Faculty recruitment	Space
Overseas program	Catalog	Clerical
Advanced placement, credit by examination	Faculty handbook	Self-paced studies
Part-time study	Registration, records liaison	Travel
Public events	Evaluation of programs	Admissions liaison
Public relations	Evaluation of faculty	Grants
Internships	Programming for Seminar Bldg. const.	Programming for Laboratory Bldg. const.
Programming for Performing Arts Bldg.		

Coordinators (leaders) of coordinated studies programs were expected to handle the "housekeeping" chores for their programs.

Rotating Deanships and Deskships

In spring 1972, the deans and the faculty (with near unanimity) proposed a major modification of policy that would subsequently lead us into some trouble. Under this policy deans would rotate after a three-year term, and the present deans would begin rotating out of office immediately, Dean B first. An associate dean, chosen by the faculty and the incumbent deans, would serve for one year as an apprentice, with the expectation of standing for deanship the following year. Concurrently, Dean C had a heart attack and, upon recovery, came back to reduced duties for only the last of the 1972–1973 academic year. New Dean D, with administrative experience elsewhere, filled in from the faculty. The situation impressed the associate dean (E) prematurely into a major desk, supervision of faculty recruitment. Being immersed thus brutally into deaning led him to decide by the end of 1972–1973 academic year that he did not like administration—at least for a while. Thus, in the academic year 1972–1973, when there were 102 faculty members, the jobs were divided this way:

Dean A	*Dean B*
Alpha group faculty	Beta group faculty
Contracted studies faculty	Coordinated studies faculty
Desks:	Desks:
Languages and overseas programs	Registration records
	1973–1974 calendar
Advanced placement and credit by examination	Evaluation of programs
	Evaluation of faculty
Public events and public relations	Curriculum planning (the four-year committee)
Workload analysis	Handbook revision
Fund raising	Coordinated studies
Arts Building	
Contracted studies internship liaison	

Dean C	*Dean D*	*Associate Dean E*
(part of the year)	Gamma group faculty	Desks:
Desks:	Group contract faculty	Faculty recruitment
Equipment orders	Desks:	Admissions
Laboratory Facilities	Planning part-time studies	Graduation
Library and AV Media	1972–1973 budget	Recruitment of minority faculty and students
Grants	Space	
Self-paced studies	Clerical	
	Travel authority	
	Group contracts	

The reader will notice that some desks have disappeared, such as public relations liaison under Dean A in 1971–1972; routine desks, which experience showed to require cursory or occasional examination by the deans, have been assigned to the deans' secretaries; the internship desk, under Dean A in 1971–1972, later became simply a liaison with the ongoing office of cooperative education.

In 1973–1974 (118 faculty members) the provost's assistant carried the admissions/registration/records desk and the Northwest Association accreditation visit. The provost handled the post-baccalaureate study and institutional evaluation desks (with Dean G). And the provost's secretary managed the clerical desk. The rest of the assignments were distributed as follows:

Dean A	*Dean F*
Gamma faculty group	Alpha faculty group
Part-time study	Faculty orientation
External programs (development)	Curricular planning
Overseas programs	Calendar
Program evaluations/histories	Catalog supplement
Faculty workload analysis	Student services liaison
Faculty handbook (with Dean F)	Counsel in humanities and arts
Catalog revision (with Dean F)	
Public events	
Individual contracts	
Counsel in humanities and arts	

Dean G	*Dean H*
Beta faculty group	Delta faculty group
Faculty recruitment	Budget
Space and facilities	Summer session
Professional travel	Self-paced learning
Institutional evaluation	Learning resources
Nontraditional credit	Grants
Graduation	Equipment
Counsel in social sciences	Phase II laboratory
	Counsel in natural sciences/ mathematics

Thus, of the original three, only Dean A remained in the deanship. To boost the experience level of the group, a faculty member powerfully equipped with administrative experience else-

where was persuaded to join the deanship for a year to complete
Dean C's term; this person became Dean H.

Failure of Rotation

As deans rotated, so also desk responsibilities tended to be
swapped from year to year. For example, Dean A was responsible
for the budget in 1971–1972, Dean D taking it over in 1972–1973.
That changing around of duties has variety to be said for it, particularly in relation to the more routine chores like collecting catalog copy from the faculty and discussing editorial revisions with
them. But for those desks requiring the experience that knows where
opportunities and pitfalls are, yearly swapping of desks hasn't
worked. Such desks bear most critically on the quality of the college: the academic budget, faculty recruitment, and curriculum
development.

The dean responsible for the budget must, during the request cycle, collate the state funding formulas relating to instruction, collect requests from coordinated studies groups and group
contracts planned for the next cycle, handle requests for equipment
developed by groups of faculty members whose work depends on
it (such as scientists and artists), add descriptive and persuasive
prose along with the numerical documentation, work with the college's budget officer and business manager to make sure the academic budget jibes with the college budget as a whole, educate the
provost and the president concerning the main issues, respond to
questions about detail from legislative and coordinating council
staffers, and attend budget hearings in case a question arises that is
too nitty-gritty for the presidential mind; then, during the spending
cycle, this dean must recommend to the provost (all the time negotiating with faculty members) how the money shall be spent and
make sure the spending has been accounted for, and if not, why
not. The spending isn't so centralized as it seems. Coordinators of
coordinated studies programs or faculty members in charge of
group contracts have substantial discretion with regard to their
respective budgets.

It is clear that developed relationships, on campus and off,
are extremely important during the request cycle. During the spending cycle, the dean uses a knowledge of how the money was spent

before, and the ability to say "no" comes only with practice. Gains to the college are obvious as the budget dean grows both in knowledge and in experiential authority. Those qualities are even more important for the other major desks, curriculum and recruitment. Although critical decisions on these matters are made in concert with the other deans, the dean with one of these desks does not have a college budget officer or a business manager to lean on. There is a provost to depend on, to be sure, but the relationship of the vice president and provost to the deans is another story, to which I will return.

Since the critical decisions on budget, programs, and hiring are made jointly by the deans after recommendation of the dean of that desk, the passing around of desks among Deans A, B, and C might have worked, if the policy of rotating the deans themselves had not been adopted. Yet the pernicious effects caused by the mutual aggravation of the two policies—desk swapping and rotation—were not clearly perceived by all at this stage, primarily because, by dint of accident or persuasion, at least someone (the number diminished from three deans in the first year to one in 1974) had had a major administrative post elsewhere, as a department chairman in a state university or a principal academic officer of a leading liberal arts college, for instance. One thing we were sure of by this time, however: the principle of the desk was not only feasible but practical.

In the academic year 1974–1975 (131 faculty members), Dean A did not rotate out as scheduled so that the deanship would have the benefit of his experience. The arrangement was as follows:

Dean A	*Dean F*
Gamma group faculty	Alpha group faculty
Budget	Curriculum planning
Grants	Modular studies
Program evaluation histories	Liaison with student services
Public events	Calendar
Workload analysis	Faculty handbook (with Dean A)
Communications Bldg. equipment	Bulletin, supplement and quarterly brochures (with Dean A)
	Liaison with admissions/registrar
	Clerical
	Counsel in humanities and arts

Dean G

Beta group faculty
Faculty recruitment
Institutional evaluation liaison
Faculty year-end wind-up
Faculty orientation
Nontraditional credit
Co-op education liaison
Self-paced learning
Learning services
Counsel in social services

Dean I

Delta group faculty
Space and facilities
Graduation
External programs (including overseas)
Academic standing
Summer session
Community workday coordination
Travel
Equipment
Phase II Lab Bldg.
Counsel in natural science

The division of labor in the following year, 1975–1976 (131 faculty members), looked like this:

Dean F

Alpha group faculty
Faculty recruitment
Visiting faculty
Clerical
Faculty exchange
Liaison with student development services (including recreation and campus activities)
Academic program maintenance
Leaves of absence (monitoring)
Affirmative action reporting

Dean G

Beta group faculty
Curriculum (summer, overseas, modules, external program, arts, business, public administration, off-campus)
External credit
Faculty assignment
Liaison with registrar, admissions, Co-op education
Academic program maintenance
Academic standing

Dean I

Delta group faculty
Budget: operational, request, capital
Space/facilities (fall/winter qtrs.)
RULE (grant)
Grants and contracts
Academic program maintenance
Workload analysis
Nonmedia technicians

Dean J

Gamma group faculty
Space/facilities (spring qtr.)
Faculty development (fall orientation, workshops, Community Day, year-end retreat)
Learning Services Center
Program assistance
Public events
Academic program maintenance

Faculty	*Academic Advisor*	*Deans' Secretaries*
Chairpersons	Academic research	Academic calendar
Professional travel	General inquiries	Faculty handbook
Public events	Advising	Bulletin, supple-
Year-end retreat		ment, quarterly
Community Day		brochures
		Logistics of modules
		Central files

In 1975–1976, two deans were in their third and last year of office; two in the second and first; all were relatively young with little or no previous administrative experience. The failure of experienced people to come forth deserves explanation, especially because one of the strong arguments for the rotation policy was that the faculty included many with long teaching and administrative experience at excellent colleges and universities. In my opinion, they did not volunteer for three reasons: they had "had" quite enough administrative experience and were very much enjoying teaching; deaning at Evergreen is a unique ordeal, for instead of working through relatively few department chairmen, the dean often deals directly with several constituencies; and deaning did not involve extra pay except for the extra months put in. (Improvements dealing with the second and third reasons will be discussed below.) The bright, young, respected members of the faculty who did step forward had to learn high-level academic administration under extremely high pressures. No matter how fast they learned—and the work of all showed talent, of some, considerable talent, in administering—even the quickest learner would fully function for two years at best.

I mentioned above that the dean at the budget desk could depend on the college budget officer for help. One might expect that the deans at the equally critical recruitment and curriculum desks could expect day-to-day help from the provost. But such support would have been superfluous in the first years, since each of the three original deans possessed considerable personal authority by virtue of experience and achievement. And at least one dean of this type remained through 1974–1975, so that decisions tended to be made by and remain in the deanship after consultation with the faculty. By this time a habit of operation had taken hold.

Since the phrase "after consultation with the faculty" raises questions about how decisions are made, I should digress briefly to answer them. To describe Evergreen's governance system in detail would go beyond the scope of this chapter; here I shall describe our system's fundamental principle and its workings, providing a sample of the kinds of decisions usually made in departments, such as those related to curriculum, hiring, and equipment purchase. The fundamental principle: a decision is made by the one person responsible for it, after consultating with the people affected by the decision. (For a detailed account, I refer the interested reader to the Kormondy report, 1976.) Experience so far indicates fairly conclusively that academic decisions can be made without the department. For example, the curriculum in a given year follows guidelines laid by a long-range curriculum planning DTF (disappearing task force, composed mainly of faculty members, with some students and staff members) which has met previously. Specific choices are made by the deans together (a single dean is responsible for overseeing the process) from the recommendations of a short-range curriculum DTF that has culled proposals made by voluntary groups of faculty members in interdisciplinary study and by individual faculty members. The process of faculty hiring is supervised by one dean, making final decisions in concert with the other deans; they are advised by a faculty-hiring DTF which had chosen those candidates who were brought to campus for interviews and participation in seminars. The opinions of faculty members in the candidates' respective disciplines have always been given weight in the deliberations, but because successful interdisciplinary work and supervision of individual contracts rests on a person's command of a discipline— and because evaluation and retention should depend more on these opinions as well—the gathering of these opinions has been formalized in the 1976–1977 version of the deanship (described below).

A few months into the 1975–1976 year, the costly effects of the rotation system, hitherto dampened by the presence of experience, became apparent to everyone: lack of collective memory, and now, a tendency for decisions to become unstuck. That these young deans themselves articulated these problems best says a great deal about their innate abilities. Unfortunately, two paid a price in health, one to the extent of having to leave the deanship for that reason, whereupon former Dean A was prevailed upon to return from the faculty temporarily.

Survival of the "Desk" Principle

When these considerable weaknesses in the keystone of our academic organization were perceived by the students, faculty members, and deans themselves, pressure for its replacement by a departmental organization would not have been surprising. But there was no such pressure, perhaps because the weaknesses were weaknesses compared to very high expectations. A more likely reason for the widespread desire to stick with the desk concept was that five years of experience had shown beyond little doubt that our academic organization was capable of reaching the goals that led us in the beginning to avoid departments. Coordinated studies at their best had proved an effective way of introducing beginning students to habits of learning. Advanced coordinated studies at their best had opened new frontiers for faculty members in their own, as well as in new, disciplines. Faculty teamwork unhindered by departmental boundaries had led to an enviable record of grant-getting. Problem-oriented projects in the field, unhampered by time constraints imposed by departmentally oriented curricula, had built an impressive record of urban planning, team research in the environmental sciences, community help in the social sciences, performances in the arts. The same freedoms when put to use by individuals had equal success; students can do full-time research for extended periods of time, and much of this research has been deemed by outside, objective observers to equal that of the most competitive master's level graduate students. Our internship program would have been hamstrung by departments, but it has built more than a thousand positions in the state of Washington and nationwide (about 25 percent of them are in use at any one time) and their holders earn more than half a million dollars in stipends yearly. And finally, the acceptance rate of Evergreen graduates in graduate schools and the job market as a whole has been excellent. No one was about to forsake the ability to get results like these. In our early years when two or three musicians, say, were seen talking together, a remark would be inevitable, witty but with a strong admixture of the apprehensive, having somewhere in it the phrase "music department." If this kind of wit persists, the apprehensiveness in it is gone, even in the midst of recent discussions regarding reorganization of the deanery.

Yet To Be Solved:
Academic Advising and Faculty Quality

But perfection eludes us. We have not yet found ways to handle academic advising and the maintenance of faculty quality as well as the departmental organization can. The fact that few colleges anywhere have been elated with the performance of the department in academic advising emphasizes rather than minimizes the comparison: given equally poor academic advising, the student will feel the lack far more at Evergreen—first, because the changing program of study compounds the need for centralized advising, which has not been available; second, and less obvious, because the very existence of a department diminishes the perceived need for advising, for where departments exist, curricula exist for all the right and wrong reasons. With curricula one seems to need little more than road signs, so that much of what passes for advising is merely traffic directing. Perhaps real advising is therefore needed just as badly in a department as it would be at Evergreen, or more, but the need isn't perceived. At Evergreen where road signs are few, if any, the student trying to suit a present to a future feels very much alone. This piece of reality is good and necessary, I think, especially in American state-supported higher education, which tends to put a job title on every curriculum, thereby lulling undergraduates into a false sense of security. Why shouldn't people, when they reach voting age, learn to live with ambiguities and uncertainties—even students? We've learned, however, that too much ambiguity too soon is not good, or at least is not tolerated by many. As they face an uncertain personal future, beginning students need reassurance as they face the choices Evergreen offers.

We see some solutions to this advising problem. The counseling office is providing more career counseling than it used to do; the placement office encourages students to think, much earlier than the last half of the senior year, about life after Evergreen. We have created the position of academic advisor, whose business it is to know what is going on in each program of study and which faculty members are especially good at what. If reducing confusion has much the same effect as better advising, we are doing that by placing under one roof all the offices that deal with a student between the time of admission and the actual entrance into the seminar. The offices of admissions, the registrar, financial aid, student accounts, academic advising, career planning and placement, and veterans' affairs will be not only in one place but under one person responsible for meshing systems and cross-training people who deal directly with students in their program planning stage, so that students will get, if not the answers they want, at least straight ones. The most promising step toward tempering ambiguity and thereby improving advising will be accomplished by advanced planning so that programs of study can be publicized two or three years in advance instead of the present one year.

I cannot yet feel quite so optimistic with regard to maintaining the quality of the faculty; we have yet to approach the level of performance of a department operating at its best. The standards embodied by the majority of the Evergreen faculty in disciplinary capability (which precedes interdisciplinary capability) and in teaching effectiveness match (it may, I hope, be said without vainglory) any undergraduate liberal arts and sciences faculty. The few who fall short of our standard glare because they are few. To students, their presence is more obnoxious than if they were in a department because a given student typically spends most or all of his or her time with a single faculty member in a given quarter. Their continued presence offends fellow faculty members, indeed hurts morale, owing to a nearly egalitarian reward system.

The system comprises seven salary grades covering twenty-seven-plus years of service. On the sole basis of experience, a faculty member proceeds to the next salary grade, in which everyone receives the same pay. There is no rank or tenure. The determination of whether a faculty member remains at Evergreen is made in the second year of each three-year contract period. Determinations on retention are made by the deans and the provost on the basis of evaluations by students and faculty members with whom the person in question has worked. The chief goal of the evaluation system is improvement through receiving the advice of others; of the pay system, true collegiality. There have been enough indications of improvements made by individuals to show that to a great extent the former goal is being met; and accomplishment of the latter is evident in the imaginatively cooperative work in gaining grants, in successful interdisciplinary program planning, in the way faculty members help others with visiting lectures or seminars, and in the general extraordinary willingness to share the work of the faculty unencumbered by competition for status in the form of rank, salary, or lower teaching loads. Pride in one's work and in the esteem of others is still very real.

We need to give a great deal more thought to developing ways of showing our esteem that do not necessarily involve money, although more money for well-deserved leaves and travel would do much good. Agreement is general, however, that the egalitarian reward system has carried us far toward our institutional goals without prejudicing quality. This system was built with the understanding that some would be better than others but that those who weren't close would be weeded out at the end of their three-year contract periods.

Why has not this necessary corollary of our evaluation and pay system worked when so much depends upon it? I suggest at least five reasons: first, in the founding years, euphoria; second, the "on-the-other-hand" syndrome—since A will eventually be evaluated by B, A writes, at worst, a noncommittal evaluation of B, full of "on the other hands"; third, the rotation of deans—the best deans in the world would not address this problem if they were to be in office no longer than one contract period. The fourth reason is the "list" syndrome; at Evergreen, if "X" people were asked to submit a list of those faculty members whose contracts should not be renewed, the resulting lists would be close to "X" number. Tongue-filled cheeks have suggested an idea they have not given Gilbert and Sullivan proper credit for, and that is to have a responsible academic officer dubbed "Collator of Lists." Most departments would not share this problem since their parameters would be circumscribed by the discipline, consideration of which leads to the fifth reason: Although we all agree that a person must be good in at least one discipline to be any good at interdisciplinary study, we have no regularized way of bringing disciplinary opinion to bear on retention decisions.

Though the need for disciplinary wisdom about faculty quality has been acutely felt only recently, when it came to making decisions about major equipment purchases and programming for facilities construction, the deans in charge have for some time turned naturally, and informally, to faculty members in the disciplines concerned. Early on, the natural sciences faculty members began meeting together for other purposes as well. Wanting to avoid the strict, often overlapping sequencing found in traditional natural science curricula, they nevertheless knew, as they fashioned interdisciplinary basic and advanced student research programs, that some sequencing was necessary. They faced earliest another problem common to all the faculty: to plan far enough in advance so that a student could plan a program of study over two or three years.

The latter problem has been addressed by faculty members in the social sciences in occasional meetings. The first meetings of the arts faculty were for the quite necessary purpose of constructing a squeaky wheel to make sure that space and equipment were made ready for them, since facilities for the arts came last in our construction plan. We faculty in the humanities have trailed, perhaps out of complacent assumptions that programs in the humanities would take care of themselves; and since that has not been the case, faculty members in the humanities have finally begun to take some halting steps. All these discussions among disciplinary groups have been intended to make sure that the right kinds of study were available for students at the right time; as yet there has been no discernible tendency to adopt the "wagons in the circle" attributes of departmentalism or divisionalism.

By mid-1975–1976 we had learned these things.

(1) The desk principle works.

(2) Frequent swapping of important desks doesn't work.

(3) Neither does rotation of deans.

(4) Deans must come to the job experienced.

(5) The deans' time must be saved for budget matters; for curriculum, especially for helping put new ideas into action and troubleshooting in some programs; and for evaluation sessions with the faculty.

(6) Minor desk tasks drain disproportionate amounts of energy from major desks; minor desks have several possible loci; some could be decentralized.

(7) The collective disciplinary wisdom of the faculty can and must be tapped for advice on curriculum, equipment, hiring, and retention—hitherto matters all handled by the department—without fear of "relapse" into departmental organization.

The Deanery at Present

With these lessons in mind we are now in the process of reorganizing the deanship, which looks like this in 1976–1977:

Academic Dean	*Academic Dean*
Curriculum and faculty assignments	Budget
	Space and facilities
Faculty recruitment	Academic personnel
Student academic standing	

Joint Responsibilities

Consultation with each other and provost on all pertinent issues
Faculty appointment and retention recommendations
Curriculum and faculty quality
Training of assistant deans

Assistant Academic Deans

No desk assignment; they serve as apprentices to deans, preferably each with tasks assigned by each dean, and over two years, they gain experience with each of the major desks (curriculum, faculty recruitment and retention, budget).

Faculty Coordinators, Chairmen/Chairwomen, Conveners
Coordinators of Coordinated Studies. Responsible for: the integrity and quality of the coordinated studies program; developing, monitoring, and reporting to the deans the operational ground rules (covenants) of the program; acculturation of new and/or inexperienced faculty members; general development of all faculty members in the program. Serve as primary liaison between the deans and the program faculty. *Coordinators of Clusters of the Group Contract Faculty and of the Individual Contract Faculty.* Responsible for: the integrity and quality of their own contract(s); reporting to the deans the operational ground rules (covenants), if any, of the

contracts in the cluster; giving such advice, counsel, and assistance as may be needed by faculty members in the cluster in carrying out their academic responsibilities; evaluation of all faculty in the cluster; serving as the primary liaison between the deans and the cluster faculty.

Chairmen/Chairwomen. Responsible for carrying out specific ongoing, committeelike activities (related to professional travel, faculty orientation, faculty workdays, and the like) ; they report periodically and are on call to the deans.

Conveners. Responsible to the deans, on call, for convening groups to address specific, usually short-term, ad hoc concerns, and then reporting the results of these deliberations to the deans.

The principal desks are divided between two deans who have four-year terms that are reviewed during the third year and renewable after the fourth year. Two associate deans, who have two year, nonrenewable terms, continue the most valuable aspects of rotation: bringing fresh views into the deanship; spreading among the faculty their knowledge of the problems and the ways of coping with them; and creating a pool of potential senior deans. The associate deans act as apprentices on the major desks and have responsibility for a few minor desks. The number of desks in the deanship has been reduced, moreover, by assigning some to "conveners," faculty members willing to contribute some time to getting the administrative job done. They are responsible for convening appropriate other faculty members to get recommendations on such matters as faculty travel leave awards, visiting faculty invitations, and students' academic standing. There is also a "convener" for each of the major disciplinary groups who acts in two ways: first, the convener contributes to the evaluation and recruitment processes his or her opinion of the given faculty member's level of expertise; and second, he or she makes sure that curriculum planning and maintenance are kept up to date so far as the disciplines are concerned.

The Possibility of Export

Whether or not Evergreen's alternative to the academic department could be exported to another institution would be controlled, in my opinion, by two factors, the first of which is size. In this respect, the department as a basic unit of governance plays an unsung role. As one faculty member put it, he could see living in a department, even with all its disadvantages, because there faculty members' political and social urges counterproductive to the academic mission find a ready, constant outlet before they become universitywide issues. In our system of governance, issues concerned with individual problems or hobby-horses find few means of expression, so that all too often they enter into and confuse debate on major concerns. Although I would not have any qualms about expressing confidence that our academic administration could be tinkered with as we grow, so that it could effectively administer a college of about four thousand, I would hesitate to name a larger figure.

The other controlling factor is the mission of the institution. In a university where furthering and maintaining disciplines takes highest priority, I cannot imagine a better organization than by departments, perhaps leavened by institutes. But if a smallish institution, especially an undergraduate one, honestly examines its goals and finds that the discipline, although very important, is not *the* most important goal, but rather that the most important is the individual student's learning, even of a discipline, then another kind of administrative organization can very well substitute for the department. Only such a college can answer the one question our history cannot: whether change requiring elimination of the department could occur amid departmental fiefdoms. The college contemplating change can take heart, however, from the fact that Evergreen's academic administration has undergone two substantial changes without disrupting the academic work for which it exists, having established that it is possible to create an atmosphere in which learning takes precedence over structure.

9

F. M. G. Willson

Department, College, or Interdisciplinary School: A British Perspective

It is unlikely that a mixed group of American and British academics, gathered together for the first time, would have any difficulty in understanding each others' references to their "departments." On both sides of the Atlantic, the organizational notion that teachers and researchers within the boundaries of a single, well-established intellectual and scholarly discipline should form a clear-cut academic and administrative unit, which should take its place alongside similar units representing other equally well-defined disciplines, has become so usual as to be regarded almost as a law of nature. Any serious questioning of it, in either country, in all but rare cases raises skepticism and hostility among the orthodox and a degree of perhaps understandable zealotry among those eager to challenge orthodoxy. In both countries, though, there are exceptions to the general institutional rule, and this chapter will briefly discuss the British exceptions. However, and with apologies to American readers thoroughly familiar with the British pattern of universities, I want to draw attention to some very basic aspects of universities in Britain which, while they do not in any fundamental sense modify the claim that the "department" is an internationally recognizable phenomenon, should enable comparisons to be both more realistic and more sophisticated.

The United Kingdom of Great Britain and Northern Ireland now has about forty-five universities. (A very long footnote would be needed to explain the equivocation fully: partial explanation follows, but in this context it would be unfruitful to pursue the detail.) In terms of student numbers, only one of them—London—looks comparable in size with the largest American universities. London, however, is a federal organization with more than forty separate teaching and research institutions enjoying varying but very considerable degrees of academic and administrative autonomy. Two of the next largest in the list are Oxford and Cambridge, but here again, though their internal relationships are closer and more complex than those in London, each university is a congeries of colleges: the colleges are legally separate from the university and from each other, are fiercely conscious of their separateness, and to a very considerable extent constitute the centers of instruction and study within the university. The University of Wales is a confederation of seven institutions—each, in effect, operating with a great deal of autonomy—scattered over the whole country, so that the figure quoted for total enrollment of students is quite misleading. In fact, if the British universities are listed in terms of the size of individual, unitary campuses—individual operating units with their own "departmental" structure—then the largest at the present time is the University of Manchester, with just less than 10,500 students. The smallest, in October 1975, not counting the separate colleges and schools of Oxford, Cambridge, London, and Wales, was the New University of Ulster with well below 2,000 students. Oxford and Cambridge have between 11,000 and 12,000 students each, but the colleges number their members only in hundreds. The largest London institutions are University College and Imperial College, the former having about 5,000 students and the latter a few hundred less.

Although the average British university has not many students by American standards, the teacher/student ratio overall is very favorable. Inevitably ratios vary by subject and are always matter for controversy, but the overall figure is 1:8, and while some "realists" and all "pessimists" expect some slippage in the future, the slippage is rarely discussed in terms "worse" than 1:10. Thus, as far as the academic staff is concerned, British university departments are not so small as the figures of student enrollment would appear to indicate. Another significant feature is the relationship of graduate and undergraduate work. Postgraduate work is undertaken at present by approximately one-fifth of the total student body in the country at large—that generalization concealing a range of from less than 10 percent in several of the smaller universities to nearly one-third in the case of the University of London taken as a whole. But it must be remembered that the usual three-year period of undergraduate work leading to a first degree in Britain is more specialized from the outset than is the American four-year exercise. Students begin their university studies about a year later than their American counterparts, have already done at least two years of fairly specialized work in a few subjects at secondary school, and have much less choice of disciplines to study when they reach the university. All these characteristics of the system have been modified in recent years and are likely to be somewhat further modified, but even allowing for such a trend, the staff members of a British university department have in many if not most cases less basic-subject teaching to do than their American opposite numbers, are less likely to be involved in considerations of "general education," and rather less likely to see as much contrast between undergraduate and postgraduate work. The British first degree has perhaps more in common with an American master's than with an American bachelor's qualification, though it is extremely easy to misinterpret such a wide generalization.

Finally, in this short catalog of background items, the political importance of the department is worth stressing. British universities are almost totally financed by the central government through the University Grants Committee and are operated increasingly as a national system. Faculty members have long been aware of themselves as a national group, and under the social and economic pressures of recent years they have become increasingly, if somewhat reluctantly, unionized professionals, negotiating with and through the universities as a group of employers in a complicated system that effectively involves the national government as paymaster. But each university, apart from Oxford and Cambridge, is governed formally by a mixed group of laymen and professional academics, and in Oxford and Cambridge government is by the academics themselves. In all of them the practical direction of academic life is firmly in the hands of the academics (though outside the ancient universities this group tends to be limited to the professoriate), influenced but not controlled by the administration, except insofar as the latter is the inescapable channel of communication with government, and to the extent that its officers may be blessed with great natural powers of persuasion.

The point here is that the very great power of the professoriate in most British universities is based, in all but a few special places, on the departmental structure. The academic politician must make his or her mark in and operate out of a department, not merely initially, but continuously until such time as he or she wishes and has the chance to take the headship of an institution. A long-established and reasonably efficient orthodox departmental structure is thus almost impregnable to attack from without. Change, therefore, in old institutions may only come from within and is likely to take the form of modest, piecemeal rearrangement rather than fundamental revision. Only in totally new ventures can different patterns be tried with any real hope of success.

Growth and Change in Single-Discipline Departments

If British universities are relatively small today, they were very small by present standards only a generation ago. The major recent change in departments, in that large part of the university system (probably at least 85 percent of the whole) in which single-discipline departments predominate, has been sheer growth, which has had no fundamental effect on basic structures or external relationships. It has brought significant changes in internal affairs, however. The normal academic arrangement of a unitary British university is to have single-subject departments as the base units. Those units are then grouped into an intermediate tier of faculties, or boards of studies, usually according to the classical connections of subject matter—the arts, natural science, social science, and so on—and each such grouping usually has a dean or chairman as leader/coordinator. The structure is topped by a representative senate or academic board. Traditionally, each department had a single professor, the rest of the academic hierarchy, in descending order, consisting of readers, senior lecturers, lecturers, and assistant lecturers. The professor was the unquestioned and unchanging head of the department: he or she was usually its main spokesman in the faculty or board of studies and its only representative on the academic board or senate.

Growth has brought a double change, still in progress. Full professorships have multiplied, so that big departments may now have three or four. In some cases the additional professorships have been regarded as purely individual appointments without reference to the headship of the department, which remains the prerogative of the holder of the original chair. In such situations, as in the remaining "one-professor" arrangements, the pressures for some democratization of the departmental regime have been increasing. Judgments of the traditional experience so far are hardly based on detached and scholarly research, but many subjective assessments are highly critical of "professorial tyranny" and see the growth of departments as leading inevitably to the introduction of rotating or elective leadership. Such a new style of leadership has indeed emerged already in many British universities and is almost certain to be further extended. But the development of something much more like the American "chairmanship" of departments, whatever it may do for internal democracy, is quite likely, at the same time, to strengthen the academic parochialism of the unit, increase the sense of professionalism and of the primacy of research and publication over teaching, and generally strengthen the defenses of the single-discipline community.

Interdisciplinary Schools

The alleged parochialism of the single-discipline unit was the starting point for some of the few outstanding recent attempts to escape from the orthodoxy of departmental arrangements. Enough concern was generated in the years after the Second World War about the supposed weaknesses of an educational system that was accused of producing increasingly overspecialized graduates to ensure that more thought was given to the potential advantages of more integrated, multidisciplinary programs of study. Two favored Oxford examples were often pointed to as models—the four-year degree course in the languages, literature, philosophy, and history of the Ancient World, known as "Greats," and its post-World War I three-year course parallel, "Modern Greats" or, as it is more widely known, "PPE"—Philosophy, Politics, and Economics. Reflection on those Oxford exercises and growing disillusion with "overspecialization" led to a considerable increase in degree courses involving the study in some depth of two or more disciplines and, much later, to the introduction of modular degree systems that enable students to exercise a much greater amount of choice than formerly, though that choice is almost always within broad fields of related subject matter and is not comparable with the much wider range of courses normally open to undergraduates in the United States.

In all universities these modifications have forced a greater interest in the relationships of disciplines to each other, especially within the broad academic categories, and have enhanced cross-disciplinary teaching arrangements and the role of coordinating faculty boards and committees. But in nearly all universities this movement has not affected the existence of the single-discipline departments or undermined their authority. Even where a fairly dramatic innovation has been made as a result of interdisciplinary enthusiasm it has not necessarily been accompanied by any structural change. For instance, Keele, opened in 1950 and called at first the University College of North Staffordshire, made obligatory a four-year, first-degree course, with a Foundation Year common to all students, who subsequently went on to three years of more specialized work. Though the whole program was infused by an idea of educational synthesis emanating from the mind and through the leadership of an elderly Oxford philosopher and master of Balliol College, A. D. Lindsay (Lord Lindsay of Birker), who died shortly after Keele opened, and although the essence of the scheme remains in being, no attempt has ever been made there to create an alternative to single-discipline departments.

An assessment of the extent to which the modern operation of the intermediate tier of academic responsibility represented by

faculties may have moderated the position of single-subject departments must wait on major institutional research. The most that
could be said, on the basis of limited past inquiries, is that the intermediate layer has developed useful diplomatic and a few service
functions but is still essentially supplementary and mediatory in
character, rather than innovative or executive. The more radical
attempts to challenge the parochialism of single disciplines have involved creating structures which, in effect, replaced both the department and the faculty by a single large, multidisciplinary unit
usually called a school. Of the few attempts to build such new
academic structures most have not survived to demonstrate the possibilities of the idea. Warwick abandoned its school concept in
favor of orthodox departmentalism after only a few years; Essex
has four schools, but each has within it several large departments
and the schools bear a close family resemblance to faculties elsewhere. Ulster also has four schools without formal departments, but
it is still small and may not yet have faced any pressure for single-
subject departmentalism. Only two new universities with enough
experience to demonstrate at least some possibilities deserve to be
looked at more closely: Sussex and East Anglia.

Sussex, which opened in 1961 and was conceived and
planned—again like Keele—in strongly Oxonian style (indeed it
was called in its early years, perhaps with friendly irony, "Balliol-
by-the-Sea"), turned its back firmly on the single-discipline department. Teaching was to be conducted in schools whose themes
were interdisciplinary, and academic staff members were to be recruited by schools to meet their special needs, so that there might
well be representatives of particular disciplines in several schools
but no organized universitywide unit covering just those disciplines.
The titles of the schools that developed are the best brief illustration of the basic notion: African and Asian Studies, Cultural and
Community Studies, English and American Studies, European
Studies, Social Sciences, Applied Sciences, Biological Sciences,
Mathematical and Physical Sciences, Molecular Sciences.

Sussex has grown relatively quickly in British terms—from
scratch in 1961 to nearly forty-five hundred students in 1975–1976.
The schools have remained the core of the university's structure,
but they were not for long without rivals. "Subject groups" were

recognized toward the end of the 1960s and stretched across schools, though more recently some persons have favored restricting the groups to within the boundaries of schools. Two "academic areas"—arts and social studies, and science—became part of the organizational picture through the existence of coordinating committees each chaired by a pro-vice-chancellor, so it might well be thought that an embryo faculty structure was being created to coordinate and support the schools. A Graduate School in Arts and Social Studies was set up, separate from the other nonscience schools and responsible for all higher degree work. Moreover, the science schools have been characterized by some unfriendly critics as simply "superdepartments" dominated by orthodox subject interests, rather than organizations operating in the spirit of interdisciplinarity, while there have been minority complaints that the arts and social studies schools do not know what a school is or is supposed to be. To the outsider, therefore, the Sussex reality is confusing and open to varying interpretations. Those convinced of the eccentricity and essential temporariness of the schools will view the appearance of subject and area organization as part of an inevitable journey back to single-subject departments and orthodox faculties. Those passionately devoted to a crossdisciplinary approach will emphasize the vigorous survival of the schools and the secondary constitutional position of the subject infrastructure. In fact, the pressure toward departmentalism may have reached its peak in the early seventies and since receded, leaving the individual subjects stronger than before but without weakening the acceptance of the schools as part of the continuing academic reality of Sussex. Given the likelihood of much slower growth or even a standstill in the next few years, Sussex will have an opportunity to discover how such a steady state affects, if at all, the school-subject dichotomy and whether sheer length of establishment will keep the scales permanently weighted in favor of the schools, or at least weighted enough to give them no less than parity with the more departmentally recognizable "subjects."

East Anglia began two years after Sussex, in 1963. Whereas the Sussex vision of interdisciplinarity embraced not only the subject matter within each school but encouraged its acceptance across all the schools, East Anglia was less comprehensive in its ambitions in this regard and has seen its schools develop with more limited and self-contained objectives. The school's names do not reveal this difference, but are worth listing to show how relatively close is the correspondence with the basic grouping at Sussex: Biological Sciences, Chemical Sciences, Computing Studies, Environmental Sciences, Mathematics and Physics, Development Studies, English and American Studies, European Studies, Fine Arts and Music, Social Studies. Perhaps because of their greater self-containment, and perhaps because of the rather slower and smaller growth of East Anglia, no serious threat to the schools from individual disciplines has yet developed, and, as in the case of Sussex, it will be particularly fascinating to see whether a period of steady state or limited growth will enable the schools to achieve and maintain an impregnable position.

Oxford and Cambridge

In the recent developments sketched so far there has been no hint of concern for any aspect of departments except the allocation to them of the academic subject matter with which they deal in the teaching and research contexts. If one takes this exclusive view of what academic organization is for, then it is not unfair to argue that multisubject schools are in effect no different, constitutionally, from orthodox departments—they only differ in having more varied subject matters to teach and to offer as potential research areas. Important—indeed, fundamental—as the difference between single disciplines and multidisciplinarity may be represented to be, it is a difference within tightly defined organizational limits. There will certainly be significant differences in the ways in which departments and multidisciplinary schools arrange their work, and there may be important organizational considerations arising from differing teaching methods, or the balance of teaching and research, or the extent to which the unit is devoted to highly specialized and professional areas such as medicine or law or music. But such inevitable variety of internal arrangement does not arouse comment: What does provoke interest is the extent to which it may be desirable and practicable to extend the responsibility of predominantly academic units to matters outside the strict definition of teaching and research.

In all the universities considered so far, the departments are indeed seen as units for teaching and research purposes only. Though there are a few very special and small exceptions, there is a clear division of responsibility within those universities between teaching and research work—seen as the business of the departments, faculties, schools, boards of studies, or other unit—and the social, residential, "general educational," nonacademic administrative and nonprofessional aspects of the lives of students and staff. The latter are entrusted, to the extent that they are accepted as desirable, to separate administrative authorities, even though ultimately most of them come under the overall policy supervision of the academically controlled senates. But there is another pattern. It is found in the ancient universities of Oxford and Cambridge and has influenced the planning of three new universities—Kent, Lancaster, and York. The basic theme of Oxbridge life is not "departmentalism," whether interdisciplinary or restricted to single subjects; it is the idea that teaching and research are only parts of the responsibility of universities to their students and teachers, albeit the most important single parts, and that such responsibility should extend to providing a setting in which the student learns not only an academic subject but how to live and develop himself or herself within a tightly knit community whose atmosphere is heavily influenced by scholarship and by sophisticated, cultured, and civilized human relationships. The setting must be small, the relations of students and teachers intimate, the coverage of subject matter wide but not too specialized—in short, the setting and the coverage claimed by their supporters to be most nearly achieved in the colleges of Oxford and Cambridge.

To correct many widely publicized, false impressions, I must emphasize that Oxford and Cambridge have not been totally "collegiate" for at least half a century. The vision of a highly residential university operating only through small colleges in which all teaching is carried on in individual tutorials, in which the teachers (college fellows) are individuals having only slight formal connections professionally with their counterparts in other colleges, and in which both the academic and social lives of students and fellows are conducted in a cultivated aura of elite and aristocratic privilege is in most respects a travesty. The current Oxbridge model is a federation: colleges are still the core and the power centers of the university, but a very high proportion of the work in individual disciplines is organized on universitywide lines through committee structures that provide a kind of departmental network across the colleges. In the sciences there are long- and well-established departments, and as graduate work and research have grown, many special subject-aligned institutions have appeared, a few in collegiate form, to take their places alongside the older colleges. Additionally, shifts in the overall financing of Oxbridge have increased the two universities' dependence on the state, and some leveling has occurred among the colleges because of centrally inspired schemes of internal redistribution of wealth. These evidences of federal or central influence should not be ignored: in any attempt, however impressionistic, to strike a correct balance, one must recognize that in the recent past the wind has been blowing more from than toward the colleges. All these developments indicate that the ancient universities nowadays work through a complex and subtle set of relationships by no means entirely collegiate in setting or attitude.

But having paid a reasonable tribute to the modern pressures of centralism versus collegiate autonomy, I should also stress how different, fundamentally, Oxbridge still is from the noncollegiate British university. Except for some specialist graduate, professional, and library facilities, and for the laboratory sciences, there are few central administrative or academic buildings and no "departmental" offices. Even the biggest colleges do not include among their fellows more than two or three people in each subject, and many colleges rely on one fellow in each field. Not only do fellows wear two hats simultaneously, but the majority, especially in Oxford, have to carry two purses, one to hold their college stipends and the other to contain their university salaries as lecturers. Students still receive a high proportion of their supervision from fellows of their colleges, though not so frequently or so rigidly as in the past through the medium of individual tutorials. Students and fellows are recruited by their colleges. Students, both undergraduate and graduate, live during part of their careers in their colleges and are dealt with administratively almost entirely by their colleges. Syllabi and examinations are formulated and operated universitywide, but the whole process is infused with collegiate attitudes, and students' academic progress and reputations are in all usual cases monitored and developed within their colleges.

Without laboring the matter unduly, one can say with confidence that, despite the modifying pressures, Oxford and Cambridge cannot be described as departmental universities and that the academic essentials are still carried on there not merely in and through the colleges in a practical sense but in a spirit of close, nonspecialized intellectual ambience peculiar to the collegiate experience. How much this situation is due only to the inertia of an old established system; how much it is influenced by the geographical scattering of colleges within the confines of two quite compact, ancient cities, so that each college retains the essence of a residential community but is always conscious of its neighbors; how much it is due to the legal separateness of colleges and university and to the divided financing that guarantees from fellows an economic loyalty to both their college and their university as well as a professional loyalty to their subject; how much it reflects a style of academic life which, despite the harsh criticisms made of it in some quarters, retains a grip on the sensitivities of men and women through its sheer urbanity and the grace and beauty of its settings and through the sense of fulfillment it can give at least to many of its members, however brief their sojourns may be—all these imply questions to which there cannot possibly be satisfactory answers. But at least this attempt to express something of the Oxbridge situation may provide a backcloth to the efforts of those newly established universities that have tried to take some of the Oxbridge collegiate system and adapt it to their own needs.

New "Collegiate" Universities

The Universities of Kent, Lancaster, and York are all located in or near old towns not dissimilar in character to Oxford and Cambridge, and superficially, therefore, it could be argued that the collegiate pattern should have guaranteed some of the advantages that have accrued to the ancient universities from the intimacy of their urban settings. But as new twentieth century institutions they had to be built on the outskirts of the towns on single large sites and could not possibly achieve the unique physical integration with the life of the towns that is found in Oxford and Cambridge. And even on the new campuses there was insufficient space to allow a generous separation of colleges from each other or from the other university buildings. All three, therefore, are quite intensively developed, and indeed at Lancaster the striking and ingenious architectural arrangements have incorporated most of the colleges in a single large complex which produces intimacy— and splendid protection from the wet northwest of England weather—but which tends to exacerbate their anonymity as living and working units. Moreover, although membership in colleges is open to staff members and students from all areas of the universities, there are no collegiate academic programs. Most of the non-laboratory teaching at Kent is carried on in the colleges, but is not their responsibility. At Lancaster and York some departments are housed in college premises, so that even though there is no direct relationship between them, it is understandable, in the absence of any college academic program, that the colleges appear to some extent as departmental headquarters with residential accommodation attached.

Like Oxford and Cambridge, the new universities supposedly reinterpreting the Oxbridge tradition revealed little enthusiasm for organized interdisciplinarity. Indeed, they and many of the orthodox single-department universities would no doubt argue that it is unfair and impossible to judge the extent of successful interdisciplinarity by reference only to academic organizational structures. And some might claim that the amount of interdisciplinary teaching and research achieved within their orthodox constitutional arrangements is as great as or greater than what has been achieved in some or all of the interdisciplinary school settings. Be that as it may, in a strictly structural context, single-subject departments were accepted as inevitable and correct from the start at Lancaster and York. Subject groups have apparently come to flourish so much, in fact, within the coordinative cover of a mixture of three faculties and a school at Kent that a report published in April 1976, while wanting to preserve the interdisciplinary approach that the university had embraced, recommended the formal recognition and strengthening of the boards of studies that have grown up and are responsible for degree programs and subject specialties—in other words, an acceptance of orthodox departmentalism within a faculty framework.

There is, therefore, little real similarity between Oxbridge and the three new collegiate universities in academic organization and practice. The "new" collegiate nature of Kent, Lancaster, and York may well be significant and even unique in the area of student affairs and—perhaps most strongly in the case of Kent—in the influence that the social and domestic pattern of residential life exerts on the character and style of the whole academic enterprise. In those contexts they might well be studied in a comparative way along with other small but highly residential universities located in or near small cities, whether "collegiate" or not, such as Durham, Stirling, Essex, or Bangor in North Wales. But in all essential academic respects, Kent, Lancaster, and York are departmental universities with student residential arrangements that may offer a better chance than elsewhere outside Oxbridge for somewhat closer academic as well as social relationships to develop among students and teachers and among at least some groups of teachers.

Some Reflections

The seeker for workable alternatives to the dominance of the single-subject department cannot be directed to many places in contemporary Britain. Sussex and East Anglia show modest but real achievements in providing interdisciplinary bases for academic organization divorced strictly from nonacademic considerations. Oxford and Cambridge are still the only strong, working examples of residential, collegiate universities in which departmentalism is kept in severe check though by no means denied a place. Kent, Lancaster, and York, whatever their other successes, are universities that experimented for a while with a quasi-departmental, collegiate structure but have developed in practice into departmental universities with special residential collegiate features. Elsewhere, the single-subject department is and has been practically unchallenged.

Recent British experience must be seen against the general economic, social, and political background of the past twenty-five years. The new universities discussed were established in an atmosphere of expansionism and optimism, yet within a very few years they were struck by the twin problems of student unrest and economic recession. The optimism and enthusiasm for innovation or for following through on the implications of innovation weakened, partly because of the onset of noisy controversy but mainly because of tighter budgets involving, particularly, fewer expenditures on physical facilities. If there was any desire to experiment seriously in a new university with college-based teaching as it was known at Oxbridge, the cost of doing so may have seemed prohibitive and the rigidity of a national system of academic salaries may have seemed an insuperable barrier to divided remuneration between college and school, faculty, or department. Ultimately, however, the difficulty either of making progress with "interdisciplinarity" or of "doing an Oxbridge" has been due to sheer lack of agreement, let alone conviction, about the educational, intellectual, and even social validity of either concept among the academic community as a whole, including the governmental and political cadres most closely concerned. And it is fair to suggest that one factor that has been particularly important in American discussion of institutional innovation has scarcely been apparent in Britain so far—the felt problems arising from the sheer size of unitary campuses. As figures given at the beginning of this chapter show, it would be impossible to find any real parallels to the huge American campuses in Britain. The need to "humanize" the campus has not been a major motive of the academic reformers; the argument has been more narrowly academic and one in which, inevitably, therefore, the element of philosophic doubt has never ceased to play a significant part.

Be that as it may, what is fairly clear from Britain's limited experience is that the way to establish viable alternatives to the orthodox single-subject departmental university is to put money, the power to appoint and pay staff members and to recruit students, and the responsibility for large, clearly defined areas of teaching wholeheartedly into the kinds of schools and colleges that have been described; to have the courage and tenacity to keep such functions in those schools and colleges for long enough to prevent the orthodox rival pattern of academic power from emerging too strongly alongside; and to have the good judgment (and the good luck) to choose and retain academic staff members with the enthusiasm and flexibility to nurture and protect the causes they were engaged to foster.

10 J. Douglas Brown

Departmental and University Leadership

$\mathbf{A}$fter years of participation as a student, professor, and dean in the day-to-day life of an old university, I find it challenging to try to analyze the reasons why such an institution maintains its effectiveness as a human organization. The more one seeks to refine experience into judgment, the more clearly the critical element for survival in a university appears to be not wealth, physical plant, alumni support, or even passing leaders but the integrity of its academic organization. Although integrity in any institution is assumed to reflect purpose and consistent standards in attaining purpose, it is the special attribute of *organizational* integrity that assures the survival of a university. This attribute arises from the way in which the academic life of the institution is ordered by a system of accepted traditions and principles that give the institution a persistent, coherent, and yet responsive personality.

Far from being an adequate answer to the question of why universities survive, the preliminary conclusion that the vitality of universities emanates from a system of accepted traditions and principles inherent in their academic organization opens up a host of queries concerning the nature of these traditions and principles and the means by which they are implemented in the day-to-day life of the institution. To understand oneself requires studied introspection. To understand institutional personality requires a similar

185

analysis of underlying assumptions, which are or should be controlling but which are far from obvious when merged into the complex of motivations found in an organized community of teacher-scholars. Even when such assumptions are fully understood, the leaders in such a community need to interpret and reinforce them in constructive ways. Effective organization involves both the understanding of principles and the art of implementing them.

Underlying Assumptions

The basic assumption of academic organization in a university is academic freedom, a concept that is far more pervasive than the outside world realizes. Academic freedom has been a powerful factor in the survival of great universities. It has promoted the development of a vast range of new disciplines. It has permitted the testing and retesting of ideas and ideals. And it has given the intellectual life of a university the flexibility to adjust to evolving knowledge, social mores, and humane values in its society when change appears to be justified and at the same time to conserve the moral, intellectual, and artistic heritage of past centuries. Unlike the church, the great university does not require conformity in religious faith. Unlike a government, it does not reward or penalize men according to their political views. Unlike a business corporation, it does not require conformity to policies because they are profitable. The university demands that its teacher-scholars be intellectually competent, honest, and responsible and assumes that they are dedicated to the advancement of knowledge and the enhancement of the potentialities of those they teach.

Despite the primacy of academic freedom, it is my experience over many years of academic administration that the preservation of this principle and the control of any possible abuse are almost entirely by-products of a mature and cohesive faculty community that lives and works together. The department provides the immediate subcommunity in which public opinion supports both freedom and responsibility. The larger faculty acts to reinforce tradition when new or small departments seem to become repressive or loose. The basic contribution of the administration is to make sure that candidates for appointment, promotion, and chairmanships are intellectually competent, honest, responsible, and dedicated people and then let them and their colleagues reinforce the assumptions of academic freedom. A lack of intellectual honesty and responsibility in a teacher-scholar is sensed far sooner by his immediate colleagues in a discipline than by a dean. The opinion of colleagues is more persuasive in setting men right or in determining status. Further, colleagues are better able to distinguish between reasoned convictions sincerely held and the subordination of intellectual integrity to ulterior ends, whether personal or political. They are also better able to distinguish between shortcomings in competence and those of character. It is the role of a dean of faculty to give confidential and understanding counsel to department chairmen on issues of academic freedom and responsibility as in all other matters affecting individual colleagues. If mutual confidence exists, most issues are solved constructively.

The character of these relationships does not imply that a president or dean of faculty is ever free of criticism concerning the views of one or many members of a faculty. For a considerable number of articulate citizens, including some alumni, the concept of academic freedom is as little understood as that of predestination. I have found that the authors of general indictments of the "radical-liberals" who "permeate" a faculty are not interested in learning either the facts or the philosophy of academic operations. When a dean or administrator receives a letter pertaining to an individual professor, he or she had best answer it with a courteous assurance that the professor in question is a teacher-scholar of competence and responsibility. The correspondence is filed without being referred to anyone, on the principle that it is far better to permit the normal internal processes of distinguishing between differences in opinion and irresponsibility to operate than to suggest dependence on the judgments of persons whose qualifications are unknown.

Within a framework of academic freedom and responsibility, it is the diversity of intellectual disciplines, interests, approaches, and determinations that gives a university ongoing life. Countervailing tensions in an academic community are normal and necessary for health and vigor. Without countervailing tensions, the human body falls into a heap, to sleep, if not to die. Without countervailing tensions in ideas, an academic community decays from sheer inertia.

It is the way in which tensions are resolved that tests the qualities of a university, not their absence. To suggest a few of the counter-vailing tensions which exist on a university campus are those involving different emphases on particular fields of learning; liberal versus professional education; teaching versus research; diverse methods of instruction, such as lecture classes, preceptorials, seminars, laboratories, and independent work; departmental and school autonomy versus centralized oversight and review; the degree of student participation in the determination of academic policy; and the appropriate roles of the faculty, the president, and the trustees. Anyone who has been a member of a teaching department can add the tensions that arise in planning curricula and in handling teaching assignments, appointments, and advancements. The reason why most successful presidents and deans come up from the professorial ranks is that an executive drawn from outside academia is frustrated not only by the tensions inherent in the life of a university but by the articulate espousal of diverse points of view by teacher-scholars schooled in the discussion of ideas.

The tensions that exist in any human organization must be resolved into constructive cooperation if the organization is to survive. The means of resolution vary widely from those that predominate in authoritarian, hierarchical organizations, such as in armies in action, to the amorphous consensus of a ladies' aid society. The underlying difference is in the command-response balance in the determination of what should be done. As organizations mature in societies blessed with democratic traditions and a relatively high level of education and well-being, the shift in the balance is toward emphasis on response. A workable premise is that the essential elements in the constructive resolution of tensions in such a society are leadership, communications, and tradition as constantly interacting factors. It is rewarding to analyze how these three elements operate in an organization as replete with counter-vailing tensions as the academic structure of a university.

Departmental Leadership

The devolution of leadership into many schools, departments, and programs is a fortunate necessity in a university. The nature of an institution comprising a wide spectrum of disciplines, educational goals, and research activities requires dependence on leaders specifically competent in the relevant field or function. Further, in a university there are leaders in terms of intellectual stature and leaders who can mold a body of teacher-scholars into an effective working unit. They are not necessarily the same. Departments vary in effectiveness from period to period according to the changing balance of intellectual leaders and organizational leaders. It is a strength of universities that such variations among departments will occur at different times. The departments with both able intellects and professors with a sense of organization help sustain the general momentum of the institution while less fortunate departments are helped by replacements and promotions to regain their strength. The primary function of a dean of faculty is to sense the rhythm of each department in terms of its growing or waning strength in order to anticipate needs several years ahead.

Although a dean of faculty is deeply concerned about the quality of every teacher-scholar under his oversight, he must take a special interest in those with some sense of organization. The dean recognizes that the senior professors in a department will be ever anxious to attract distinguished colleagues to enhance the reputation of their department throughout the country. But a collection of prima donnas becomes a source of distress for all concerned, including themselves. And thus the dean must keep an eye out for those relatively rare individuals who make good chairmen—it has been said that not more than one full professor out of five functions well in this capacity. Nevertheless, a much larger proportion of the senior members of a department should be expected to form a cohesive core of those who are concerned with the corporate effectiveness of the department and willing and able to assume some function in departmental leadership. Experience has shown that even departments that have suffered heavy losses through retirements, deaths, or other causes can be brought back to strength if three strong members remain. That this renewal can be accomplished suggests the survival qualities of a departmental unit within an ongoing academic structure. To the outside world, the strength of a university is an impressionistic summation of many undifferentiated attributes. To a dean of faculty, its academic standing is a series of mental ratings of departments ranging from excellent to those in a rebuilding stage.

In the demanding task of assuring effective leadership in the various academic units in a university, one should avoid the error of relying on any form of election of chairmen, rump or official. The central leadership of a university should have the authority to select its subleaders. After informal consultation with a number of the senior members of a department, the president, with the advice of the dean of faculty, should combine his knowledge of people and his sense of what is needed to select a chairman who will be both a leader in the department and his representative in communicating university policy. The normal tensions in a department which might lead to conflicting interests in the selection of a chairman should be subordinated to the integrating principle that he or she represents the *whole* department as a *continuing* organization which must, to be effective, have impartial and judicious leadership in the consideration of personnel actions, budgets, curricular programs, and research projects. Since departmental recommendations on all these matters must be approved at higher levels of administration, the chairman must simultaneously interpret university policy to his colleagues in the department and convey departmental needs and goals to the central administration. It might be said that the chairman must learn how to resolve tensions on both a horizontal and a vertical plane in academic organization.

The selection and continuing evaluation of department chairmen is a fine art. Fortunately, it can be improved by experience. In assessing the essential qualifications of an effective chairman after years of varying success, I would put intuitive integrity first. This means not merely being honest and fair in day-to-day dealings with others, but possessing a personal system of values that affords a basis for judgment of issues which is more sensitive than logic alone. A chairman deals with people. His understanding of people, their purposes, potentialities, values, and effectiveness, is enhanced by an introspective understanding of his own qualities. Intuitive integrity is an essential attribute of leadership, not only in judging others, but also in gaining the continuing respect of a group of colleagues with differing interests and opinions. Countervailing tensions in any organization are far more often resolved through respect for a leader of tested integrity than by clever compromises. The chairman of a department should be such a leader and not merely a skillful mediator of opposing factions.

Another essential qualification for a chairman is a sense of organization. This is the ability to think of an organization as a structural combination of people whose functions are differentiated but whose activities are coordinated by leadership, intercommunication, and tradition to serve a common end. Many intellectuals prefer freedom from the restraints of organization, although they appreciate the support it provides. In particular, they resist accepting the persistent obligations of the leadership that makes organization possible. But there are others, equally able, who find the challenges of building and leading an organization a source of satisfaction which supplements rather than replaces the satisfactions of teaching and scholarship.

Such a person should find leadership in the organization interesting and rewarding, but not so that it impairs his zeal to advance his other professional abilities. Again, it is the balanced resolution of countervailing tensions within himself that creates a good chairman. If he permits himself to become too occupied with the details of organization, his standing and respect as a teacher-scholar suffers. If, on the other hand, he permits his department to lose momentum and drift while he concentrates his energies on learning, his rising distinction as a scholar is no justification for his continuance as chairman. The resolution of the tensions is aided by his willingness and ability to delegate functions to others, yet retain responsibility for leadership and oversight. A good chairman, like a good quarterback, soon learns that he will not last the game if he insists on carrying the ball when others are available.

An effective leader demonstrates his sense of organization in many ways. He shows an interest in and an understanding of people, not a tolerant acceptance, but an instinctive appreciation of what men and women are and what they can do. Further, the leader has sufficient humility to seek advice, delegate functions, and weigh relevant considerations rather than have too much confidence in his own judgment. But balancing humility is a willingness to accept responsibility when decisions must be reached and actions taken. A self-determined chairman, no matter how efficient in get-

ting things done, leaves a department in a shambles once he is
gone. Consensus becomes smothered under a climate of lazy tolerance. A chairman who hates to make decisions can let his department become a debating society.

Other qualities of a good chairman are expressed in his art
of leadership. He exercises foresight in anticipating problems before
they become acute. He encourages informal discussion of issues so
that a middle ground of accommodation begins to be accepted
rather than awaits formal debates in meetings after sides have been
taken. If a chairman avoids joining one side or another, he is free
to carry on preliminary private conversations with those colleagues
whose judgment he respects. What causes the most serious problems
is not the members' disagreements but their inability to discuss
differences without emotion. A good chairman not only encourages
full discussion but makes sure that all members of his department
have as complete information as possible on any important question
of policy. A sound principle is to give them more than they need to
know rather than less. It is a human trait to enjoy having "inside"
information, but this pleasure is more likely to lead to suspicion
than to confidence among those affected. The best means of communication is oral discussion, when this is possible. A mimeographed
circular may transmit words accurately, but it does not necessarily
assure understanding.

The art of leadership can be illustrated by describing the
best way for a chairman to handle a departmental meeting when
an important issue must be resolved. First, as mentioned above, the
chairman has made sure that all relevant information on the issue
has been circulated. To gain a better insight, the chairman has
discussed the issue with several members without revealing his own
tentative judgment. He should come to the meeting with some
fairly clear idea of a wise and feasible solution of the issue, but
should repress any inclination to present his views early in the
meeting. This is rather the time to be sure that all the considerations are presented by members of differing views. If some considerations are overlooked, especially those of feasibility and cost,
the chairman should raise them. Long experience has shown me
that the extreme views of some members will be gradually neutral-
ized in, perhaps, the first two-thirds of the meeting period. Then

the chairman can begin to lead discussion toward a workable consensus. But if consensus does not seem possible because the opposing sides are close to balance, it is time for the chairman to express his judgment. Better he should support one side or the other, as long as either supports a feasible solution, than encourage continuing debate on less consequential points. Once a chairman takes a position, he should support it vigorously and persuasively. A leader must lead and not merely arbitrate. He is not a passive moderator, but the chief operator in an ongoing organization. In all organizations, no matter how democratic, indecisive leadership creates confusion and doubt. The trumpet must give forth a certain sound when the time for decision has come.

One of the most important functions a department chairman should perform is assuring a proper balance in the diverse approaches to learning and the varied subareas of instruction and scholarship represented in his discipline. In history, there are periods, areas, and specialized approaches to consider, from medieval to modern, Russian to Spanish American, and constitutional to diplomatic. In physics, there is the balance between theoretical analysis and experimental research. In economics, econometrics may crowd out the study of complex issues in policy. Every discipline appears to attract some professors who cling to the current "inner mystery" of the discipline, whatever it may be in approach, coverage, or methodology, and seek to strengthen the manpower and curriculum of the department in the field they embrace, at the expense of less popular but still significant fields. It is again the chairman, with the help of the central administration, who must support a proper long-range balance in his department, no matter what his own predispositions may be. This task is not easy, since scholarly enthusiasm often approximates theological zeal.

When a chairman has demonstrated the qualities and arts of leadership that have been suggested as ideal, one is strongly tempted to permit him to continue in office as long as he is willing. But succumbing to this temptation is usually a mistake. No matter how much such a chairman has learned to delegate and no matter how adequate his supporting staff, the responsibility for leadership and administration does take its toll on the intellectual energy and the personal freedom needed to advance a scholarly career. Further, an able chairman, over time, is bound to encourage other senior members of the department to enjoy a lesser degree of responsibility than is conducive to true partnership in the determining of policies in a department. Rotation of the chairmanship of a department involves some risk, but it also encourages the sense that the department is a body of colleagues in which leadership is shared. Moreover, because successful departments tend to become smug and cozy, they benefit from new leadership. Disciplines do change, and fresh ideas may be wholesome stimulants to progress. Even the best symphony orchestras do better if different conductors test their capabilities from time to time. A new chairman, judiciously selected, may encourage a reconsideration of those goals, policies, and judgments concerning personnel and curricula which are more tested by past experience than challenging for the years ahead.

In balancing the advantages of having experienced chairmen and the need for rotation to encourage participation and new approaches, experience appears to support an average tenure in office of five years. A useful pattern is the three-year appointment subject to a single reappointment of three years. If a chairman does not come up to expectations, replacement at the end of three years should cause no ill feeling. The reasons for reappointing a successful chairman are sufficiently obvious to discourage adverse comment. It is usually the case that professors who want most to be chairmen are not those most wanted by either their colleagues or the central administration in filling the assignment.

Nature of the Creative Teacher-Scholar

Successful leadership at any level in a university, or in any other organization, must be responsive to those led. In a factory or a bank, one would not normally give much space to the analysis of individual employees. They are too diverse in character, background, education, responsibilities, and aspirations. But the teacher-scholars in a mature and distinguished university are a very special group. To organize them effectively, one must know a good deal about them as individuals. They are appointed, professional colleagues and *not* employees. They participate in academic management. In many ways, they are a self-governing body. Academic freedom and responsibility combine to form traditional and pervasive mores. Able teacher-scholars can be led, but not coerced or satisfied by remuneration alone. In sum, to understand how an academic organization operates requires an understanding of the creative teacher-scholar without whom a university would be an educational factory. Over the centuries, great universities have survived because they have accommodated themselves to the attributes and concerns of these talented individuals.

A native quality of a creative teacher-scholar is an inquiring mind, enhanced from childhood onward through all stages of his education. A true love of learning is not confined to a narrow field, but reaches out in both breadth and depth as life proceeds. This fundamental motivating drive in a long career of study and teaching is stimulated and reinforced by interaction with colleagues and students with a similar bent, in formal sessions and in informal conversation. Both freedom and opportunity are essential in sustaining an enthusiasm for inquiry sufficient to find new truth rather than, year by year, to wear out the old. Since both interaction and freedom are needed in balanced rhythm, the ideal climate for inquiry is one in which periods of teaching are interspersed with periods of study and research of varying length during the weeks, months, and years of an academic career. This climate is the justification for the usual arrangements of university life—both lecture halls and libraries or laboratories, seminar rooms and private studies, days of teaching and days for research, short vacations and long, and successive terms of teaching and periodic leaves for scholarship. Creative teacher-scholars do not flourish under the nine-to-five, five-days-a-week schedule of a bank or office. The rhythms of an inquiring mind do not fit into a neatly ordered timetable. An academic administrator knows this from his own experience. He is not the manager of a department store.

Another attribute of a creative teacher-scholar is a close combination of the powers of analysis and accumulation. The gathering of unanalyzed knowledge produces a pedant whose mind is like a crowded attic full of unsorted and unorganized recollections. It is when knowledge and ideas are first analyzed and evaluated and then added to one's intellectual resources that they become useful in further inquiry and discovery. But again analysis and evaluation are greatly enhanced by interaction with colleagues who have similar interests and also by the need to explain and discuss knowledge and ideas with students even less inclined to easy acceptance. The members of a community of scholars and students help each other in the process of analysis and accumulation in which all, at different stages, are engaged. This colleagueship is a great advantage of a university over isolated centers where scholars or scientists are removed from constant contact with either students in their own field or scholars in other fields. A "think-tank" may be a helpful retreat for a professor on leave, but it lacks the interactive stimuli of a teaching community.

The most distinctive attribute of the creative teacher-scholar is intuition, a mysterious quality of the subconscious association of ideas—the combination of ideas to form new ideas. It is creation *from* and not *against,* since it requires a vast complex of accumulated knowledge and ideas which have been assembled by an analytical and inquiring mind. Such knowledge and ideas are by no means confined to a narrow discipline. An intuitive scholar draws upon his whole lifelong range of study and experience. Ideas and suggestions arise by the marvelous powers of association that make the human brain both a vast and ordered library of total experience and a powerful and subtle instrument for the retrieval of relevant (or irrelevant) memories. Intuition transcends the logic of conscious analysis although supported by it. As in the take-off of a jet aircraft, logic may create the momentum to gain flying speed, but intuition is necessary to leave the ground and gain a vastly wider perspective.

One might assume that a teacher-scholar with a persistently inquiring mind, the powers of analysis and accumulation, and an ability to supplement logic with intuition would be an ornament to any faculty, respected by his peers. And indeed he might be a stimulating catalyst in suggesting scholarly projects for others, but a further attribute is needed if he is to be a truly creative teacher-scholar in his own right. This attribute is *self-discipline,* the willingness to balance the intuitive discovery of likely ideas with a sustained concentration on testing and retesting them to be certain that they have validity. In the excitement of discovery, it requires a deep sense of responsibility and personal integrity to delay any announcement of one's findings until every possible error has been checked. The teacher-scholar in a university is helped in this process by his early training, by his willing colleagues, and even by his more articulate students. The most powerful motive for thoroughness, however, is the possible adverse criticism of scholars throughout the world when findings are published. The publication of scholarly papers adds to the pool of knowledge, but it also encourages responsible scholarship, if the author wants to be respected in a community of creative teacher-scholars.

Other less formidable attributes of the creative teacher-scholar must also be recognized by those who participate in academic organizations. They vary in some degree from person to person, but are more norms than exceptions. One is the tendency toward time-consuming perfectionism which can become irritating to administrators and outsiders, and even to colleagues and spouses. An idea-man seeking truth abhors sloppiness in thinking, but not necessarily in material surroundings. Further, a creative teacher-scholar is likely to be introspective. Most creative people are. They test their ideas in the laboratory of their own minds. A by-product of such introspection is that they tend to judge policy, as well as truth, for themselves. Trained in exposition and discussion, they are fond of debate, in private conversation and in meetings of committees, departments, and faculties. Perfectionism and introspection, joined with a proneness to discussion, may become a problem in gaining consensus on academic policy if some members of a department or a faculty do not remember that stubbornness in defending a scholarly premise does not need to be exercised in defending an academic policy uniquely one's own.

From this analysis of the creative teacher-scholar, it is a sound conclusion that concepts of time and authority in a distinguished university are distinctly different from those in industry and business. The creative teacher-scholar tends to resist the judgments and criticisms of others unless he respects their standing in his terms. He is likely to discount advice from any person who assumes that hierarchical status will automatically give credence to his suggestions. He abhors suddenness and prefers to analyze the reasons for a policy rather than to accept it at face value because it is promulgated by a president or dean. The wise academic officer well knows the limits upon whatever authority is assigned to him in the bylaws of the university and learns to develop policy through leadership rather than command. He is sensitive to the large area in which colleague authority is the source of effective administration. In this sense, universities are systems of partnerships coordinated and integrated through leadership, intercommunication, and tradition. Academic freedom and the nature of the creative teacher-scholar have combined over the centuries to establish a special but workable pattern of administration.

Role of the General Faculty and Its Committees

As universities have grown in size and coverage, wide differences have developed in the degree to which the members of a university faculty participate in academic administration in a specialized school rather than in a university as a whole. There are many devices to assure that both levels of participation are possible, such as elected senates and the representation of schools on appropriate universitywide committees. It is true, however, that most of the considerations involved in assuring effective academic organization and administration through faculty participation at a level above that of the department are essentially the same whether one is discussing a semiautonomous school or the university as a whole. To avoid repeated references to variations in the titles and functions of academic officers and committees among universities of differing size and structure, I have found it best to use the titles and functions customary at Princeton University. Although some of the procedures of an old but smaller university may not be appropriate for many other institutions, I believe the experience I have gained in their use will illustrate general considerations in academic administration.

Committees are essential in any organization dependent on the response of its constituents rather than on the limited insights of an authoritative leader or board. A university is peculiarly dependent on the response of its faculty and students, as well as many other supporting groups. Fortunately for the reader, the present discussion is restricted to faculty participation in academic administration. Further, the simplest and most concise way to summarize experience in respect to the structure and operation of faculty committees is to express some hard-won convictions concerning what works.

The persistent error in academic administration is to have too many committees. Faculty complaints about wasted time are often justified. But if participation in developing essential policy or in weighing decisions affecting individuals is denied, far greater complaint would ensue. Experience has shown that only three types of general committees are worth the time they take: advisory, legislative, and quasi-judicial. Advisory committees should not legislate, nor should legislative committees judge individual cases. An advisory committee assists a dean or president by communicating faculty attitudes or suggestions concerning policies. It should, therefore, meet with the officer advised and not otherwise. A legislative committee assists the faculty by formulating in precise language any proposal deemed worthy of faculty consideration. A quasi-judicial committee interprets faculty rules, policy, and standards in specific cases, particularly concerning individuals, whether faculty members or students. To clarify these conclusions, we might well consider the functions of certain key committees and to indicate where an overlap of function may occur.

A type of faculty committee that is basic to the educational as well as the financial integrity of a university is that on the curriculum or course of study, undergraduate or graduate, whether within a school or throughout the university. Such a committee must help resolve the persistent countervailing tensions arising from excessive differentiation and specialization within a curriculum as opposed to the restraint needed to assure a close-knit structure of offerings conducive to the best possible education of the student. Sound economy in building a curriculum is not only an educational requirement but a necessary means in assuring the best use of faculty manpower and university funds. But it is in the nature of a teacher-scholar to seek approval of a course on a segment of his discipline which most interests him and on which he is especially prepared, even though the segment is too specialized to warrant the time of students or the cost of instruction involved in a full course. If a young Ph.D. has worked long on the events related to the War of 1812, he may seek authorization of a course in American history from 1810 to 1815. If an older professor has spent years in the study of Roman roads, he may propose a course that will examine them mile by mile. Though the professor's department should seek to dissuade him, it often passes the buck to a central committee, which is less exposed to the sentimental tolerance and subtle logrolling to which a department is susceptible.

The job of a committee on the course of study is to be tough, to see the forest of educational and financial economy for the trees of individual interests and enthusiasms. Various approaches are possible. One is the setting of departmental course quotas that may require the elimination of an active existing course to offset any new course approved. Another is to require the chairman of the department concerned to appear before the committee and express his personal judgment as the officer of the university directly concerned with the long-run effectiveness of his department. A third approach is to suggest a one-time seminar to test interest in the given subject, with a limit on size or on the qualifications for enrollment. A more drastic solution may be a directive from the committee to the department to restudy *all* its offerings and develop a program that more fully reflects the current state of its discipline, the qualifications and interests of its faculty, and the best pattern of instruction for its students. A course-of-study committee should be chaired by a senior dean who should lift discussions to the level of educational philosophy and economy, rather than that of short-run compromise. When new departments, rather than new courses, are concerned, special committees may be necessary, inasmuch as the problems of manpower and costs are even more evident.

A committee on the course of study is essentially *legislative,* since it weighs proposals from the departments and determines how far and in what form they should be approved by the faculty. In the area of curriculum, the faculty is operating within its principal jurisdiction, educational policy. It may, likewise, consider changes in the methods of instruction or in the requirements for a degree. But in a different but equally important area, a faculty committee may need to become a *quasi-judicial* body, reviewing the recommendations of departments for the appointment and advancement in rank and salary of individual members of its own body. This review involves a sharing of responsibility with the president and the board of trustees, since a faculty cannot expect to set its own salaries, whether piecemeal or in general. Therefore, a faculty committee established to review the appointments and advancements of individual members is also *advisory* to the president. It can, however, be a very valuable instrument in the wise and effective manning of a university and in the avoidance of errors of judgment at both the departmental and the university level. Where this type of committee has evolved over the years, it has become respected by faculty members, administrators, and trustees alike. Many other institutions would profit greatly by its existence.

Ideally, the faculty should elect an advisory committee on appointments and advancements by a special ballot. To assure that its members have experience and judgment concerning both personnel and the proper manning of a teaching department, it is wise to restrict nominees to the current chairmen of departments, with voting arrangements requiring that all the major divisions of the university are represented, even though all eligible faculty members vote on all candidates. By this means, the committee represents the whole faculty and yet contains members cognizant of the special problems arising in particular areas of learning as well as the general problems of building a strong department. The appointments and advancements covered by such a committee can be adjusted to institutional size. Ideally, they should include, at least, all those in which tenure is involved, whether by outside appointment or by promotion from within. Promotions to full professor should be covered. Since it is very difficult to separate status and salary in personnel administration, the committee should review not only the salaries recommended in cases where changes in status are involved, but also the general schedule of salaries in the department covered.

An advisory committee on appointments and advancement should meet with the president in strict confidence after it has had a full opportunity to study all departmental recommendations. The dean of the faculty normally acts as secretary and presents the cases. Other deans may be present to provide advice and judgment, but only the elected members of the committee should vote. If the president needs further advice from a dean, he can secure it at other times. The president should not feel bound by the verdict of the committee and may postpone decision, but with full discussion based on extensive data, both from the department and from outside sources, he should normally be ready to make his decision. The role of the dean of the faculty throughout the whole period in which changes in faculty status or salary are being considered is to counsel with chairmen concerning individual cases, available positions, salary levels, and departmental balance in age and field. He acts as a leader in attaining a fair and feasible working balance of all the interests and aspirations which, over time, serve as dynamic forces in the development of a strong, effective faculty.

These kinds of faculty participation in determination of educational policy and faculty manning should go far to indicate that a university faculty is and should be an essential element in academic management. But two other committees, one strictly advisory and the other both quasi-judicial and advisory, may illustrate how the various levels of university administration and authority can be welded together. The first is a faculty advisory committee on policy, which meets only with the president. The other is a faculty committee on conference that meets with the educational committee of the board of trustees. Both are two-way channels of communication. The committee advising the president should be elected from the total faculty to permit representation of both old and young. It should meet whenever either the president or its own members request such a meeting. The committee on conference with the trustees should include those older members in whom the faculty as a whole has great confidence. It should have longer, overlapping terms. The reason for the quality and stability of a committee on conference is that it should serve not only as a channel of communication, but also as a channel of appeal for any faculty member who has a grievance regarding status, salary, or other conditions that has not been resolved at an appropriate administrative level within the university. It is this committee that holds hearings to consider such cases and transmits its findings to the educational committee of the board for such action as the board deems proper. Although appeals to the conference committee and the board may be rare, the availability of an open and active channel of communication from the faculty to the board on all matters of faculty concern affords a subtle but enduring satisfaction.

One could discuss innumerable other committees which a

president, dean, or faculty could appoint. A few dogmatic conclusions will suffice. A committee should not be appointed unless it is vitally necessary, has a clearly defined function, is chaired by a responsible officer, will not waste time, and is not larger than seven members, if at all possible. A committee is a poor device if executive action is sought rather than policy or judicial interpretation of policy. Committee meetings should never last more than two hours. The chairman of a committee should know what he and his committee are doing, should discourage wordy diversions, and secure definite and clearly expressed results. If information is required for intelligent consideration of a problem, it is the obligation of the chairman to provide it, preferably well in advance of a meeting. It is a waste of a committee's time to argue about a fact rather than a judgment. When a faculty committee makes a report to the faculty, it is the responsibility of every member of the committee who has shared in the recommendation to help the chairman in supporting it. This conclusion is a counsel of perfection not usually accepted by those who love to see a dean "in the middle" in a strenuous faculty debate.

Role of Dean

The upper reaches of academic organization in American universities vary so widely that it is sometimes difficult to designate who is the chief officer under the president *primarily* responsible for the quality and effectiveness of a faculty. Such an officer may exist for a core area of arts and sciences while the deans of professional schools have parallel functions for their schools and a provost coordinates policies across the university. Having served as a dean of the faculty and as a provost in a smaller university, I find the former title much preferable, even though a dean of the medical school might object if he must report to the president on matters concerning his faculty through a general dean of the faculty. In an area as vital to the organizational integrity of a university as the quality, effectiveness, cooperation, and morale of its total faculty, some senior officer is bound to gain most influence through his understanding, experience, and sense of responsibility.

The functions of a provost may be too much spread over budgets, supporting services, such as libraries, laboratories and

computer centers, and planning to permit him to keep abreast of
the current problems related to faculty personnel, morale, curriculum, and educational policy, except in terms too broad to
satisfy the faculty that he has their continuing interest at heart.
The title "dean of the faculty," on the other hand, suggests, as it
should, that the officer so designated is the focus of the relations
between the faculty of a university and the corporate entity as
represented by the president and the board of trustees. If there is
no such officer, there should be one, no matter what his title. If the
provost is too busy, the president is even more so. Meanwhile, the
countervailing tensions between all other concerns (such as finance,
grounds and buildings, fund raising, and alumni and public relations) and the concerns of the university's precious cutting edge, its
faculty, may be inadequately resolved. Effective organization requires that where tensions exist there should be clearly defined
channels for their expression and resolution. The best channel in a
human organization is a person, not a committee or a complicated
organization chart with solid and dotted lines.

Under this interpretation of the office, the dean of the
faculty of a university should be both the chief representative of
the president to the faculty through the schools and departments
and the recognized representative of the general faculty in the
higher levels of university administration. He should have direct
access to the president and to all other chief officers reporting to
the president. He should, however, religiously avoid expressing
policy judgments to the board of trustees, either in meetings or
with single members, except with the president's specific approval.
He can argue with the vice presidents in charge of finance or facilities but should accept the decision of the president concerning any
representation to the board. His job is to be a leader in the educational functions of the university. Ideally, not only all the heads of
departments reporting to him, but all area and functional deans as
well, should consider him their friend in court in his area of jurisdiction. However, a dean of the faculty is wise to encourage any
academic officer to see the president or any other senior official
directly if his problem suggests the need to do so. Yet if possible,
the dean should advise the president in advance of the issues involved and even of possible solutions. Leadership is enhanced not

by jealousy about one's jurisdiction, but by ready and willing help to anyone with a problem.

All organized operations require routine reports, recommendations, directives, and correspondence. The constant temptation is to expand the flow in order that all contingencies are fully covered. But a dean of the faculty is dealing with professors who abhor bureaucratic practices. Therefore, every form or questionnaire used should be trimmed down and simplified. Only in the evaluation of personnel should economy of effort give way to thoroughness. Reports providing many other kinds of information can be prepared and analyzed by administrative assistants for consolidation into summary comparisons. But in weighing the qualifications of individuals, much can be learned from a close reading of extended analyses and even casual comments.

The most valuable insights a dean of the faculty can gain about senior officers, chairmen, and faculty members are those developing in face-to-face discussion. Direct contact is also the most effective way of assuring an understanding and implementation of policy. A good schedule of work is to confine one's handling of paper work to mornings and to leave afternoons available for a long series of half-hour appointments with chairmen and other officers. A tested format is to use the first fifteen minutes of such interviews to deal with the problem presented and the second fifteen minutes for a relaxed discussion of general developments in the visitor's area of concern or in the university generally. An idea casually suggested at such times often ripens into action. Ideas, like children, seem to do better when their parents aren't around and especially when the ideas are transmitted as assumptions rather than as preachments. A dean of the faculty is in an excellent position to act as a clearinghouse of ideas and experience across departmental lines. It is better to illustrate one's conclusions with the experiences of others than to appear as an omniscient judge. There are times, however, when convictions should be bluntly expressed, especially when ethical standards are involved. When time does not permit face-to-face discussion, a telephone conversation is preferable to a written communication. In any transmission of ideas or policy, the oral response of the recipient is far more indicative of understanding and attitude than a carefully composed acknowledgment.

The toughest jobs of a dean of the faculty are not the oversight of educational policy and curriculum or the handling of faculty appointments and advancements. These become opportunities for creative leadership. The toughest job is the pruning out of error, whether in personal behavior or in departmental administration. With regard to individuals in the junior ranks, the dean can give firm advice to a chairman. But with professors on tenure, there comes a time when he should take on the job himself. An individual in trouble can be helped in many ways, including medical treatment, leaves for rehabilitation, or just good advice. It may seem a paradox, but a dean of the faculty has greater influence with a tenured professor needing help than with a junior faculty member *because* the former is on tenure. The dean's presumed long-run interest in the individual allows him to put his recommendations more forcibly. Nothing in the tradition of tenure prohibits a confidential, face-to-face presentation of a calm but penetrating analysis of a professor's errors when these are injurious to himself, his colleagues, and the university.

When a chairman proves to be a poor administrator, a dean of the faculty can give him special help. The dean should not dwell on past mistakes, but provide "preventive medicine" by reviewing the considerations that should affect his future decisions. If such help proves insufficient, the time may come for removal. In such a case, it is far more considerate of the man and of his future contribution to the university to enlarge on the advantages of freedom from diversion from teaching and scholarship than to review his shortcomings in a position for which he has less talent. Faculty morale is a vital part of a dean's business. It develops from a multitude of relationships and conditions.

Role of the President

Overseeing the academic organization and administration can receive, in modern times, but a limited part of the time, thought, and energy of a university president. Unfortunately, the acute problems of financial solvency, governmental regulations, alumni and public relations, large research projects, and a complex support structure have increasingly made academic direction a precious and satisfying diversion rather than the major thrust of a most demanding position. It might be rewarding, therefore, in a discussion of the academic organization as a whole, to indicate the most essential functions to which the president can assign such time as he has available for the advancement of the educational program of his university and the building of its faculty.

Regardless of other duties, the president remains the chief exponent of the educational mission of the university, the philosophy of education that undergirds this mission, the goals sought, and the quality of performance that is required to attain those goals. An organization or an institution is bound to reflect, in some degree, the personality and values of its leadership. The outside world, as well as the faculty, administration, and students of a university, is always prone to personalize leadership. Even in a very old institution, the president cannot fade back into an amorphous "they." Rather, he is assumed to have a more immediate influence on the day-to-day academic affairs than the nature of a university permits. But in the longer run he *has* a persistent and lasting effect.

(1) In both formal speeches and informal discussions, the president must state and restate repeatedly the educational mission of the university in terms appropriate to his audience. What is said or written for outside consumption has influence inside as well. Educational philosophy is not an easy subject to communicate because most people are not philosophers, and because they assume themselves to be educated, they are inclined to accept an autobiographical norm. Likewise, they confuse an institution's goals with their own. For example, if that aim is to make money, a university should help people make more money. No matter how busy the president is in balancing the university's books, he must continually take time and occasion to put first things first—to remind all those participating in the life or support of the university that its great central purpose is the advancement of learning and the enhancement of talent. The faculty members of a university need to be confirmed in their conviction that they remain, as they have been over the centuries, at the cutting edge of the university's mission.

(2) In upholding the traditions of a university, the president must make clear by words and actions that the concept of academic freedom will be wholeheartedly and courageously sus-

tained. Nothing has a more insidious influence on faculty morale and performance than the suspicion or knowledge that the president will not stand up to pressures to limit academic freedom.

(3) The president can have the most direct influence on the academic standing and effectiveness of his institution through the selection of his senior faculty and, from among the senior faculty, his choices of deans and chairmen. Unlike most other enterprises, a university is selecting a member of *management* every time a tenure appointment is approved. Therefore, the president must not only find time to review proposed appointments and promotions under firmly established procedures, but should assess and reassess, from time to time, the strength and effectiveness of all teaching units.

(4) Because of the wide diversity of educational programs in the modern university, the president must depend heavily on his deans and chairmen, and on the wisdom of the faculty and its committees, to handle curricula and instructional methods. The president is more likely to become involved in major changes, such as the establishment of new schools and departments or the approval of major research programs and facilities.

(5) Although presidents of universities can and do perform many other functions that enhance the effectiveness of the academic organization, space permits but one important addition. It is that a president of a university should know and be known by as many of his colleagues as time and energy permit. He is the leader of the faculty as well as of the university. Teacher-scholars, as herein discussed, respect people for what they are rather than for the titles they bear. The time a president invests in knowing his faculty personally, and not merely as an audience in formal meetings, pays good dividends. Human organizations remain human, no matter how large and impressive they become. Cohesiveness is an attribute gained through human contacts and attitudes. It is peculiarly a function of leadership to enhance the humanness of an institution.

Toward Humane Organization

In a time when American industry and government are becoming increasingly impersonal because of bigness, layers of specialized administrators, computers, and "cost-effectiveness" account-

ing, the American university may be fighting a rear-guard action to preserve the humane climate that I assume to be the basis of an effective academic organization and administration. It is my deep conviction that industry and government have become less effective rather than more effective because they heavily discount the importance of human motivation and human relations in any organization, no matter how large. Industry and government may be able to operate under conditions wherein their workers must increasingly conform to precise and predetermined roles. But this possibility increases the challenge faced by American universities, as centers of creative discovery and creative teaching, to avoid the dulling influence of conformity to principles of organization that ape science and technology rather than implement human understanding. In no aspect of university life does this challenge have more critical significance for the future of our country and the world than in academic organization and administration.

11 Dean E. McHenry

Toward Departmental Reform

M any years ago I chose the title "professor of comparative government" because I thought it best described my field and method of inquiry. In this volume, my associates and I have sought to analyze a problem of comparative *college and university* government: the internal organization or departmental structure of academic institutions.

Colleges and universities, like all other organizations, cannot exist without some subdivisions or units. The major structural problem they face—and the major question of this book—is whether the disciplinary department as we have known it is the best model for these subdivisions. Are there other forms of academic organization that can achieve educational purposes equally well and possibly better? To analyze this question, we have sought the views of departmental advocates, critics, and reformers in both British and American settings. All the authors of this book, as students and practitioners of academic administration, would agree that some internal structuring of colleges and universities is not only inevitable but desirable. Yet major differences exist among them, as in higher education at large, about the discipline as the basic organizing principle for this structuring.

We recognize that disciplinary departments are a predominant force in higher education. Even the professional schools rely on them for their intellectual underpinnings. Nor would most authors argue that the claims of the disciplinary department as an elemental unit of academic polity are not strong. As Andersen and Trow note in the opening chapters of this book, conventional departments offer several advantages for being the basic unit.

Most obviously, if least importantly, disciplinary departments are familiar. After nearly one hundred years of widespread experience with them, not only academics but the educated laymen are well acquainted with them. Today's professors and students, in contrast to those of earlier centuries, have grown up through the departmental system even in secondary schools, which have themselves grown increasingly departmentalized along disciplinary lines.

Beyond familiarity, disciplinary departments offer simplicity of structure: parallel and equal organizational units based on the commonly accepted divisions of knowledge, a clear hierarchy of authority, and a relatively agreeable division of labor between units.

They also afford convenience by grouping faculty members and students on the basis of their particular interest in a field of knowledge. They stimulate conversation and cooperation on these interests, and they permit judgments to be made about student admission and graduation and about faculty appointment, promotion, and tenure by specialists knowledgeable about this subject matter.

Moreover, they are tied, in Trow's phrase, to the "international fraternity" of scholarship and learning. Indeed, they are the institutional manifestation of the intellectual movements within the academic world at large.

But perhaps most important, as Trow points out in Chapter Two, because the disciplines embody the ultimate academic value of truth, departments organized by discipline are driven to be self-correcting. As moral communities based on the norms and canons of verification, they possess a particular capacity for self-renewal. Recall Trow's point:

> The academic disciplines embody, in their methods of work, procedures designed to force their practitioners to confront inconvenient facts. Indeed, it may be said that only the disciplines care whether an assertion is empirically or logically true and are concerned with the evidence on which it is based. Other

approaches to issues, outside the constraints of a discipline, are
more concerned whether a statement is plausible or interesting
or useful or morally or politically virtuous (for example, "progressive"). . . . It is not an accident that we are most likely
to see academic work highly politicized in those courses furthest removed from the constraints of the academic disciplines.
And indeed, those persons who wish to politicize higher education are very often those most hostile to the autonomous norms
and values of the academic disciplines, and for good reason.

Those who champion the abolition of existing departments
must recognize these strengths, and those institutions that forego the
constraints of the academic disciplines must find other means to
protect their teaching and research from devolving into indoctrination and dilettantism. Indeed, as one reviews the early chapters of
this book, one may well feel that the arguments for accepting conventional departments as they now exist, or at least with only
modest tinkering, are so strong that few will be likely to venture
along the uncertain roads of reform.

Yet even the proponents of disciplinary departments concede at least some of the weaknesses that Benezet and Harrington
in particular emphasize. All departments, by definition, are subject
to parochialism and segmentalism. Naturally they tend to look inward rather than outward. As a result, disciplinary departments
that operate as the only organizational unit of colleges or universities may prove efficient for teaching their particular subject matter
but less than effective for helping students learn about overarching
cross-disciplinary relationships. They impose territoriality in what
should be a seamless web of knowledge and encourage the erection
of defenses against the "uninitiated" and the "ignorant."

In addition, they neglect the major issues of human life,
none of which lies in only one discipline. They imply to students as
well as faculty members that the increase of knowledge is more
worthy than the application of this knowledge to the conduct of
life and that expertise about facts is more important than relationships among facts.

Perhaps most important, they substitute structural rigidity
for intellectual fluidity. They impose an intellectual straitjacket on

the development of teaching and research. Robert Straus, for example, from the perspective of professional education, contends (1973, p. 896):

> There is nothing intrinsically permanent about disciplines; they are merely convenient subdivisions of tentative knowledge, concepts, and methods that at particular times have appeared meaningful and functional. As man's knowledge changes, it is logical and necessary that the boundaries of disciplines should change accordingly. Indeed, the change is constant, and it is reflected today in the significant amount of multidisciplinary activity between and among scholars. Most such interchanges, however, take place outside of and in spite of the formal organization of universities. The formal organization exerts great force toward maintaining the status quo and is a major barrier to any change in the traditional and entrenched departmentalization of academic activity.

And thus, although ideally they are intellectually self-correcting and self-renewing, in practice they all too frequently tend toward structural ossification and obstructionism. When only the members of the department have the supposed expertise to have a voice in departmental policy, mediocrity can spiral downward into pedantry and decay.

To imply that the pros and cons of departmental organization, as weighed in the opening chapters of this book, form merely two opposing points of view for partisan debate would be wrong. Rather than a bimodal distribution of the advocates and opponents of departments, there is a fairly even distribution along a continuum between the two views. Even the staunchest proponents of disciplinary departments, such as Andersen and Trow, admit that some improvement in their operation is possible; and most everyone would agree that some improvement is needed. The differences occur over the extent of these improvements.

For example, as I read the authors of our opening chapters, I sense that Andersen has the greatest confidence in departments, assuming they are well run. In Chapter Two, Trow finds them indispensable in carrying out the training and research functions of universities, but he confesses they may not be the best unit for providing a liberal and unspecialized education or for resolving the most important questions about life and society. Benezet's finely balanced consideration in Chapter Three distinguishes between college and university departments; he also deals with the "coordinating department" or "field committee" through which departments of a particular discipline within a complex university system or a group of cooperating institutions can approach common problems. And in Chapter Four Harrington advocates a variety of alternatives, such as the experiments described in Chapters Five through Eight, because of his conclusion that traditional departments, however useful in the past, now tend to obstruct needed change and are ill suited to deal with such issues as overexpansion, student unrest, faculty unionism, and internal quality control.

For anyone who desires some improvement in the present system, needed changes may range from minor and informal palliatives to complete radical revision. But by and large, all potential improvements can be grouped into two main categories, depending on their extent. A number of them, ameliorative in nature, retain the disciplinary department as the core element of academic organization and as "home base" for the faculty and students. They make only some adjustments in departmental operations or supplement departments with subsidiary units to correct specific deficiencies and increase their effectiveness. The more drastic reforms transform the departmental system itself by devising other affiliations, teams, or organizational units that either supersede conventional departments or cross-cut them as equal competitors. Let us consider these two major types of change in turn.

Amelioration

A number of ways exist to make changes in disciplinary departments without disturbing their role as the basic organizational structure of academic institutions. The most immediate, as Andersen and Brown suggest in earlier chapters, is to improve departmental leadership. The quality of departmental administration is crucial for the constructive resolution of tensions, Brown points out, and essential for a humane climate in academic life. And Andersen is correct that many departments need a full-time administrative assistant or executive secretary to save the chairman for teaching, research, and major policy decisions.

Increasingly, training opportunities for new chairmen are developing, and some institutions have gone so far as to create training periods for incoming chairmen—similar to the inservice role of the dean-elect of the School of Social Science at Hampshire College. The selection of departmental leaders can take several forms, ranging from the appointment of heads who remain in office until retirement or death to the election of chairpersons for short terms and even the rotation of leadership among all departmental faculty members, with each member assuming the chair for a year or other brief period. But regardless of form—and some large institutions employ more than one form—most observers agree that to assure effective working relationships, if heads are appointed by a dean or other senior officer, the appointment should follow consultation with department members; and if chairpersons are chosen by their departmental colleagues, their nomination should typically lead to pro forma administrative appointment. Depending on such factors as the mode of selection, duration of the appointment, and the standing and abilities of the incumbent, the position can be made a powerful and vital executive role and a force for departmental progress rather than a mere "choremanship," involved with running errands for a group of colleagues or higher-level administrators who themselves make the important decisions.

Beyond such improvements in departmental administration, several administrative techniques at higher levels can help overcome departmental rigidity. One such policy can prevent departments from assuming that when one of their faculty positions is vacated, whether because of retirement, death, resignation, or other termination, they have the right not only to fill the slot but also to retain its same rank for the next occupant. An alert provost or dean will bring each such vacated position back to a central pool and authorize its reallocation only after proof of need.

Similarly, in the filling of faculty positions, particularly at senior levels, a department ordinarily should not have the sole power to initiate recruitment and nomination. A preferable pattern for such appointments is to have a search committee composed of members of related departments as well as the recruiting department. In major appointments, scholars from other institutions might well sit as advisors, and the committee should be charged not merely to recommend candidates but first to assess the direction of the discipline and the department, project their future needs, and select nominees only on the basis of these projections.

Another possibility that has gained support as budgets have become tight is to take financial administration largely out of departmental hands and place it in the dean's office. At Santa Cruz, for example, academic support funds (except those for the colleges) are allocated to the divisions, and expenditures are controlled from there, thus eliminating the need for a fiscal staff in each discipline and providing expert fiscal management at the divisional level. Similarly, the provision of stenographic services for faculty members in conveniently located "pools" rather than in departments can both save money and provide better service. The consolidation of fiscal and stenographic functions is one way to make better use of scarce resources.

To guard against ossification, some institutions such as Harvard maintain permanent visiting committees to the departments, composed of outside scholars and knowledgeable laymen and charged to assure continued strength and progress. And if slippage appears, institutional officers should not hesitate to call in recognized leaders of the field for objective fact finding and frank advice about revitalization.

To reduce isolation and parochialism, several other policies can be considered. Some institutions are encouraging faculty members to develop more wide-ranging interests and abilities, not by changing the departmental structure as such but by helping individuals improve themselves through faculty development programs and more flexible rewards for the mastery of allied fields and for participation in team teaching at intradepartmental and interdisciplinary levels.

Some institutions, such as the University of Wisconsin–Green Bay and the University of Texas of the Permian Basin, are assigning faculty offices by other than disciplinary affiliation to stimulate interdisciplinary interaction. More of them are underwriting informal opportunities for discussion across disciplinary boundaries at faculty clubs, retreats, and colloquia. One example is Columbia University's program of over a hundred ongoing University Seminars, open to faculty members of Columbia and other colleges and universities and to selected nonacademic associates and graduate students. Begun in 1945 under the inspiration of history professor Frank Tannenbaum, four of the original seminars—The State, The Problem of Peace, Studies in Religion, and The Renaissance—are still in existence, having been joined more recently by groups on such topics as Labor (1948), Public Communication (1951), American Civilization (1954), Communism (1960), The City (1962), Pollution and Water Resources (1967), Death (1971), Women and Society (1974), and The History of the Working Class (1976). Participants receive neither remuneration nor credit, but obtain the opportunity to meet over lunch or dinner once or twice a month with colleagues sharing similar interests.

Beyond such informal interdisciplinary programs is the interdisciplinary research institute or center, which provides supplementary appointments to faculty members on a part-time basis and to research associates as full-time staff members. Well-enough known and studied (for example, by Ikenberry and Friedman, 1972) to warrant little more than mention here, these centers leave the hegemony of the disciplinary department secure in terms of basic decisions about student and faculty progress while giving both faculty members and students some opportunities for cross-disciplinary scholarship. Institutes are confined mainly to larger and more prestigious universities. Typically an organized research unit will "buy" a portion of a faculty member's time in order to facilitate participation in a particular research project. The faculty person enjoys some release from teaching and often welcomes the chance to spend more time on research which, when completed, may enhance his value in the academic marketplace. Some critics argue that such use of the faculty by research institutes accentuates the flight from teaching. Though it may help the faculty member secure a desired advancement, it may also disrupt the teaching program of his department. When research units "buy" the time of faculty members, the department often must hire temporary help to carry the teaching load. Other supplements to the departmental framework for wide-ranging faculty members include joint appointments by departments and an occasional institutionwide appointment as a "university" or "distinguished" professor.

Supplements to departments for students similarly range from the informal to the highly organized. At the most informal level, infinite possibilities exist for assuring students (especially freshmen) fellowship, motivation, and orientation through extracurricular as well as curricular means. Among successful efforts was that of Florida State University, where, after the idea of an experimental college was abandoned in the early 1960s, small groups of freshmen were formed around faculty advisers. Members of these groups enrolled through block registration in all or some of the same courses, and engaged in common social activities. It was succeeded at Florida State by The Freshman Learning Experience, which combined block registration with cross-disciplinary plenary sessions of students and faculty. A similar attack on impersonalism has been launched as a regular program at Berkeley, following successful experimentation with it in 1972–1973 and 1973–1974. Called the Freshman Cluster Program, it brings together groups of between fifteen and seventeen freshmen who share similar academic or career interests to meet regularly with a faculty member and a graduate student with the same interest. Members of Berkeley's clusters take several courses together during their first term and receive academic advice and vocational counsel from their mentor and his or her graduate assistant. Although Berkeley's clusters tend to be disciplinary in nature, there is no strong reason why students should not be grouped on the basis of other interests.

More formally, freshmen as well as sophomores and upperclassmen can pursue a specialized topic in seminar programs built around the individual interests of a faculty member rather than the agenda of a department. These seminars can demonstrate to freshmen the excitement of scholarship and the rigor of intellectual investigation unrestricted by disciplinary boundaries. Harvard's Freshman Seminars, forecast by E. H. Land in 1957 and inspired by the New College Plan of 1958, remain the best-known example of this effort, now found at more than 150 institutions, including Hampshire and some of the colleges at Santa Cruz.

At a more advanced level, further supplements are possible,

the most obvious being the opportunity for students to concentrate their studies in areas or on topics beyond the academic disciplines and across departmental boundaries. They can break the lockstep of departmental majors through double majors and their own independently designed and approved programs.

Finally, the most formal supplements to departments for students are full-fledged nondepartmental undergraduate colleges, such as Michigan State's "University College," which enroll their own students and retain their own faculty to offer general education, and cluster colleges manned either by faculty members on joint appointment or by a separate staff—among the most recent being "Strawberry Creek College" (formally, the Collegiate Seminar Program) of the University of California, Berkeley. For teaching and learning unrestricted by the disciplinary department, such colleges parallel the research and scholarly opportunities of interdisciplinary research institutes as supplements to the departmental structure.

Transformation

In contrast to these various attempts to ameliorate the limitations of traditional departments while retaining them as the basic element of college and university organization, other efforts aim at ending their dominance by creating replacements for them or equal alternatives to them. These include the sample of innovations reported in the case studies of American and British institutions in Chapters Five through Nine. The simplest, for a small institution, is exemplified by Hampshire College, as described by Charles Longsworth in Chapter Seven. Hampshire shunned disciplinary departments by taking four major divisions or schools as its basic academic units. These four schools are more than "departments writ large": they serve as a unifying structure for student progress and interdisciplinary faculty participation. In England, two new universities launched in the 1960s—Sussex and East Anglia—have chosen and retained interdisciplinary schools as their basic units, as F. M. G. Willson notes in Chapter Nine. Three other new British universities have chosen a collegiate form of organization, although they lack collegiate instructional programs comparable to those of Oxford and Cambridge.

The interdisciplinary schools of Hampshire, Sussex, and East Anglia are not far different from the pattern of a number of other colleges that have used divisions without departments as their organizing unit. In liberal arts colleges and community colleges, the most common of these divisions have been humanities, social sciences, and natural sciences. Hampshire's four schools of humanities and arts, natural science, social science, and language and communication appear to offer a model organization for an independent small college where the proliferation of departments results in one-, two-, and three-person units. Few institutions have been launched under more favorable circumstances, and none with which I am familiar had as careful planning as Hampshire.

A second possibility is to organize departments on some other basis than the disciplines. The University of Wisconsin–Green Bay, where problem-based departments are not the exception but the rule, provides an excellent example, as Edward Weidner describes it in Chapter Five. Instead of forming departments in the usual way, Weidner and his colleagues have organized them about broad issues, most often related to long-run environmental concerns, such as population dynamics and regional analysis. Green Bay's departments are composed of faculty members trained in several different fields, and the evaluation of the academic progress of both faculty members and students is multidisciplinary. Weidner concedes that this problem-based approach poses some difficulties: the theme or issue around which a department is built must be a long-term one if continuity is to be maintained. As new intellectual and social problems emerge, adjustments must be made in the alignment of tenured faculty members. Professors trained in a particular discipline but lodged in a multidisciplinary unit may sometimes long for closer association with colleagues of their own background. Young faculty members may suffer a lack of research productivity during their years of transition from graduate school specialization to problem orientation. And some students, concerned about the utility of an unconventional degree, want a degree with a conventional label—a wish satisfied at Green Bay by the option of a joint major, one problem-oriented and the other disciplinary. Yet although such pitfalls exist, they can be successfully overcome, as Green Bay illustrates.

Perhaps the most radical alternative of all is illustrated by The Evergreen State College, which has abandoned all pretense of departmentalism as such. As Charles McCann tells its story in Chapter Eight, its best-known curricular innovation—year-long coordinated studies programs, in which four or five faculty members work intensively with some hundred students on a common topic or concern—has been supported by an even more radical administrative organization, in which faculty are grouped into alpha, beta, delta, and gamma units to work with particular deans who have specific administrative responsibilities or "desks." As of 1976, the Evergreen deanships feature less rotation of responsibility and more stability of desk assignments than in previous years, but the arrangement of faculty members and deans in nondisciplinary groups continues as an antidepartmental model not previously seen in higher education. Its evolution and outcomes will be followed closely by all those interested in innovative organization and administration. Even now, Evergreen has proven that a college can indeed operate without departments, divisions, or even schools.

A less radical solution is illustrated by the University of California, Santa Cruz. As noted in Chapter Six, Santa Cruz represents the disciplines as "boards of studies" but cross-cuts them with thematic colleges—producing an organizational matrix in which faculty members and students hold membership in both a disciplinary group and a college.

The roots of the matrix idea are deep in American higher education. As Benezet and other authors have indicated, coordinating departments, field programs, interdisciplinary research institutes, and occasional cluster colleges have permitted at least some wide-ranging professors and a limited number of students to collaborate on cross-disciplinary topics. But in almost all American institutions, these interdisciplinary units have tended to be mere addenda or appendages to the dominant departmental structure—a convenient but seemingly stopgap approach to inconvenient intellectual issues that cut across departmental boundaries. Thus joint professorships have been the exception among faculty appointments, interdisciplinary majors have been allowed in "special" circumstances, and cluster colleges have been the alternative for a limited few. Even the most famous adaptations of the Oxford and Cambridge col-

legiate system—Harvard's "houses" and Yale's "colleges"—have
primarily supplemented the disciplinary departments of Harvard
and Yale by playing an informal and extracurricular educational
role rather than standing as equal to the departments.

Since the 1960s, however, a number of institutions have
begun to ask whether joint appointments and interdisciplinary opportunities needed to be limited only to the exceptional scholar and
the exceptional student. Could they instead become the normal
expectation? At Santa Cruz we sought to answer this question in
the affirmative by organizing the campus so that each faculty member holds a joint appointment, half time in a disciplinary board of
studies and half time in a college. Both boards of studies and colleges participate in evaluating faculty members for advancement,
and both may offer courses and majors for students. We viewed this
matrix as a way to transplant to an American state university the
matrix relationship of Oxford and Cambridge colleges with their
universities. Our intent was to provide both exceptional educational
opportunities for undergraduates through the residential colleges
and a solid foundation for graduate study and research through
the disciplines.

The Santa Cruz matrix is not a radical departure from the
American departmental norm. It is unusual only in the extent to
which colleges take a genuine part in teaching and play a substantial role in evaluating potential and existing faculty members.
Its almost universal practice of joint faculty appointments provides
the colleges with the power to make a case for the faculty members
who teach undergraduates well and against those who do not. The
difficulties in making a theoretical fifty-fifty split in responsibility
between college and discipline also fifty-fifty in practice admittedly
are considerable. The boards of studies, using well-tried disciplinary yardsticks, tend to be surer about their judgments on academic
personnel than the collegiate authorities, who must develop standards almost de novo. And a matrix organization necessarily creates
divided loyalties and bifurcated obligations in contrast to the simple
and single allegiances of a one-dimension departmental system.
Nevertheless, although the Santa Cruz matrix has aroused much
controversy both within and outside the institution, it appears to

have helped attract and retain an outstanding faculty and student body.

Other American institutions have been experimenting with variations of the matrix idea. When Drexel University organized its first doctoral programs in 1965, it cross-cut its undergraduate departments with new interdisciplinary programs on the environment and on humanities and technology. The University of Texas at its Dallas and Permian Basin campuses has sought to avoid traditional departments by maintaining disciplinary groups called "faculties" for purposes of faculty recruitment and program development, while using its colleges—for example, science and engineering, management, and arts and education at Permian Basin—for basic academic operations. And Ottawa University in Kansas is balancing its departments with four interdisciplinary centers concerned with communication, expression, and value clarification; the study of organizational and cultural issues; issues of individuality and personal values; and studies of human interaction with the environment. These centers offer portions of the university's general education program, advise students, teach interdisciplinary courses, and conduct depth-study majors. Each unit has a five-year authorization; if not extended, it will "self-destruct."

In essence, these matrix plans set up equal but opposite alternatives to the disciplinary department and challenge faculty members and students to choose both a disciplinary home and an interdisciplinary base of operation. They raise the field program, the interdisciplinary research institute, and the cluster college to a level competitive with the department without in the process abandoning the department.

Summation

Among those who feel that improvement in the departmental system is needed, some may wish to undertake—or be able to accomplish—only limited amelioration of specific problems. Others may seek the actual transformation of the departmental system itself. For them, the achievements of Hampshire, Green Bay, Evergreen, Santa Cruz, and other institutions should prove instructive. But at least from this observer's perspective, the accomplishments of Hampshire, Green Bay, and Evergreen offer more direction for the creators of the next generation of new institutions than for those who seek to reorganize existing ones. Abolition of conventional departments is likely to prove impractical if not impossible at an already departmentalized college or university. For existing institutions, movement toward a matrix organization seems more realistic. Placing a second organizational stratum across the present departmental structure, although difficult, is less threatening than abolition, yet it promises similar benefits. Indeed, it offers institutions the means to greatly expand degree programs on important topics, whether urban affairs, international relations, American studies, or East Asian culture, without creating new departments to offer the programs. It provides a way to extend education without the overextension of resources and commensurate expansion of the faculty.

In short, sweeping reform of the departmental system may need to await the creation of new institutions, but in the meantime many lesser improvements can be considered and implemented. Disciplinary departments, useful as they have been and as they still are, can be made less parochial and more supportive of the overall goals of their institutions. Small changes are possible even in times of restricted resources; and these changes can open the way to broader reforms or even overcome enough departmental limitations that the abolition of departments will prove unnecessary.

Bibliography

American Council on Education. *American Universities and Colleges.* (7th Ed.) Washington: The Council, 1973.

ARNEST, B. M. "The Colorado College Plan: An Academic Program Changes, But a Commitment Does Not." *The Colorado College Magazine,* 1970, *5* (Winter), 4–16.

ASHBY, E. *Technology and the Academics.* New York: St. Martin's Press, 1958.

BAKER, R. S. *Woodrow Wilson: Life and Letters, Princeton, 1890–1910.* Garden City, N.Y.: Doubleday, Page, 1927.

BARBER, C. L., and others. *The New College Plan: A Proposal for a Major Departure in Higher Education.* Amherst, Mass.: The Four Colleges, 1958.

BARZUN, J. *The American University: How it Runs, Where it is Going.* New York: Harper & Row, 1968.

BELL, D. *The Reforming of General Education.* New York: Columbia University Press, 1966.

BEN-DAVID, J. *American Higher Education: Directions Old and New.* New York: McGraw-Hill, 1972.

BIRNEY, R. C., and others. *Report of the Educational Advisory Committee to the President of Hampshire College.* Mimeo. Amherst, Mass.: Hampshire College, April 13, 1966.

BLAU, P. M. *The Organization of Academic Work.* New York: Wiley, 1973.

BOLTON, C. K., and BOYER, R. K. "Organizational Development for Academic Departments." *Journal of Higher Education,* 1973, *44* (May), 352–369.

225

BRANN, J., and EMMET, T. A. *The Academic Department or Division Chairman.* Detroit: Balamp, 1972.

BROWN, J. D. *The Human Nature of Organizations.* New York: AMACOM, 1973.

BRUBACHER, J. S., and RUDY, W. *Higher Education in Transition: An American History, 1636–1956.* New York: Harper & Row, 1958.

BRUCE, P. A. *A History of the University of Virginia.* Volume 1. New York: Macmillan, 1920.

Cambridge University. "Report of the Syndicate on the Relationship Between the University and the Colleges." *Reporter,* 1962, *92,* 1075–1150.

CAPLOW, T., and MCGEE, R. J. *The Academic Marketplace.* New York: Basic Books, 1958.

Carnegie Commission on Higher Education. *Priorities for Action: Final Report of the Carnegie Commission on Higher Education with Technical Notes and Appendixes.* New York: McGraw-Hill, 1973.

CARR, R. K., and VAN EYCK, D. K. *Collective Bargaining Comes to the Campus.* Washington: American Council on Education, 1973.

Claremont University Center. *The Claremont Colleges: Progress and Prospects.* Claremont, Ca., 1972.

CLARY, W. W. *The Claremont Colleges.* Claremont, Ca.: Claremont University Center, 1970.

COHEN, M. D., and MARCH, J. G. *Leadership and Ambiguity.* Report for The Carnegie Commission on Higher Education. New York: McGraw-Hill, 1974.

Commission on Academic Tenure in Higher Education (Keast Report). *Faculty Tenure: A Report and Recommendations by the Commission on Academic Tenure in Higher Education.* San Francisco: Jossey-Bass, 1973.

CONANT, J. B. *Shaping Educational Policy.* New York: McGraw-Hill, 1964.

CORSON, J. J. *The Governance of Colleges and Universities.* New York: McGraw-Hill, 1960, 2nd ed. 1975.

COX, H. *The Secular City.* New York: Macmillan Co., 1965.

CURTIS, M. H. *Oxford and Cambridge in Transition, 1558–1642.* New York: Oxford University Press, 1959.

DARKENWALD, G. G., JR. "The Department Chairman Role in Relation to the Social Organization of Colleges and Universities." Doctoral dissertation, Teachers College, Columbia University, 1970.

DETOCQUEVILLE, A. *Democracy in America.* New York: Harper & Row, 1966.

DEWEY, J. *Democracy and Education: An Introduction to the Philosophy of Education.* New York: Free Press, 1966.

DOYLE, E. A. *The Status and Functions of the Departmental Chairman.* Washington: Catholic University of America Press, 1953.

DRESSEL, P. L., and FARICY, W. H. *Return to Responsibility: Constraints on Autonomy in Higher Education.* San Francisco: Jossey-Bass, 1972.

DRESSEL, P. L., JOHNSON, F. C., and MARCUS, P. M. *The Confidence Crisis: An Analysis of University Departments.* San Francisco: Jossey-Bass, 1970.

DRESSEL, P. L., and REICHARD, D. J. "The University Department: Retrospect and Prospect." *Journal of Higher Education,* 1970, *41* (May), 387–402.

DURYEA, E. D. "Evolution of University Organizations." In J. Perkins (Ed.), *The University as an Organization.* New York: McGraw-Hill, 1973.

DYKES, A. R. *Faculty Participation in Academic Decision Making.* Washington: American Council on Education, 1968.

Education at Berkeley. Report of the Select Committee on Education, Academic Senate, University of California at Berkeley. Berkeley and Los Angeles: University of California Press, 1968.

EHRLE, E. B. "Selection and Evaluation of Department Chairmen." *Educational Record,* 1975, *56* (Winter), 29–38.

EPSTEIN, L. D. *Governing the University: The Campus and the Public Interest.* San Francisco: Jossey-Bass, 1974.

ETZIONI, A. *A Comparative Analysis of Complex Organizations.* New York: Free Press, 1961.

EVANS, R. I. *Resistance to Innovation in Higher Education: A Social Psychological Exploration Focused on Television and the Establishment.* San Francisco: Jossey-Bass, 1970.

The Evergreen State College. *The Evergreen State College Bulletin 1971–72.* Olympia, Wash.: 1971.

The Evergreen State College. *Faculty Handbook.* Olympia, Wash.: 1971.

FARICY, W. H. "Grouping Departments." *Journal of Higher Education,* 1974, *45* (Feb.), 98–111.

FELLMAN, D. "The Department Chairman." Paper presented at the 22nd National Conference on Higher Education, American Association for Higher Education, Chicago, March 6, 1967.

FLEXNER, A. *Universities: American, English, German.* New York: Oxford University Press, 1930.

GAFF, J. G., and Associates. *The Cluster College.* San Francisco: Jossey-Bass, 1970.

GERTH, H. H., and MILLS, C. WRIGHT (Eds.). *From Max Weber.* New York: Oxford University Press, 1946, p. 147.

GILMAN, D. C. *University Problems in the United States.* New York: Century, 1898.

GLASS, H. B. *Science and Liberal Education.* Baton Rouge: Louisiana State University Press, 1959.

GROSS, E., and GRAMBSCH, P. *Changes in University Organization, 1964–71.* New York: McGraw-Hill, 1974.

HALSEY, A. H., and TROW, M. *The British Academics.* London: Faber, 1971.

Hampshire Reports. No. 1. Hampshire College, Winter 1976.

HARTNETT, R. T. "Strengthening Institutional Quality Through Institutional Research." *New Directions for Higher Education,* 1975, *12* (Winter), 61–70.

HASKINS, C. H. *The Rise of Universities.* New York: Henry Holt, 1923.

HAWKINS, H. *Pioneer: A History of Johns Hopkins University (1874–1889).* Ithaca, N.Y.: Cornell University Press, 1960.

HEFFERLIN, JB *Dynamics of Academic Reform.* San Francisco: Jossey-Bass, 1969.

HENDERSON, A. D. *Policies and Practices in Higher Education.* New York: Harper, 1960.

HODGKINSON, H. L. "The Next Decade." In H. L. Hodgkinson and L. R. Meeth (Eds.), *Power and Authority.* San Francisco: Jossey-Bass, 1971.

HODGKINSON, H. L., and MEETH, L. R. *Power and Authority: Transformation of Campus Governance.* San Francisco: Jossey-Bass, 1971.

HOFSTADTER, R., and METZGER, W. P. *The Development of Academic Freedom in the United States.* New York: Columbia University Press, 1955.

HUBER, V. A. *The English Universities.* (2 vols.) Translated by Francis W. Newman. London: W. Pickering, 1843.

HUTCHINS, R. M. *The University of Utopia.* Chicago: University of Chicago Press, 1953.

IKENBERRY, S. O., and FRIEDMAN, R. C. *Beyond Academic Departments:*

The Story of Institutes and Centers. San Francisco: Jossey-Bass, 1972.

JENCKS, C., and RIESMAN, D. *The Academic Revolution.* Garden City, N.Y.: Doubleday, 1968.

KEATS, J. "John Keats' letter of February 19, 1818 to John Hamilton Reynolds." In D. Bush (Ed.), *Selected Poems and Letters.* Boston: Houghton Mifflin, 1959.

KEETON, M. *Shared Authority on Campus.* Washington, D.C.: American Association for Higher Education, 1971.

KERR, C. *The Uses of the University.* Cambridge: Harvard University Press, 1964.

KORMONDY, E. J. "Governance and The Evergreen State College." Report prepared for Lilly Endowment Project in College and University Governance, John D. Millett, Project Director and Senior Vice-President, Academy for Educational Development. Washington, D.C.: Academy for Educational Development, 1976.

Liaison Committee of the State Board of Education and The Regents of the University of California. *The Need for Additional Centers of Public Higher Education in California.* Sacramento: California State Department of Education, 1957.

Liaison Committee. *A Master Plan for Higher Education in California, 1960–1975.* Sacramento: California State Department of Education, 1960.

MCCONNELL, T. R. "Faculty Government." In H. L. Hodgkinson and L. R. Meeth (Eds.), *Power and Authority: Transformation of Campus Governance.* San Francisco: Jossey-Bass, 1971.

MCGRATH, E. J., NYSTROM, W. C., and PATMOS, A. E. "A Study of Divisional Organization." *Association of American Colleges Bulletin,* 1943, *29* (Dec.), 477–497.

MCKENNA, D. L. "A Study of Power and Interpersonal Relationships in the Administration of Higher Education." Doctoral dissertation, University of Michigan, 1957.

MAIER, R. H., and WEIDNER, E. W. "Creating and Encouraging an Innovative Academic Environment in Higher Education." *Higher Education* (Elsevier Scientific Pub. Co., Amsterdam, Netherlands), 1975, *4,* 61–68.

MEETH, L. R. "On the Dangers of Teaching Too Well." *Change Magazine Report on Teaching: 1,* 1976, *8* (March), 2.

MEIKLEJOHN, A. *Education Between Two Worlds.* Freeport, New York: Books for Libraries Press, 1972.

MEIKLEJOHN, A. *Political Freedom: The Constitutional Powers of the People.* New York: Oxford University Press, 1965.

MOODIE, G. C., and EUSTACE, R. *Power and Authority in British Universities.* London: Allen and Unwin, 1974.

MOONEY, R. L. "The Problem of Leadership in the University." *Harvard Educational Review,* 1963, *33,* 42–57.

MORRISON, S. E. *Three Centuries of Harvard, 1636–1936.* Cambridge, Mass.: Harvard University Press, 1936.

MURRAY, R. K. "On Departmental Development: A Theory." *Journal of General Education,* 1964, *16* (Oct.), 227–236.

MYERS, W. S. (Ed.). *Woodrow Wilson: Some Princeton Memories.* Princeton, N.J.: Princeton University Press, 1946.

National Science Foundation. *Federal Support to Universities, Colleges and Selected Nonprofit Institutions, Fiscal Year 1974.* NSF #75-325, 1975.

NEWMAN, J. H., CARDINAL. *The Idea of a University.* New York: Longmans, Green, 1947.

ONCKEN, G. R. "Organizational Control in University Departments." Technical Report 71–20. Seattle: University of Washington, Department of Psychology, June 1971.

Oxford University. *Report of Commission of Inquiry.* (2 vols.) Oxford, 1966.

PATTERSON, F., and LONGSWORTH, C. R. *The Making of a College: Plans for a New Departure in Higher Education.* Cambridge: M.I.T. Press, 1966.

PERKIN, H. J. *New Universities in the United Kingdom.* Paris: Organization for Economic Co-operation and Development, n.d.

PERKINS, J. A. *The University as an Organization.* New York: McGraw-Hill, 1973.

PIERSON, G. W. *Yale: The University College, 1921–1937.* New Haven, Conn.: Yale University Press, 1955.

PIMENTEL, G. C. "Addendum—A Minority Report." In *Education at Berkeley.* Report of the Select Committee on Education, Academic Senate, University of California at Berkeley. Berkeley and Los Angeles: University of California Press, 1968, pp. 195–221.

PLATO. *The Apology of Socrates.* Edited by Adela Marion Adam. Cambridge: Cambridge University Press, 1914.

PLATO. *The Republic.* English translation by Paul Shorey. Cambridge: Harvard University Press, 1943.

QUINCY, J. *The History of Harvard University.* Cambridge: Harvard University Press, 1840.

Regents Commission on Doctoral Education, R. W. Fleming, Chairman. *Meeting the Needs of Doctoral Education in New York.* Report to the New York State Board of Regents. Albany: State Education Department, 1973.

RIESMAN, D. *Constraint and Variety in American Education.* New York: Doubleday Anchor Books, 1958.

ROURKE, F. E., and BROOKS, G. E. *The Managerial Revolution in Higher Education.* Baltimore: Johns Hopkins Press, 1966.

RUCKER, D. *The Chicago Pragmatists.* Minneapolis: University of Minnesota Press, 1969.

RUDOLPH, F. *The American College and University.* New York: Knopf, 1962.

RUML, B. *Memo to a College Trustee.* New York: McGraw-Hill, 1959.

RUSSELL, B. *Education and the Good Life.* New York: Boni and Liveright, 1926.

RYAN, D. W. "The Internal Organization of Academic Departments." *Journal of Higher Education,* 1972, *43* (June), 464–482.

SALANCIK, G. R., and PFEFFER, J. "The Bases and Use of Power in Organizational Decision Making: The Case of a University." *Administrative Science Quarterly,* 1974, *19* (Dec.), 453–473.

SANFORD, R. N. *The American College.* New York: Wiley, 1962.

SHATTOCK, M. L. (Ed.). *University Administration in a Period of Expansion.* British Council course on University Administration, 1970. London: British Council, n.d.

SHILS, E. "The Hole in the Centre: University Government in the United States." *Minerva,* 1970, *8* (Jan.), 1–7.

SHUART, J. M. "Some Value Orientations of Academic Department Chairmen: A Study of Comparative Values and Administrative Effectiveness." Doctoral Dissertation, New York University, 1966.

SIKES, W. W., and others. *Renewing Higher Education from Within: A Guide for Campus Change Teams.* San Francisco: Jossey-Bass, 1974.

STAFFORD, R. A. "Green Bay's Interdisciplinary Faculty." *Change,* 1972, *4* (April), 20–22.

STEWART, C. "The Place of Higher Education in a Changing Society." In N. Sanford (Ed.), *The American College.* New York: Wiley, 1962.

STORR, R. J. *Harper's University: The Beginnings: A History of the University of Chicago.* Chicago: University of Chicago Press, 1966.

STRAUS, R. "Departments and Disciplines: Stasis and Change." *Science,* November 30, 1973, pp. 895–897.

THWING, C. F. *A History of Higher Education in America.* New York: D. Appleton, 1906.

TOURAINE, A. *The Academic System in American Society.* Carnegie Commission on Higher Education. New York: McGraw-Hill, 1974.

TROW, M. "The Public and Private Lives of Higher Education." *Daedalus,* 1975a, 2 (Winter), 111–127.

TROW, M. (Ed.). *Teachers and Students: Aspects of American Higher Education.* New York: McGraw-Hill, 1975b.

TROW, M. "The American Academic Department as a Context for Learning." *Studies in Higher Education,* 1976, 1 (March), 11–22.

TROW, M., and FULTON, O. "Research Activities in American Higher Education." In M. Trow (Ed.), *Teachers and Students.* New York: McGraw-Hill, 1975, pp. 39–83.

TUSSMAN, J. *Obligation and the Body Politic.* New York: Oxford University Press, 1960.

University of California, President. *A Proposed Academic Plan for the University of California.* Berkeley, 1961.

University of California, President. "San Diego and Santa Cruz: Some Comparisons." Berkeley, 1972.

University of California, Santa Cruz, Chancellor. *A Provisional Academic Plan for the Santa Cruz Campus, 1965–1975.* Santa Cruz, 1962.

University of California, Santa Cruz, Chancellor. *Santa Cruz Campus Academic Plan, 1965–1975.* Santa Cruz, 1965.

University of California, Santa Cruz, Chancellor. *Academic Quality at Santa Cruz: Report of the Chancellor's Self-Study/Accreditation Commission.* Santa Cruz, 1975.

University of Kent. *Reports of the General Committee Working Parties.* Canterbury, April 1976.

University of Sussex. *Final Report of the Committee of Inquiry into the Organization of the University of Sussex.* Sussex, May 1973.

University of Wisconsin. *The University of Wisconsin-Green Bay Preliminary Academic Plan.* Approved by the Board of Regents, March 10, 1967.

University of Wisconsin. *The University of Wisconsin-Green Bay Statement of Philosophy and Undergraduate Program.* Approved by the Board of Regents, February 16, 1968.

VEYSEY, L. R. *The Emergence of the American University.* Chicago: University of Chicago Press, 1965.

VEYSEY, L. R. "Stability and Experiment in the American Undergraduate Curriculum." In C. Kaysen (Ed.), *Content and Context.* Carnegie Commission on Higher Education. New York: McGraw-Hill, 1973.

WALKER, D. E., and HOLMES, D. C. "The University Professor and His Department." *The Educational Record,* 1960, *41* (Jan.), 34–36.

WALTZER, H. *The Job of Academic Department Chairman.* Washington: American Council on Education, 1975.

WEIDNER, E. W. "Problem-Focused Education: The Environment." *Educational Record,* 1971, *52* (Fall), 314–320.

WEIDNER, E. W. "A Case Study on The University of Wisconsin-Green Bay." Prepared for The Center for Educational Research and Innovation of the Organization for Economic Cooperation and Development. Paris, July 1973a.

WEIDNER, E. W. "Environmental Education: Implications for Institutional Structure." *Environmental Education at University Level: Trends and Data.* Paris: OECD-CERI, 1973b.

WEIDNER, E. W. "Interdisciplinary and Higher Education." *International Journal of Environmental Studies,* (Gordon and Breach Science Publishers, England), 1973, *5,* 205–214.

WHITEHEAD, A. N. *The Aims of Education and Other Essays.* New York: Macmillan, 1929.

WILBY, P. A series of articles on new universities in the *Times Higher Education Supplement.* London, February–May 1976.

YUKER, H. E. *Faculty Workload: Facts, Myths and Commentary.* Higher Education Monograph #6. Washington, D.C.: ERIC Clearinghouse on Higher Education, 1974.

Index

A

Academic freedom, and leadership, 186–187, 207–208

Administration, without departments, 147–169. *See also* Leadership

Advising: at Evergreen, 163–164; as school function at Hampshire, 132–133; at UC Santa Cruz, 115

American Council on Education: Freshman Survey by, 113–114; SAT scores compared by, 113n

Amherst College: and Five-College cooperation, 139–145; and Hampshire College, 117–119

ANDERSEN, K. J., x, xii, 1–11, 13, 35, 211, 213, 214

Arkansas, University of, chairman's role at, 59–60

ARMACOST, P. H., xvi

ARNEST, B. M., 150, 225

ASHBY, E., 150, 225

B

BABBITT, I., 55

BAKER, R. S., 92, 225

BARBER, C. L., 117, 118, 119, 122, 139–140, 225

BARRY, D., 150, 153

BARZUN, J., 58, 225

BELL, D., 121–122, 225

BENEZET, L., xii–xiii, 34–52, 62, 95, 212, 214, 221

BLAISDELL, J. A., 94

BOLTON, C. K., 62, 225

BOYER, R. K., 62, 225

Brandeis University, freshman SAT scores at, 113n

BROWN, J. D., xv, 116, 185–209, 214, 226

BRUBACHER, J. S., 4, 226

BRUCE, P. A., 3, 226

BRUNO, M., 136

BURNS, R. E., 95

C

CADWALLADER, M., 150, 153

California, University of, Berkeley: biology departments at, 101; Freshman Cluster Program at, 218; Strawberry Creek College at, 219; undergraduate education at, 45–46

California, University of, Santa Cruz: academic advising at, 115; boards of studies at, 101–107; colleges' academic role at, 107–110; development of, 86–88; grading system at, 111–112; models for, 91–98; organizational matrix at, xiv, 86–116, 218, 221–223;